Stuck at the Airport

A Traveler's Survival Guide

HARRIET BASKAS

A FIRESIDE BOOK
PUBLISHED BY SIMON & SCHUSTER
NEW YORK   LONDON   TORONTO   SYDNEY   SINGAPORE

FIRESIDE
Rockefeller Center
1230 Avenue of the Americas
New York, NY 10020

Designed by Christine Weathersbee

Manufactured in the United States of America

10 9 8 7 6 5 4 3 2 1

Library of Congress Cataloging-in-Publication Data

Baskas, Harriet.
    ·Stuck at the airport : a traveler's survival guide / Harriet Baskas.
        p. cm.
        1. Airports—United States—Guidebooks.   2. Airports—Canada—
Guidebooks.   3. Travel—Handbooks, manuals, etc.   I. Title.

TL726.2 .B373 2001
387.7'36'0973—dc21   2001023160

ISBN 0-7432-0539-1

For Ross, partner in flying and all else

Acknowledgments

Enthusiastic thanks are due to:

The staff members and information booth volunteers who revealed secrets about their airports and generously shared their on-site knowledge;

Rose Pike, who first cleared "Stuck at the Airport" for takeoff;

Expedia.com crewmembers Mary Brisson Redmayne, Renee Russak, Mark Morris, and the hardworking team that keeps "Stuck at the Airport" on-line;

Anne Depue, literary agent, for dedicated service en route;

and Kristine Puopolo, Andrea Nelsen, copy editor Liz DeRidder, and others at Simon & Schuster for a safe landing.

Contents

Introduction

"The Devil himself had probably re-designed
Hell in light of information he had gained
from observing airport layouts."

—Anthony Price,
The Memory Trap, 1989

I once spent eight hours at a Kentucky airport waiting for a connecting flight to Seattle. I read the newspaper, finished my book, mailed some postcards, ate too much bad food, and inspected the three model airplanes in the terminal lobby—twice. Only in the sixth excruciating hour, when the orange plastic bucketchairs became just too much, did I notice a tiny green sign sporting a faded arrow and the words "Obs. Deck. This Way." Feeling just a bit like Alice picking up the bottle labeled "Drink Me," I pushed open a heavy door, climbed a short flight of stairs, and entered a glass-walled room with comfortable leather chairs, a lovely countryside view, display cases full of historical artifacts, and a great snack bar! If only *someone* had clued me in to this oasis earlier, my time spent "stuck at the airport" would have been easier to handle, and perhaps downright pleasant.

Since then, I've been aggressively investigating airports. Not just looking for observation decks, but for art and cultural exhibits, well-stocked bookstores, restaurants with creative menus, shops with reasonably priced, gift-worthy inventory, and spots where a weary traveler can catch a nap, take care of business, or just get a breath of fresh air.

I knew other travelers would be curious about my findings because flight delays are increasing, passengers are being ordered to arrive earlier and earlier for flight check-in, and "dwell time"—the amount of time airline passengers spend in airports during layovers—is lengthening by about 5 percent a year. Whether we're traveling or just picking someone up at the airport it seems we've all experienced being stuck at the airport at one time or another. We may not be able to do anything about the amount of time a flight is delayed, but we can certainly do something about how we spend our time "dwelling."

So how can you dwell well? In some airports it's nearly impossible unless you're toting your own toolkit: a long book, a laptop, a CD player with headphones, packaged snacks, extra cash, a toothbrush, individually wrapped Handi Wipes, and a charged cell phone. In many airports, however, it's surprisingly easy—and getting easier—to do your banking, get a haircut, pick up a gift, and sit down for a massage. Without going too much out of your way, it's also possible to find safe and snuggly places to take a nap, clean places to shower, and covered straightaways to sneak in a run, or at least an energizing walk. In some airports, you can even get a dentist to take a look at that troublesome tooth, a shoemaker to fix that wobbly heel, or a doctor to perform that much-needed physical.

Shopping at many airports is getting to be a more pleasant experience as well. At one time, it seemed airport concessionaires literally banked on the fact that air travelers would pay exorbitant prices for last-minute souvenirs, gifts for kids, and even a pack of gum once they were in the airport. Not anymore. In the mall-like settings at the Pittsburgh and Orlando international airports, for example, the shops are so plentiful (and familiar) that it's easy to forget you're even in an airport. At London's Heathrow Airport there are personal shoppers on hand who will not only shop for you but also escort you past security so you can shop duty-free in other terminals. I even know folks who schedule special trips to Oregon's Portland International Airport just to shop sales-tax-free along a tree-lined "street" filled with branches of many of the city's top specialty stores. The fact that many airports now impose a "street pricing" policy means that those airports' shops can no longer inflate their prices just because you're shopping at the airport. So don't get irritated, go Christmas shopping in July.

It's not only the shopping that has gotten more enjoyable at many airports—there are now more choices for what to eat. There's still fast food everywhere, but now it's easier to find fruit juices and smoothies, healthy veggie wraps, salads with something other than wilted lettuce, great barbecue, sushi, and, of course, that much-needed good cup of coffee. Detroit (of all places) has a Tequilaría; Orlando has an on-site brewery; Dallas/Fort Worth sports a licensed winery and wine-tasting room, and most airports have at least one sit-down restaurant that uses cloth napkins and full-size plates.

Once you've showered, shopped, and eaten, why not see some art? Many airports own top-notch art collections and priceless historical artifacts. The Smithsonian Institution may house the *Spirit of St. Louis* monoplane, for example, but Lindbergh's personal airplane is suspended from the ceiling in the Main Terminal at the Lambert–St. Louis International Airport. San Francisco International Airport's Bureau of Exhibitions, Museums, and Cultural Exchange organizes more than 40 exhibitions a year, ranging from documentary photography and kitsch collectibles to significant exhibitions on loan from museums and private collections. At Seattle-Tacoma International Airport you'll find pop-can quilts in some bathrooms, works by Louise Nevelson and Frank Stella, and a display of weapons and drug paraphernalia collected at security checkpoints.

A few notes about the airports included here and how they've been evaluated: For the most part, the airports in this volume are those that serve the highest volume of US travelers. A few, California's Burbank and San Jose airports, for example, are "up-and-coming" facilities that are increasingly being chosen as alternative destinations for folks heading to major cities and are thus experiencing rapid growth. While I have not yet visited every airport that exists (I'm working on that), I have spent time at each airport in this book. I have tried to assess the facilities with a wide variety of travelers in mind, from families taking that once-a-year vacation to harried road warriors making that weekly business trip.

I've also tried to ensure that the information listed in this book is correct. However, many airports are undergoing refurbishing and expansion, so you may encounter changes in some of the vendors, services, and facilities. Call ahead if you want to be absolutely sure a service or vendor will be available, and don't be shy to ask for help on-site from the information booth staff.

So, next time you find yourself "stuck at the airport," rejoice. Store your carry-on in a locker, pick up a map of the airport, and open up this book. And if you find something I've missed, or something that has changed, please let me know. You can e-mail me at: airstuck@aol.com

Stuck at the Airport

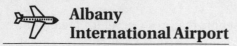

Albany International Airport

Albany, New York
Airport Code: ALB
Web Address: http://www.albanyairport.com

In 1927, when Charles Lindbergh touched down at Albany's first airfield on his triumphant 48-state tour, 10,000 people showed up to greet him—and one fan stole the aviator's laundry, presumably as a souvenir. Later, Lindbergh's motorcade was halted at a railway crossing, not because a train was coming but because the railway crossing guard insisted on shaking Lindbergh's hand.

Despite the delays, city officials succeeded in having Lindbergh visit the Shaker-owned farmland chosen as the site of the city's first commercial airport. One year later the Albany Municipal Airport opened for business and Albany became known as the "aerial crossroads of the great Northeast."

These days, Albany International Airport (ALB) serves more than 1 million passengers each year. Very few of them get their laundry lifted.

Get Oriented

- Luggage carts rent for $1.25. You'll receive a $.25 refund when you return a cart to the rack.
- There are no lockers at the Albany International Airport.

The terminal at Albany International Airport is shaped like an inverted T with the concourses lined up side by side. Concourse A serves American, Northwest, and United. Concourse B serves US Airways and Delta. In Concourse C you'll find flights for Continental and Southwest. It should take just a few minutes to go from the security checkpoint to the end of any concourse.

Take Care of Yourself

► **Eat**

The airport's main food court features Carvel ice cream, the Coffee Beanery, and the Saranac Brew House, which serves lunch and dinner in an "Adirondack Mountain" atmosphere. You can get pizza at Arrezio's in Concourse A, breakfast and light entrées at the Capital Deli & Pub in Concourse B, and coffee and light snacks at the Coffee Beanery in Concourse C.

Best Healthful Nosh

Salads at the Saranac Brew House.

Best Sinful Snack

An ice cream banana boat from Carvel.

► **Relax and Refresh**

You'll find some comfortable overstuffed chairs in the "rest area" of Concourse B and a courtyard just outside the west end of the terminal. If you need a truly quiet place to relax, head for the meditation room in Concourse C. Or grab a seat just past the security checkpoint, in the area airport officials call "Times Square," and watch all the other travelers rush by.

If you'd like to freshen up, the unisex Albany International Airport Barbershop is located on the first floor of the terminal in the baggage claim area. It's open Tuesday–Friday, 9 AM–6 PM and on Saturdays until 4 PM. Just across the street from the airport there's a Hilton Garden Inn (518-464-6666) that offers day rates that include access to the hotel's pool and fitness center.

Sorry, smokers, no smoking is allowed in the terminal.

Take Care of Business

• All airport phones are equipped with data ports.

The airport's business center is located on the second level of the terminal in Concourse C and is open Monday–Friday 7 AM–7 PM. This is the place to head for if you need to send a fax, make some copies, or get access to the Internet. The business center also rents computers and printers (518-242-4488).

Explore the Airport

► **Shop**

Owned by Albany County Airport Authority itself, Departure–The Museum Shop is an unusual airport concession filled with a tempting array of crafts and historic items gathered from more than 40 museums in New York's capital region. A good place to pick up that last-minute Adirondack basket or special piece of Shaker furniture. Your other airport shopping choices include Capital Book Sellers in Concourse C and a news and gift shop in each concourse.

► **Sightsee**

On the third floor of the airport you'll find an art gallery featuring rotating exhibits of work by contemporary regional artists, collections from area museums, and national traveling exhibitions. The gallery is open from 6 AM to 11 PM. Past shows have included Pulitzer Prize–winning photographs, whimsical sculptures, children's art, and selections from the National Museum of Racing and Hall of Fame in Saratoga Springs. Elsewhere in the terminal, keep your eyes open for historic regional photographs along Concourses A and C and the flock of brightly colored birds hanging from the ceiling in Concourse B.

To get a good view of the airfield, head to the observation deck on the third floor of the terminal. This area is equipped with a radio that lets you listen in on control tower chatter.

► **Play Around**

There's a kids' play area on the second level of Concourse A. Kids might also enjoy a visit to the observation deck on the third floor where they can watch planes come and go and eavesdrop on the conversations between the control tower and the pilots. Older kids might also enjoy whatever art or cultural exhibit is currently being featured in the third-floor gallery and the historic regional photographs along Concourses A and C.

Go into Town

A taxi ride to downtown Albany will cost about $14 and take about 20 minutes. Saratoga Springs is about a 30-minute trip. If you want to try public transportation, the Capital District Transit Authority bus service charges $1.25 for the trip to Albany and $1.60 for the ride to Troy.

Other Information

If you need more information about Albany International Airport before you arrive, call the Airport Information Center at 518-242-2222.

 # Amsterdam
Airport Schiphol

Amsterdam, Netherlands
Airport Code: AMS
Web Address: http://www.schiphol.nl

"Once," an airport hostess exclaims, "Amsterdam Airport Schiphol was just an ordinary place for starting or ending a trip. But now it's a real airport city, where travelers can do pretty much anything!"

Hostess-hype? Not really. Amsterdam's Schiphol Airport (AMS) has a casino, a supermarket that stays open every day until midnight, top-drawer artwork, the cheapest duty-free in Europe, and a kids' play area with (free!) Nintendo games. Not too long ago, one of Amsterdam's sex clubs even applied for a license to open a "relax-club" here, but their application was turned down.

"Relax-club" notwithstanding, Amsterdam Airport Schiphol expects to provide service for more than 37 million passengers this year.

Get Oriented

- Free baggage carts are scattered throughout the terminal.
- Self-service lockers are located in the main departure lounge areas and in Schiphol Plaza.

Schiphol has a logical, well-marked layout. There's one main terminal with three departure areas (1, 2, and 3) before security and three lounge areas (South, Central, and West) after security with concourses, or piers, labeled B, C, D, E, and F.

KLM is the predominant airline here and you'll find it operating out of Departure Hall 2. Of the other 90 or so airlines that fly through here, you'll find Air France, British Airways, and SAS in Departure Hall 1, Northwest in Departure Hall 2, and Continental, Delta, and United Air Lines in Departure Hall 3.

It should take you just about 5 minutes to travel between concourses, but it can take 15–20 minutes to walk from one end of the terminal to the other. More, if you get lured into the casino.

Take Care of Yourself

►Eat

Café Amsterdam, located on the upper floor of the West Lounge area (postsecurity), is a good example of a traditional Amsterdam-style "brown café," and the Network bar, on the upper level of the Central Lounge area, is an example of a more modern Internet café.

You'll find a seafood bar serving caviar, oysters, and other delicacies in the South Lounge area near the D gates, and a colorful sandwich bar called the Nautilus Bar serving light meals in the West Lounge area.

For other choices, head out to Schiphol Plaza, where you'll find several 24-hour food outlets, including Delifrance, the Juggle Sandwich Bar, the Juggle Juice Bar, and Burger King.

Best Healthful Nosh

Sandwiches from Sandwich Island on the upper level of the West Lounge area.

Best Sinful Snack

Chocolate, from any of several shops appropriately marked "Chocolate Store."

►Relax and Refresh

To escape the hustle and bustle, head for the upper level of any of the departure lounge areas, which also offer good people-watching perches.

There is no on-site health club, but there is a massage kiosk (Back to Life) in the departure lounge area between Piers E and F. At the Hotel Mercure Schiphol Terminal, located behind customs in the Departure Hall 3 area, you can get a sports massage, take a sauna, or use the shower. Phone: 31-20-604-1339. The hotel also rents single rooms for day use for 90 guilders, or about US$36.

The night rate is 105 guilders, or about US$42. Doubles rent for a bit more.

Other hotels on airport property include the Hilton Amsterdam Airport (31-20-603-4567) and the Sheraton Amsterdam Airport (31-20-316-4300).

If you need the services of a dry cleaner or a hairdresser, head for Schiphol Plaza, the shopping center/transportation hub connected to the airport. You'll also find a shoe repair shop and 1-hour film-developing services.

If gambling is your form of relaxation, you'll be delighted to know there's an airport casino, located in the departure lounge between Piers E and F. Gaming options include roulette, blackjack, and slot machines. You'll need to be over 18 and in possession of a boarding pass to get in.

And if you need a truly quiet spot you can also visit the meditation room on the second floor of the lounge section between Piers E and F.

Take Care of Business

- You'll find Internet terminals on the second floor of the Central Lounge area at the post office and at the Network bar. (Rates at the post office are cheaper.) Otherwise, phones with data ports are scattered throughout the terminal.

There are public fax machines in the West Lounge and South Lounge areas, postsecurity. These are coin-operated machines that accept only Dutch coins. You can also send and receive fax messages at the post office. Banks, currency exchange, and ATM machines are located in the departure lounges (postsecurity) and in Schiphol Plaza.

For more serious business, you'll find a business center, which rents mini-offices by the minute, in the Central Lounge, and workrooms for rent in the business center (on the mezzanine level between the E and F gates) that include a personal computer, telephone, and fax machine. Hours: Monday–Friday, 8:30 AM–5:30 PM. The Hilton Amsterdam Airport and the Sheraton Amsterdam Airport, both on airport property, also have business centers.

Explore the Airport

►Shop

If you're in Schiphol on a layover, you're in luck—Schiphol is reputed to have some of the best duty-free prices in Europe. For non-duty-free shopping, head for Schiphol Plaza—the shopping center connected to the airport, the railway station, and the Sheraton Hotel. The 40 shops here are open from 7 AM until 10 PM and offer everything from books and chocolate to lingerie, leatherwear, toys, and watches. There's also a supermarket here open from 6 AM until 12 midnight.

►Sightsee

Artwork is a delightful and integral part of the Schiphol landscape, from the giant clogs featured in Mark Brusse's piece "I Meet You," in the Arrival Hall 3 area, to Kees Franse's sliced-wood "Apple" in the Departure Hall 3 area. My favorites: a neon piece called "HaHa HiHi" by John Körmeling in the West Lounge area, and Hugo Kaagman's piece "Nice Trip," a Delft-inspired tile wall near the departure lounge area between Piers E and F. Elsewhere in the airport you'll find work by American artists Dale Chihuly, Jenny Holzer, and others.

To get a great view of the airfield activities, head for the Panorama Terrace. Take the elevators or the stairs in the middle of Departure Halls 1 and 2 up to the third level of the terminal. Hours: 9 AM–6 PM; free admission. The Panorama Terrace also features an Astrojet flight simulator. Fee: 5 guilders or about US$2.

►Play Around

Younger kids will enjoy the children's play area (postsecurity in the departure lounge area between Piers E and F), which features climbing structures, a video machine, and a bank of Nintendo games.

Next door to the play area is a baby-care center, complete with cribs, changing areas, and facilities for warming bottles. Baby-care facilities are also available presecurity on the upper floor of the Departure Hall 2 area, near the Touch Down restaurant, and on the upper floor of the Departure Hall 3 area, next to the Color Café.

Older kids will enjoy a visit to the Panorama Terrace between Arrival Halls 1 and 2, where there are not only great views of airplanes and airfield activity, but also an Astrojet flight simulator ride.

Also, be sure to have kids keep an eye out for all the wonderful art scattered around the airport.

Go into Town

A taxi ride to the center of Amsterdam will cost about 60 guilders (about US$24) and take about a half hour, depending on traffic and time of day. You can use your credit card to pay in advance at the Schiphol taxi counter in Schiphol Plaza.

Less expensive options include a 20-minute train ride to Central Station (CS), which costs just 6 guilders (about US$2.40) or the KLM hotel bus service, which stops at a variety of hotels in town. Check with the information desk for details on these services and for the routes of the public buses.

Other Information

If you've exhausted all these activities, try a visit to the Schipholscoop Visitors Center, at Arrival Hall 1, which features information about Schiphol's plans for expansion and general information about the development of the airport. It's free. Hours: 10 AM–5 PM weekdays, 12 noon–5 PM weekends. The folks at the Visitors Center can also point to you toward the Avidome Museum, which contains information about the history of Schiphol and of aviation in general. The museum is about a 10-minute walk from Schiphol Plaza (you'll pass the Sheraton and Hilton hotels and the Trade Center). Admission is 10 guilders, or about US$4.

If your layover is 4 hours or more, store your luggage and take in some Amsterdam sights. You can take the train into town or stop by the Holland Tours Schiphol kiosk and choose a guided minibus tour that can include everything from a tour of a cheese or clog factory to a ride on a canal boat.

Need more information? There are five airport information desks located throughout the airport. Ask for a timetable booklet, which includes a great deal of detailed information about the airport facilities.

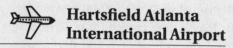

Hartsfield Atlanta International Airport

Atlanta, Georgia
Airport Code: ATL
Web Address: http://www.atlanta-airport.com

Built in 1925 as Candler Field on the site of an abandoned auto racetrack once owned by Coca-Cola magnate Asa Candler, the facility known today as William B. Hartsfield International Airport (ATL) serves more than 79 million passengers a year and recently wrested the title of "World's Busiest Airport" from Chicago's O'Hare International Airport.

No question about it, ATL is big and busy, but thanks to a $250 million makeover inspired by Atlanta's spruce-up for the 1996 Centennial Olympic Games, the facility is fairly easy to navigate and full of amenities.

Get Oriented

- Luggage carts rent for $2.50.
- Storage lockers are located on each concourse, postsecurity.

To get your bearings, pick up a copy of the airport directory from one of the information racks. You'll find that the airport consists of a main terminal and six concourses: T, and A through E. Concourse E serves international flights, the others serve domestic flights. Concourse T is directly connected to the main terminal. Concourses A through E are accessible via an underground "people mover" transportation system.

Atlanta is the hub airport for Delta Air Lines, with most Delta gates bundled in Concourses A and B. All other concourses serve a variety of airlines, with America West, Continental, Northwest, TWA, and US Airways grouped in Concourse D. An underground mall connects the main terminal and the concourses. You can walk, ride the moving sidewalk, or hop on one of the airport's nine automated trains that travel along a 3.5-mile loop.

Time between trains at any of the airport's 13 stations is usually no more than 2 minutes. It's an easy 5-minute walk or ride from the main terminal out to Concourses T, A, and B. If you're heading from the main terminal out to Concourses C, D, or E, however, you'll get there faster on the train: it's a 2.5-mile trek between the main terminal and Concourse E.

Take Care of Yourself

▶ Eat

In the main terminal atrium, you can get a down-home meal with biscuits or barbecue at Paschal's Southern Cuisine, or opt for a more straightforward menu of soups and sandwiches at the Atlanta Bread Company. If you're up for it, there's also a piano bar at Houlihan's.

The centerpoint of Concourse A features Chili's Too, Great Wraps, the Wall Street Deli, and another branch of Paschal's Southern Cuisine. In Concourse B, look for Charley's Steakery, Mo' Better Chicken, and the Magnolia Bar & Grill. Out in Concourse C you can satisfy your sweet tooth at either Ben & Jerry's or Pecan Street Sweets. Best bets in Concourse D are Au Bon Pain or Chili's Bar & Bites, and in Concourse E, it's either something from the food court or potluck from the vending machines.

Best Healthful Nosh

Sandwiches from the Wall Street Deli or a wrap from Great Wraps, both in the Concourse A centerpoint.

Best Sinful Snack

Ben & Jerry's ice cream (in Concourses A and C) or candy from Pecan Street Sweets, in Concourse C.

▶ Relax and Refresh

For true peace and quiet, stop in at the chapel, located on the west side of the main terminal's central atrium, or grab a seat in the three-story atrium itself. Designed as an easily accessible central point where people can meet one another, grab a bite to eat, shop, or relax, the atrium features a 100-seat lounge area, lots of interesting stores, a full-service restaurant, a food court, a full-service shoe repair shop (Heel Quik), and a business center. One frequent traveler reports that while the seating area is lovely, it's often full, so don't bank on getting a spot here. You can also rent a portable DVD player and a movie at InMotion Pictures, located in the main terminal, Concourse A, and Concourse B.

If you need more serious rest or some freshening up, head to the baggage claim area, where you'll find courtesy phones for a variety of nearby hotels. One of the closest, the Renaissance Concourse, has a day rate that includes access to the health club and exercise facilities (404-209-9999).

Smokers will find smoking lounges at Gates T3 and T13, A14 and A23, B7 and B24, C17 and C26, and E8, E15, and E30. For some reason, Concourse D seems to be smoking-lounge-free.

Take Care of Business

- The US Postal Service operates its first and, airport officials claim, only official airport postal store in the southwest corner of the main terminal atrium.

Business travelers rejoice: the Atlanta airport has a wide variety of spots where you can get down to business:

The Executive Conference Center on the third floor of the main terminal atrium has meeting rooms, workstations, fax and copying services, secretarial support, and a notary service (800-713-1359). The Concierge Center, the Cellular Travel Communications shop, and a travel agency (World Travel Partners) are also located in the main terminal and offer faxing and copying services.

In the concourses you'll find business centers, which rent fully equipped offices by the minute, just above the center food court in Concourse A, at Gate 15 in Concourse B, and at the midpoint of Concourse T next to the Delta customer service center. Keep an eye out as well for self-service BTS business centers that provide ATM machines, Internet access kiosks, copy and fax machines, as well as package drop-off points. Many areas in Gates C, D, and E also feature Internet kiosks and phones with data ports.

Explore the Airport

► Shop

In the main terminal atrium, shop for souvenirs of Atlanta's best-known export at the World of Coca-Cola store, or pick up T-shirts, key chains, and other mementos of Atlanta at the City Store. The atrium also features branches of the Body Shop, the Museum Company, Electronics Innovations, and Waterstone's Booksellers. Sports enthusiasts will enjoy the Pro Shop (golf) and the Great Sports shop in nearby Concourse T, which also has a branch of the Disney Store, Genuine Golf, and Bare Escentials (which offers bath products, cosmetics, and aromatherapy products).

In Concourse A you'll find additional branches of the Disney Store, Waterstone's Booksellers, Better Golf, and the Body Shop as well as a Silverworks kiosk showcasing Native American jewelry. Concourse B has branches of Bally, Bath & Body Works, Genuine Golf, the Disney Store, Benjamin Books & Café, and a shop called Magnolia Place, where you can pick up Vidalia onion dressing, candy-coated pecans, peach syrup, and other Southern delicacies.

Concourse C features the Book Corner, another branch of Great Sports, and Erwin Pearl (jewelry), and Concourse D sports branches of Magnolia Place and the Book Corner. In Concourse E you'll find the Georgia International Marketplace, Wilsons Leather, and branches of both The Wall (CDs) and Waterstone's Booksellers.

► Sightsee

While there is some art and several cases filled with historical memorabilia in the main terminal atrium, art lovers will want to make tracks for Concourse E (the international terminal), where more than $1 million was spent on public art. The collection's centerpiece is the 54-foot-tall, 2.5-ton sculptured light installation titled "Ascension in the Millennium," created by a team of Atlanta artists as an interpretation of the mythical phoenix and of Atlanta's rise from post–Civil War ashes. You'll find "Ascension" between the escalators leading to and from the underground transit system.

Concourse E also features permanent artwork by at least 18 Georgia artists, including Craig Nutt's "Corncorde," a 10-foot-long flying ear of corn; David Hubbard's eight "flying machines" made from recycled objects and bits of machinery; and many display cases filled with objects and artifacts from Atlanta-area art institutions, including the High Museum of Art, the Center for Puppetry Arts, the Atlanta History Center, and others.

The best spots to watch airfield activity are the north and south ends of Concourse E and the midsections of other concourses.

►Play Around

Kids enjoy waiting for the atrium clock tower to chime, riding on the people mover, or searching for the art exhibits in Concourse E, especially the figures from Atlanta's Center for Puppetry Arts museum that represent twentieth-century puppetry in China, Indonesia, Germany, Egypt, the former USSR, and the United States.

Go into Town

The 10-mile cab ride to downtown Atlanta takes about 20 minutes and costs $18. A bus or shared shuttle van ride takes a bit longer but costs only $12. For a faster and cheaper ride to town, try the subway. The Metropolitan Atlanta Rapid Transit Authority (MARTA) subway station is located inside the airport terminal, at the west end, near other ground transportation services. MARTA trains arrive at and depart from the airport every 8 minutes. The ride downtown costs $1.50 and takes about 30 minutes.

Other Information

For general information about the airport before you arrive, call the airport concierge at 404-768-4100.

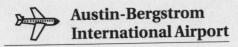

Austin-Bergstrom International Airport

Austin, Texas
Airport Code: AUS
Web Address: http://www.ci.austin.tx.us/newairport

The decommissioning of an air force base is usually an economic hardship for the local community. Not for Austin: when Congress closed Bergstrom Air Force Base, city officials realized they could finally replace an inadequate in-city airport with something much bigger and better on the outskirts of town.

The new Austin-Bergstrom International Airport (AUS) opened in May 1999 with a bright, airy passenger terminal named for the late Barbara Jordan, the three-time congresswoman from Houston who was the first black woman elected to the Texas senate. The terminal features a great deal of Texas-made artwork, a wide variety of Texas-flavored restaurants and shops, and a live-music stage that showcases the work of Austin musicians. Even the piped-in music heard throughout the airport is a specially commissioned Austin mix.

Get Oriented

- Luggage carts rent for $2. A $.25 "reward" is given when you return a cart to the rack.
- There are no lockers at the airport, nor is there any baggage check service.

Austin-Bergstrom has only one terminal with 25 gates laid out in a logical line. Southwest and American Airlines use the center gates (7–19), and all other airlines are clustered on either side. It should take you no longer than 10 minutes to walk from one end of the terminal to the other, providing you don't get sidetracked by one of the enticing shops.

Take Care of Yourself

►Eat

Most airport restaurants are branches of well-known Austin eateries, so browse carefully before making your decision. In the west food court, look for Amy's Ice Cream, the Salt Lick (BBQ), Schlotzsky's Deli, and Matt's Famous El Rancho, which serves enchiladas, quesadillas, and traditional Mexican breakfasts. Word has it that the original Matt's was a favorite of the late President Lyndon Johnson. The west concourse also features a coffee bar in a newsstand named www.news.austin and the Hill Country Bar, which serves Texas-made wines and beers.

The east food court boasts the Armadillo Café & Cantina, Harlon's BBQ, and Wok & Roll. The Highland Lakes Bar in the Central Marketplace features live entertainment on Thursdays and Fridays.

Best Healthful Nosh

Salads and sandwiches from Schlotzsky's Deli in the west food court.

Best Sinful Snack

Any flavor from Amy's Ice Cream in the west food court.

►Relax and Refresh

A good spot to escape the airport hustle and bustle is the seating area in the west concourse next to the Sister Cities exhibit or at the gate areas at the far ends of the terminal. If you'd rather be in the thick of it all and perhaps hear some live music, grab a spot in or next to the Highland Lakes Bar in the Central Marketplace. Live music ranging from jazz and pop to mariachi and marimba is presented on Thursday and Friday afternoons. On the fourth Sunday of each month, there's a "Jazz Brunch" that runs from 10 AM until 1 PM.

If you—or your pet—need a breath of fresh air, visit the landscaped dog-walk area, just outside of the baggage claim area. Drinking fountains are set at both pet and people height and there are complimentary plastic "poop-scoop" bags.

The Hilton Austin Airport offers travelers a day rate and is located on airport property in the former administration building and officers' headquarters for Bergstrom Air Force Base (512-385-6767). The nearby La Quinta Austin Airport Inn and Suites also offers a day rate and has both a pool and fitness center (512-386-6800).

Sorry, smokers. The airport is entirely smoke-free. You can light up outside the terminal, but you must be at least 15 feet from the doors.

Take Care of Business

- Many public telephones have data ports, and Austin-Bergstrom is the first airport to be set up for wireless Internet access. A two-level business center is located across from the Southwest Airlines ticket counter, at the east end of the terminal building. Head here for computer station rentals, Internet access, currency exchange, language translation, video-conferencing, and assorted other services. You can also buy office supplies and lottery tickets here. Hours: 5 AM–10 PM, daily.

Both American and Continental Airlines have club lounges here and will let nonmembers use their facilities for a fee ranging from $35 to $55.

Explore the Airport

►Shop

Like the restaurants, retail outlets at Austin-Bergstrom International Airport offer many local items. Austin City Limits offers CDs, tapes, and souvenirs from the well-known PBS TV program of the same name. Stars of Texas, Blue Bonnets, Austin Attitudes, Austin Artifacts, and the Austin Market offer Austin- and Texas-inspired clothing, artwork, food items, and souvenirs. Look for wildflower-emblazoned stationery, chili-pepper dishware, Dallas Cowboys memorabilia, and boxes of Armadillo Droppings—good candy with a funny name.

Golfers will enjoy the cozy Tour Golf Club, and travelers of all stripes will be delighted with the travel accessories, books, games, and travel information provided by the Travelfest shop.

► **Sightsee**

Practically everywhere you look at Austin-Bergstrom International, you'll find a piece of art, a historical display, or an exhibit relating to an educational resource in the city. My favorites include the "big hair" and cowboy hat etchings on the mirrors in the baggage claim area restrooms and the maps of Texas rivers and Austin circa 1839 imbedded in the floor of the baggage claim area.

A complete list of all the artwork commissioned as part of the airport's construction is included in the airport "Visitor Guide." Just be sure you don't miss the ceramic tiles in the concourse restrooms, the series of paintings above the west ticket counters, and the exhibit case that bridges the back wall of the two bookstores.

In addition to all the artwork, take notice of the displays in the pylons along the concourse. Each acts as a mini-museum, showcasing the highlights of a local cultural, educational, or historical facility. Of particular interest is the pylon describing how one of Austin's downtown bridges became home to millions of bats. (Turns out that's a good thing!)

You can get a great view of airfield activity from most any spot by the gate waiting areas, but note that Gate 2 faces the left runway and Gate 25 faces the right runway.

► **Play Around**

While there's no official kids' play area, there's plenty here to keep kids entertained. In the baggage claim area, for example, kids can learn geography by walking along the maps imbedded in the floor. Also, the mirrors in the baggage claim area bathrooms feature etchings of cowboy hats (men's room) and "big hair" (women's room), so kids can try on some new looks.

On the concourse level, a series of cast-metal medallions above the drinking fountains "discuss" the Texas mystique in humorous ways, while 10 pylons feature exhibits highlighting Austin-area cultural organizations ranging from the Austin Children's Museum to the work of Bat Conservation International.

Kids might also enjoy visiting the Austin Sister Cities display, at the west end of the concourse level, which features cultural artifacts from Austin's eight Sister Cities in Australia, Germany, Peru, Lesotho, Japan, Mexico, Taiwan, and Honduras.

Go into Town

The 15-minute cab ride to downtown Austin will cost about $13. A shuttle van makes the 8-mile trip for about $8. The city bus (Capital Metro) serves the airport with routes 46 and 100. The fare is $.50. The bus stop is located on the upper concourse level on the island at the eastern side of the terminal. For schedule information, stop by the Visitors Center information desk on the baggage claim level.

Other Information

In addition to the great art, good food, and interesting shopping, Austin-Bergstrom International Airport has another plus: it's the first Texas airport (and the fourth in the United States) to install Public Access Automatic External Defibrillators (AEDs). Eight publicly accessible, battery-operated devices are located on the concourse level and in the baggage claim area.

Austin-Bergstrom International Airport also has an "Airport Ambassador Program," which features red-vested folks who roam the airport greeting travelers and helping them find their way. If you need information before you arrive, call 512-530-2242 during business hours.

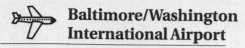

Baltimore/Washington International Airport

Baltimore, Maryland
Airport Code: BWI
Web Address: http://www.bwiairport.com

When President Harry S. Truman dedicated this airport, back in June 1950, it was called Friendship International Airport. The name changed to Baltimore/Washington International Airport (BWI) in 1973, "not because we weren't friendly anymore," an airport official is quick to explain, "we just wanted to make it clear that we were determined to serve both the Baltimore and Washington communities."

BWI is still a friendly place, with historical displays and interactive exhibits scattered throughout the terminal and an award-winning garden, complete with a flock of flying metal geese, tucked in between the main terminal and the parking garage.

Get Oriented

- Luggage carts rent for $2.
- Lockers are located on Piers A, B, C, and D, postsecurity.

BWI's layout includes one main terminal building and five concourses, called "piers," laid out in a straightforward manner. The few gates in Pier A are used by United, and Pier B is used mostly by Southwest Airlines. Pier C services American, America West, Continental, Delta, Frontier, Northwest, and Southwest. US Airways and TWA are the major airlines over in Pier D, and Pier E is reserved for international flights.

It will take just a few minutes to walk from one pier to the next, but it can take up to 10 minutes to walk from Pier A (the southernmost pier) to Pier E (the northernmost pier).

Take Care of Yourself

► **Eat**

Top picks for sit-down meals at BWI are CK's Restaurant (between Piers B and C) and the Wild Goose Ale House (at the top of Pier B), where the specialties include crab cakes, crab soup, Chesapeake-style gumbo, and locally brewed beers. To combine eating with a great view of the airfield, head to the Flight Deck Café on the upper level of the Observation Gallery. There are also numerous fast-food outlets and snack vendors throughout the terminal and on Piers D, C, and B.

Best Healthful Nosh

Salads at CK's or the City Deli (between Piers B and C) or a fruitshake from Flying Fruit Fantasy, near the City Deli.

Best Sinful Snack

Ice cream from Flying Fruit Fantasy (between Piers B and C).

► **Relax and Refresh**

BWI's Observation Gallery (located between Piers B and C) is a two-story airport oasis. If the downstairs children's play area is too noisy, head upstairs and grab a seat on one of the couches arranged along the 147-foot-long window that overlooks three intersecting runways.

Other spots to help avoid the hustle and bustle include the meditation room just before the entrance to Pier E (hours: 6:30 AM–10:30 PM daily); the sunken "Garden Court," outside the security checkpoint for the E gates; and a spot off the connecting corridor just past the restaurants on your way to Pier D.

The USO operates a lounge on the lower level of the terminal between Piers E and D where military travelers can get free coffee, store their luggage, watch TV, read, or, for a small fee, rent a recliner in a "quiet room."

There are no barbershops or massage kiosks at BWI, but if you need to nap or freshen up the Sheraton International Hotel is on airport property (410-859-3300) and offers a day rate for those who check in after 9 AM and are out by 5 PM. Other nearby hotels are listed in the airport guide brochure (available from the information booths in the main terminal) and in the baggage claim areas.

If it's a nice day, go outside: between the main terminal and the parking garage you'll find the award-winning Chesapeake Garden. Designed to reflect an Eastern Shore wetlands area, the garden features ornamental grasses, flowers—including Maryland's state flower, the black-eyed Susan—and a flock of 150 flying metal geese.

Smokers are welcome in CK's Lounge (between Piers B and C), in the Oriole Lounge (at the top of Pier D), and in the Wild Goose Ale House (at the top of Pier B).

Take Care of Business

- A business center is scheduled to open in the international terminal.
- Data phones are located throughout the terminal.

BWI operates a "Friendship Center" between Piers C and D on the upper level of the terminal where a $10 fee gets you access to a cash bar, TV, a small lounge, restrooms, phones, data ports, and a meeting room.

If you need to send a fax, make copies, or rent a workstation with Internet access, stop at one of the Travelex (Mutual of Omaha) business centers located at the top of Piers C and E. There are also Internet kiosks at the entrance to Pier B and in Piers C and E.

Explore the Airport

►Shop

If you left your souvenir shopping for the airport, you're in luck: each of the Celebrate Maryland shops (by the lower level of the Observation Gallery and in Piers C, D, and E) carries crab cakes, seasonings, crab-oriented cookbooks, kitchenware, and clothing, along with all manner of Chesapeake Bay paraphernalia. Crab and Chesapeake Bay souvenirs are also available at the

Market Walk (also by the Observation Gallery lower level), where I found Utz Crab Chips, a potato chip with—you guessed it—crab seasonings.

The Book Corner has two locations at BWI: near the top of Pier B not far from the Bon Voyage Travel Store and in Pier D. You'll find a toy store called Just Plane Kids between Piers C and B, and branches of the Body Shop and the Museum Store in Pier D. In Pier C (by Gate 12) you'll find all manner of caps at Lids.

►Sightsee

The upper level of the Observation Gallery, located in the ticketing concourse between Piers B and C, has several interactive exhibits highlighting air travel, weather, takeoff and landing, and air control. Time will "fly" as you monitor weather conditions at airports around the country, sit in a flight simulator and try to navigate a landing, or follow planes on the exact same radar system used by the FAA.

The Observation Gallery also features a disassembled Boeing 737-200 airplane, offering a close-up look at assorted plane parts, including the nose cone, cockpit, landing gear, fuselage section, wing, and a vertical stabilizer.

Want to learn more? Head over to the upper level of Pier E (the international pier), which features a 170-foot-long, 28-foot-high photo timeline of Maryland's aviation and space history, from the first balloon flight over Baltimore to NASA's Goddard Space Flight Center's involvement in space exploration.

On the Pier E lower level, you'll find the Freedom Shrine, which features copies of many important documents in American history, including the Declaration of Independence, the US Constitution, the Bill of Rights, and the Gettysburg Address.

The best spot to see takeoffs and landings is from the upper level of the Observation Gallery, which features a 147-foot-long window overlooking three intersecting runways.

►Play Around

Younger kids will enjoy the play area on the lower level of the Observation Gallery (between Piers B and C), which features a

51-foot-long porcelain mural offering a bird's-eye view of the world and a carpeted play area with a make-believe airplane, baggage cart, fuel truck, and tug. Plans are in the works to expand this space further and make the play area more interactive.

Older kids will enjoy the hands-on interactive aviation exhibits and disassembled airplane parts on the upper level of the Observation Gallery, the aviation time line at the entrance to Pier E, and the game room near the entrance to Pier D.

Go into Town

A cab ride to downtown Baltimore will cost about $18 and take 10–15 minutes. A cab ride to Washington, DC, will cost $55 and take about an hour. Shared van service to downtown Baltimore and other areas is offered by Supershuttle (800-258-3826), but BWI is also served by MTA light rail service, which will take you downtown for $1.35. For the schedule call: 410-539-5000.

Both MARC and Amtrak trains stop at BWI's rail station. MARC riders pay $5 to go to Union Station in Washington, DC, while Amtrak riders pay $16 for the same ride. Be sure to check the schedules: MARC operates weekdays only, while Amtrak operates daily but with less frequent service. A free BWI shuttle bus services both rail stations. (MARC: 800-325-RAIL, or 800-325-7245; Amtrak: 800-USA-RAIL, or 800-872-7245.)

Other Information

The Tom Dixon Aircraft Observation Area is located at the end of one of BWI's main runways and features picnic tables, drinking fountains, a tot-lot, and aircraft descriptions. This observation area is a popular access point for the 12.5-mile BWI Trail, which runs around the perimeter of the airport. To get there, ask one of the folks at a BWI information booth for directions.

If you need additional information about BWI you can call ahead: 800-I-FLY-BWI (800-435-9294). Or ask at one of the on-site information booths for a copy of the "Terminal Map and Guide."

Logan International Airport

Boston, Massachusetts
Airport Code: BOS
Web Address: http://www.massport.com/logan

Boston Airport, as this site was originally known, began operations in 1923 as nothing more than a mail stop and a home base for small planes. In 1944 the airfield was dubbed Commonwealth Airport, but in 1952 it was renamed Logan International Airport (BOS) in honor of General Edward Lawrence Logan, a Harvard Law School graduate who served in the Massachusetts House and Senate and as a municipal court judge.

Get Oriented

- Luggage carts rent for $1.50. You'll receive a $.25 refund when you return a cart to the rack.
- Lockers are located in Terminals A, B, C, and E, postsecurity.

Logan has five passenger terminals (A, B, C, D, and E) laid out in a horseshoe pattern, each serving a variety of airlines. Terminal A serves Continental, the Delta Shuttle, Midwest Express, Frontier, and Cape Air. In Terminal B you'll find service for America West, American, MetroJet, Midway, and US Airways. Terminal C services TWA, Delta, and United, and Terminal D serves AirTran, Alitalia, and charter flights. Terminal E serves all Northwest Airlines flights and international arrivals. Shuttle buses run on a continuous loop between the terminals and can usually get you from one terminal to another in about 10 minutes.

Logan is in the midst of a major modernization program, so while the recently completed parking garage now connects to the terminals via skybridges, there is still quite a bit of construction (and detours) to come.

To get your bearings ask an "Airport Ambassador" for a map or stop at one of the information booths located on the ground level of Terminals A, B, C, and E. The booths are staffed 7:30 AM–11:00 PM.

Take Care of Yourself

►Eat

Legal Sea Foods, a popular local chain, has a full-service restaurant in Terminal C, a café in Terminal B, and express branches in Terminals A and C. Bella Boston is located in Terminal B. After sampling the local seafood, you can move on to local and regional beers. You'll find Killian's Boston Pub in Terminal B, Sam Adams Brewhouse in Terminal C, Shipyard Brew Port Restaurant in Terminal E, and branches of the made-famous-by-TV Cheers Bar & Grill in Terminals A and B.

In addition to the Legal Sea Foods Express, Terminal A has a food court (Bean Town) featuring the Bean Town Deli, and a variety of fast-food outlets. Terminal B sports a branch of Au Bon Pain (which is also in Terminals C and E), the Boston Deli, and Sbarro's (which is also in Terminal E). Terminal C has the main Legal Sea Foods Restaurant, Baldini's, Last Minute Eats, Samuel Adams Brewhouse, and Taste of Boston Deli. Over in Terminal E, you'll find a Campbell's soup kiosk, Arigato Sushi, and the Portside Bar & Café.

Best Healthful Nosh

Fresh seafood (or raw clams) from the Legal Sea Foods raw bar in Terminal A or C.

Best Sinful Snack

Chocolates from the candy store (Truffles) in Terminal C.

►Relax and Refresh

For a truly quiet spot, head for the Our Lady of the Airways Chapel, which opened in 1952 as the first airport chapel in the country. It's located just off the walkway between Terminals B and C and is open from 7 AM to 11 PM daily. Terminal C has a big open central area that's usually quite busy but is also a good place to grab a seat and watch other travelers rush by.

For a little professional help, stop at Classique Hair & Nail Salon on the departure level of Terminal C or Nailport (in Terminal A on the departure level and in Terminal E), which offers manicures and pedicures. Or stop at the massage kiosk (A Relaxed Attitude) located on the upper level of Terminal A.

If you need to nap or want a workout, head over to the brand-new Hilton Boston Logan Airport Hotel, directly accessible from both Terminals A and E. Ask about a day rate if you'd like to catch a few hours of sleep, or pay just $15 and get access to the hotel's health club, pool, whirlpool, and showers (617-569-9300). The Hyatt Harborside Conference Center & Hotel (617-568-1234) is also on airport property. They offer day rates for rooms and make their health club and pool facilities available for guests checking in on a day rate.

Smokers can light up in designated curbside smoking areas.

Take Care of Business

- All airport pay phones have data ports and there are fax machines on the lower level of each terminal.

There are Internet kiosks in Terminals A, C, D, and E and a FleetBoston Full-Service Bank branch in Terminal D. Terminal A has a communications center where you can send faxes and take care of e-mail. Staples, the office supply store in the Terminal C "Boston Landing" shopping area, offers faxing, photocopying, and cell-phone battery recharging services as well.

Full-service business centers are at the Hilton Boston Logan Airport Hotel, which is connected to Terminals A and E by moving walkways, and at the Hyatt Harborside Conference Center & Hotel, which is also on airport property and accessible by shuttle.

Explore the Airport

►Shop

Street pricing is in effect at Logan, which means prices here should be comparable to prices downtown. Head first for Termi-

nal C (the "showcase terminal"), where you'll find Boston Landing: 14 specialty stores and kiosks. Highlights include: Brookstone, Waldenbooks, Lids, Staples, the Museum Company store,
the Children's Museum store, a PGA Tour shop, Travel 2000, and a
shop called Touch of New England.

Over in Terminal A you'll find Benjamin Books and a variety of
newsstands and gift shops. In Terminal B, look for AltiTunes (CDs
and small electronics), Boston Marketplace, and Anthony's Pier 4
Lobsters. If a box of live lobsters in the overhead bin doesn't ap-
peal to you, you can opt for frozen Boston clam chowder from the
Legal Sea Foods restaurants.

► **Sightsee**

Artwork at Logan is part of Artport, the airport's public art
program. As part of each construction project, new pieces are
added, so be sure to stop by a terminal information booth for directions and updates on what's where.

For now, Terminal C has two giant mirrored-wall sculptures
by James Seawright (on the north and south walls of the terminal)
that fragment and reflect the image of each passerby. There's also
a ceiling sculpture by Susumu Shingu that moves gently with the
air patterns in the terminal and a pair of nine-foot glass cubes
created by George Rhoads that contain Rube Goldberg–type devices that send lacrosse balls careening through an entertaining
maze of chutes, jumps, and bridges. Kids love this!

If you're traveling on the elevated walkway that connects Terminals A and E with the central parking garage, you might notice
lots of folks looking down. They're not all incredibly shy—they're
probably looking at the underwater images Jane Goldman embedded in the terrazzo floors to celebrate New England's rich
marine history. Look carefully and you'll see everything from
seashells to deep-sea creatures.

For a historical perspective on the airport, spend a few minutes with two exhibits that trace the history of air travel in New
England and the growth of Boston's airport. One exhibit is in the
walkway between Terminals B and C, the other in the new parking
garage on the fourth-level walkway heading toward Terminal E.

If you've got a bit more time before your flight, take the free shuttle bus (on the lower levels of all terminals) to the water shuttle dock (see "Go into Town"). Inside the pavilion there's a set of twelve paintings by Mela Lyman ("Transported") which feature scenes of water and swimmers. Outside the pavilion, there's a steel wind sculpture with wind wheels, vanes, and cups. Walk along the waterfront path and you'll find Carlos Dorrien's 30-ton sculpture, consisting of a granite portal and three granite slabs with carved images centering on East Boston's immigration, trade, and maritime history.

You'll be able to get good views of the airfield from the top of the Terminal B garage, the Terminal C food court, and the glass walkway between Concourses B and C. The Kidport play area in Terminal C not only offers a great view but has helpful signs along the window ledge that help identify the various personnel and pieces of equipment out on the tarmac. To get a view of the city, head for the elevated walkways that connect Terminals A and E to the Central Parking Garage.

►Play Around

Logan has two Kidport play areas, located in Terminals A and C in the departure level of the main terminal area.

The one in Terminal C is larger than the one in Terminal A and is attached to the Boston Children's Museum shop. At the Terminal C Kidport you'll find a baggage slide, a toddler playspace, an interactive cockpit, and a good view of the airfield. Kids will also enjoy watching balls make their way through the wacky intricate metal sculptures in Terminal C.

Go into Town

- The folks at the concierge-style information booth on the lower level of Terminal C can help you make dinner, theater, concert, or hotel reservations before you leave the airport.

A cab ride to downtown Boston will cost you $15–$20 and might take anywhere from 20 minutes to more than an hour, depending on traffic and time of day. If you're headed downtown to Boston's financial district you can take an airport water shuttle. The 7-minute trip from Logan to Boston's Rowes Wharf will cost you $10 each way. The service runs weekdays, every 15 minutes, from 6 AM to 8 PM; and on Friday and Saturday nights the hours are extended to 11 PM. Saturday and Sunday departures are every 30 minutes. There are also "on-call" water taxis from Logan Dock to 11 wharves throughout Boston Harbor. Pay your fare on board.

Six different private bus companies provide service between Logan Airport and South Station. The buses depart Logan every 15–30 minutes from the lower-level terminal curbs. Fares run about $7–$9.

At $.85, the "T" (what locals call Boston's subway transit system) is a bargain. Shuttle buses take you to the airport's Blue Line Station stop where trains to downtown Boston and other points leave every 7 minutes. Hours: 5:30 AM–1:00 AM. Public buses also run from the airport to Boston's South Station. The CT3 bus runs every 20 minutes and stops at the lower-level curbs of Terminals A and E and on the upper levels of Terminals B and C.

Other Information

If you need more information about the airport before you arrive, call 800-23-LOGAN (800-235-6426).

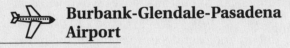

Burbank-Glendale-Pasadena Airport

Burbank, California
Airport Code: BUR
Web Address: http://www.burbankairport.com

In the 1930s and 1940s, the Burbank-Glendale-Pasadena Airport was the primary passenger air terminal for Los Angeles. It was a glamorous place, too, where early aviation stars such as Amelia Earhart and Charles Lindbergh were likely to drop in.

Then, during World War II, the airport sort of disappeared: the entire field was camouflaged and used by Lockheed to produce B-17 bombers, P-38 fighters, and Hudson bombers while the terminal continued to serve civilian passengers.

Today, freeways, commuter rail lines, and maps on the Internet make it easy to find the airport, but the majority of travelers bound for the Los Angeles area head instead for bustling LAX. Still, more than 5 million savvy travelers each year choose the Burbank Airport (BUR) because it's low-key, uncrowded, and just 13 miles from downtown Los Angeles.

Get Oriented

- Luggage carts rent for $2. You'll receive a $.25 refund when you return a cart to the rack.
- There are no storage lockers at the airport.

Burbank Airport is a single building with two wings, or terminals. United and Alaska Airlines use Terminal B; Southwest, American, and America West use Terminal A. It should take you no longer than 3 minutes to get from one end of the airport to the other.

Take Care of Yourself

►**Eat**

The airport's single sit-down restaurant is called Air Hollywood Bar & Grill, a comfortable venue that serves breakfast, lunch, and dinner. Airport personnel recommend the Cobb salad, the Chinese chicken salad, and the wraps.

There are also snack bars and lounges in each terminal. No Starbucks outlets here, but the restaurant and snack bars make coffee and espresso drinks with Wolfgang Puck's special blend.

Best Healthful Nosh

Barbecue chicken salad, served at Air Hollywood in the central terminal area.

Best Sinful Snack

Dark chocolate cake à la mode, also served at Air Hollywood.

►**Relax and Refresh**

The best place to relax is on the outdoor patio between the main terminal area and the United Air Lines gates in Terminal B. If you enjoy golf, stop by the PGA Tour Shop in the airport's central area and take a few practice swings on the putting green.

To freshen up, stop by the unisex barbershop at the main entrance to the terminal.

Sorry, smokers, no smoking is allowed anywhere in the terminal.

Take Care of Business

There are no phones with data ports, nor any place at this airport to make a copy or send a fax. Your airline membership cards won't do you any good here either, because there are no clubrooms.

Explore the Airport

►**Shop**

There are limited shopping opportunities at Burbank Airport: just a PGA Tour Shop and a couple of news-and-gifts shops that specialize in Hollywood-related souvenirs, everything from Beverly Hills shot glasses to statuettes declaring your best friend this year's "Best Actress."

►Sightsee

During the 1930s, Amelia Earhart lived in nearby North Hollywood and came by Burbank often to test and repair planes she purchased from Lockheed. Other early visitors included Charles Lindbergh, Wiley Post (who made the first solo flight around the world), and aerospace tycoon Howard Hughes. Photos and memorabilia relating to these and other noted guests are in display cases in the Terminal A corridor, just before the security checkpoint. Exhibit cases in Terminal A also display scale-model airplanes from the airport's collection.

In Terminal B, you'll find photos of the airport between 1942 and 1945, when the facility was hidden from aerial view under acres of canvas and chicken wire painted to resemble grain fields, sunflowers, roads, and houses. The folks at Disney Studios helped with this transformation, teaching airport personnel the art of camouflage and helping to build "houses" out of plywood and burlap. The trees and bushes? They were made out of wire with green spray-painted chicken feathers glued to the branches. To complete the disguise, workers even moved pretend cars around pretend streets every few days and, each Monday, workers hung real clothes out on clotheslines.

These days airport decorations are a bit more up front. On the walls along the corridor in Terminal A you'll see life-size color cutouts of film and TV stars, including Jerry Seinfeld, the guys and gals from *Friends,* Jay Leno, and others. Ask a passerby to snap a shot of you and a celebrity—or hang around and snap photos for others. And keep an eye out for the real thing: many celebrities avoid the hustle and bustle of LAX and catch flights out of Burbank Airport.

If you'd rather spend your time spotting jets, grab a seat pretty much anywhere in Terminal A and you'll get a good view of airfield activity. The best views of the airfield, however, are from the top floor of the airport parking structure.

► **Play Around**

Southwest Airlines has a small play area for kids in Terminal A. Kids might also enjoy looking at the historic photographs, model airplanes, and memorabilia displays in the Terminal A corridors or taking a trek up to the top of the parking structure to get a bird's-eye view of the airfield.

Go into Town

A cab ride to downtown Burbank will cost about $10 and take just a few minutes. The 13-mile cab ride to downtown Los Angeles, however, will cost between $30 and $40 and take anywhere from 20 to 30 minutes. A shared shuttle ride to downtown Los Angeles will cost between $12 and $15.

This is also one of the few airports in the country with its own Amtrak/commuter rail stop: the Burbank Airport Rail Stop is at the south end of the airport, about a quarter mile from the terminal. It's an easy walk if you don't have much luggage, but if you need a lift, the airport provides a courtesy shuttle.

The airport is located near major bus lines, but buses do not come directly to the terminal.

Other Information

To get additional information about the airport before you arrive, call 818-840-8840.

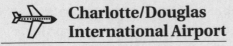# Charlotte/Douglas International Airport

Charlotte, North Carolina
Airport Code: CLT
Web Address: http://www.charlotteairport.com

One of Charlotte's early airfields doubled as the polo grounds. Another, near the site of the present-day airport, featured weekend air shows filled with daredevil aerial feats by former war pilots, barnstormers, and stunt pilots. Today, a tamer but much busier Charlotte/Douglas International Airport (CLT), named in honor of Mayor Ben E. Douglas Sr., is US Airways' largest hub and serves more than 23 million passengers a year.

Get Oriented

- Luggage carts rent for $1.50. You'll get a $.25 refund when you return a cart to the rack.
- Lockers are located in the terminal and in each concourse.

Charlotte/Douglas International Airport has one terminal with four concourses (A, B, C, and D). Construction of a new concourse and expansion of two others began in summer 2000, and, for a while, will disrupt traffic flow for travelers using the airport's commuter services.

For right now, Concourse A serves Delta, United, American, TWA, Northwest, Continental, and Air Canada, and Concourses B and C serve US Airways. Concourse D serves all international flights (US Airways and British Airways) and all commuter flights through US Airways Express.

It's approximately a 10-minute walk from one concourse to another, and all concourse entrances are centrally located around the airport's atrium, which has restaurants, lounges, and shops.

Take Care of Yourself

► Eat

In the main atrium, you'll get table service at Chili's Bar & Bites and at the Cheers Bar & Restaurant. For something a bit more "racy," pull into the Stock Car restaurant in Concourse B, where you'll find NASCAR racing décor and a souvenir stand offering hats, T-shirts, and all sorts of NASCAR collectibles. Down in Concourse C, A Taste of Carolina serves locally brewed beer.

Best Healthful Nosh

Fresh fruit or healthy sub sandwiches at Miami Subs, or salads from the Chili's restaurant, both in the atrium.

Best Sinful Snack

Hot chocolate-chip cookies from Mrs. Fields Cookies or candy from Candy Express, both in the atrium.

► Relax and Refresh

The white rocking chairs in the atrium were originally part of a "Porch Sitting" art exhibition. Travelers so loved the chance to rock away traveling-tension that the rockers are now a permanent airport feature. In fact, if you'd like one of these rocking chairs to take home, airport officials will put you in touch with the North Carolina shop that makes them.

"Official" entertainment centers around the piano in the middle of the atrium each Thursday and Friday evening from 3 PM until 7 or 8 PM, but if you're in the mood to tickle the ivories any other time—go right ahead! In fact, until recently, two baggage handlers used to spend their lunch hours playing jazz duets on this piano. Gifford Cordorva and Vernon Smith became so popular that they recorded a CD (on sale in the airport gift shops) and, under the name Ten2Ten, joined Lou Rawls on tour.

If music isn't your bag and you'd rather be outside, head down to the baggage claim area and outside to the Queen's Courtyard, located between two of the airport's parking structures. Here you'll find a series of historical markers, benches, grassy areas, a fountain, and the 15-foot-tall bronze Queen Charlotte sculpture by Raymond Kaskey.

The Quiet Zone, located under the staircase in the atrium and behind the First in Flight lounge, is a great place to take a nap, read a book, or get some work done. Or for true peace and quiet, head for the chapel (meditation room) just outside the Concourse B security checkpoint.

Charlotte/Douglas International Airport has no on-site health clubs or hotels. However, there's a barbershop operating on the baggage claim level; a "nail technician" stationed at the dry cleaners (The Valet) in the Concourse D connector; and massage therapists on duty some weekday afternoons at the Body Shop in the atrium, near Concourse C.

For more serious freshening up, ask for a day rate at one of the nearby hotels. The Sheraton Airport Plaza Hotel (704-392-1200), for example, has a day rate that entitles you to use the pool, hot tub, and exercise facilities.

Smokers will either need to head outdoors to light up or patronize one of the restaurants or bars that feature a smoking section.

Take Care of Business

- Phone banks with data ports and self-service fax machines are located on all concourses.

US Airways and British Airways both have clubrooms here. The US Airways Club/Business Center is located next to the atrium between Concourses C and D. You don't need to be a member to use the business center here (or at any of their clubs) but you'll have to pay a $50 day fee. US Airways clubrooms are also located in Concourse B and by the international gates in Concourse D.

Non–club members will find data ports, self-serve fax machines, and comfortable seating areas in the main atrium "Quiet Zone." If you need to take care of banking or mail a letter, you'll find a full-service branch of the First Citizens Bank in the ticketing lobby of the main terminal, ATMs in the atrium near Concourse A, and stamp machines in the Concourse D connector.

Explore the Airport

►Shop

Shopping highlights include Simply Books (in the atrium), Erwin Pearl (jewelry), and Bernard's (clothing) next door to each other at the beginning of Concourse C, and The Gathering (at Gate B4), which offers upscale gifts, gift baskets, cigars, hot sauces, souvenir-sized lighthouses, and other North Carolina–themed items.

►Sightsee

In the center of the main atrium you'll encounter a piece of artwork titled "First in Flight" hanging, appropriately enough, over the First in Flight bar. The whimsical kinetic sculpture by artist George Greenamyer incorporates gears, model airplanes, mythological images, a clock, and even a paper airplane made out of the letter commissioning the artwork.

Out in the Queen's Courtyard (accessible via the baggage claim level) you'll find Raymond Kaskey's 15-foot-tall bronze sculpture of Queen Charlotte and a series of historical markers containing information about the airport, the region, local transportation, the North Carolina gold rush, the Mecklenburg Declaration of Independence, and Queen Charlotte, the namesake for the county and the county seat.

The atrium provides great views of airfield activity, while the end of Concourse D offers good views of the city.

►Play Around

Kids will enjoy picking out all the whimsical elements in the "First in Flight" sculpture in the main atrium and, depending on the current show, inspecting the art-filled boxes scattered around the atrium and other spots throughout the airport. If you've got a layover of more than 2 hours, ask the folks at the information booth (on the ticketing level) or the Welcome Center (on the baggage claim level) for directions to the nearby Carolinas Aviation Museum. Admission: $2.

The Mindwork store, in the Concourse C connector, offers a

wide range of educational toys and projects. Or just give in and take the kids to the Disney Store and/or the Candy Express shop in the atrium, on the way to Concourse D.

Go into Town

Charlotte/Douglas International Airport is located seven miles from uptown Charlotte. There are set fees for cab rides to a variety of areas around the city, but a ride to the city center will cost about $20 and take anywhere from 15 to 25 minutes.

A shuttle ride (Carolina Transportation Airport Express: 704-359-9600) to the uptown area will cost $8. Public buses (fare: $1) run to and from downtown once an hour.

Other Information

You can call ahead to the airport's multilingual 24-hour recorded information line at 704-359-4910, or call the folks at the Airport Welcome Center at 704-359-4027. The information counter is located on the ticketing level and is open daily from 7 AM to 9 PM. Their number is 704-359-4013.

 **Chicago O'Hare International Airport**

Chicago, Illinois
Airport Code: ORD
Web Address: http://www.ohare.com

This bustling air traffic hub, which just recently lost the title of "World's Busiest Airport" to Atlanta's Hartsfield International Airport, was originally called Orchard Place and was home to a giant wooden-roofed factory producing Douglas C-54 troop and cargo carriers for use during World War II. Renamed O'Hare International Airport (ORD) in 1949 to honor Lieutenant Commander Edward H. "Butch" O'Hare, a Chicagoan killed during the war, the facility remains true to its roots by retaining "ORD" as its official abbreviation.

Get Oriented

- Luggage carts can be rented for $1.25 throughout the terminals.
- Storage lockers were recently removed from all terminals.

Today, O'Hare has four terminals: Terminals 1, 2, and 3 primarily serve domestic flights, and Terminal 5 hosts international flights. United and United Express use Terminals 1 and 2; Terminal 2 also serves Northwest, Continental, Trans World Airlines, America West, and several other carriers. Terminal 3 serves American Airlines, Delta, and others. The walk between each of the domestic terminals can take up to 15 minutes, and a ride from the domestic terminals to Terminal 5 on the airport transit system can take 5–10 minutes.

To get your bearings, ask for a terminal map at one of the four information booths located on the lower level of each domestic terminal and on the upper level of the international terminal.

The booths are staffed by people who, collectively, speak 26 languages.

Take Care of Yourself

► **Eat**

Dining options in Concourse C in Terminal 1 (the United terminal) include the Chicago-based Berghoff's, Panda Express, and the sushi kiosk at Gate 20. In Concourse B, look for Chili's (Gate 14) and the Wolfgang Puck Café at Gate 6. In the main hall of Terminal 2, your choices include Edy's Ice Cream, Cinnabon, Juice Works, and the Fresh Departure Deli. Over in the Terminal 3 rotunda you'll find the Chicago Tap Room, Great American Bagel, Panda Express, Momo's Pizza, and Butch's Grill.

Best Healthful Nosh

Juice Works in Terminal 1 (Gate B15), in the main hall of Terminal 2, and in the Terminal 3 rotunda has healthy sandwiches, juices, and yogurt. There's also a sushi kiosk at Gate C20 in Terminal 1.

Best Sinful Snack

Chocolate from Fanny May Candies in Terminals 1, 2, and 3.

► **Relax and Refresh**

- O'Hare's bathrooms feature a hygienic and strangely entertaining "Sani-Seat," an ingenious gadget that wraps plastic around the toilet seat after each use. Restrooms also feature sanitary hands-free flushers.

O'Hare is usually too crowded to offer many genuinely quiet spots, but there's a small parklike area in the connecting corridor between Terminals 1 and 2 that affords a good view of the airfield. You'll also find comfortable seating near the Children's Museum just past the security checkpoint in Terminal 2, and at the exhibit area sponsored by the Chicago Museum of Broadcast Communications at the end of Terminal 2, toward the rotunda. For a peaceful spot, try the chapel in Terminal 2, on the second-floor mezzanine above the TWA counter. Or hoof it on over to the lobby area of the O'Hare Hilton, which is just a 5-minute walk from the terminals via an underground pedestrian tunnel. If you want to check in, the Hilton offers a day rate on a space-available basis (773-686-8000).

The folks at Back Rub Hub in Terminal 3 specialize in relaxing massages, and the unisex Francolynn Hair Salon on the lower level of the O'Hare Hilton offers haircuts and manicures.

If walking the terminal concourses isn't enough exercise, you can purchase a $10 day pass for the health club located on the lower level of the Hilton, with its coed sauna/steam room, swimming pool, whirlpool, and weight rooms. It's open Monday–Thursday, 5 AM–11 PM; Friday until 10 PM; and 6 AM–10 PM on weekends (773-601-1722).

If you overdo it, stop by the University of Illinois at Chicago Medical Center's clinic in Terminal 2, just past the security checkpoint, open daily 6 AM–10 PM. And if you *really* overdo it, you'll be glad to know that O'Hare was the first airport to provide publicly accessible defibrillators throughout the terminals.

Take Care of Business

- Telephones with data ports are located throughout the airport.

The Skybird Business Center, upstairs in the rotunda in Terminal 2, contains desks, computer hookups, and facilities for mailing packages, sending faxes, and holding meetings. The airport is also home to a pair of business centers (in Terminal 1, across from Gate B6 and in the underground walkway between Concourses B and C) where you can rent a fully equipped mini-office on a per-minute basis.

Explore the Airport

►Shop

Browse the bookstores in Terminals 1, 2, and 3 and the Beanie Baby store (Ty-riffic) in Terminal 3. Terminal 1's Concourse B houses

Michael Jordan Golf, which purveys shirts, chocolate golf balls, and other golfing paraphernalia, and a branch of the Field Museum Store. Chicago Sports Section located in Terminals 1 (Gates B6 and C9), 2 (Gate F1), and 3 (Gate L4) offers team trinkets, and Brookstone has shops at Gate C11 and in the main hall of Terminal 3.

► **Sightsee**

Students from Gallery 37, an award-winning Chicago arts education program, created the painted benches placed throughout O'Hare's terminals, including the benches and mosaic planters near the player piano in Terminal 2. Down the hall is an exhibit of vintage radio and television sets, courtesy of the Chicago Museum of Broadcast Communications.

Running along the tunnel connecting United's two concourses is Michael Hayden's "The Sky's the Limit," the world's largest neon sculpture, whose undulating lights are paired with a peppy sound track. Terminal 5 features a museum-quality collection of 43 stained-glass windows and 19 wooden sculptures by Jerzy S. Kenar, a Polish-born artist who lives in Chicago.

Wherever you are in the airport, listen up. When the sound system isn't being used to announce gate changes, lost kids, or the prohibition on smoking, it broadcasts music by some of Chicago's best-known jazz, blues, classical, folk, and rock musicians. If you hear something you like and need to know the name of a tune, you can look it up at www.airportmusic.org.

Finally, for impressive views of O'Hare's facilities, hop on the people mover. The Automated Transit System travels a total of 2.7 miles on a single trip, making stops at the domestic and international terminals and at the long-term parking facility.

► **Play Around**

Stop by the cheery "Kids on the Fly" activity center sponsored by the Chicago Children's Museum in Terminal 2. At flight-related play stations, kids can tag and weigh baggage, load cargo, and take the controls in a simulated control tower and jet cockpit. Just make sure the "pilot" steers clear of the 10,000-piece Sears Tower made of Legos.

Also, be sure to take the kids to visit the airport's dinosaur: a four-story-high, 72-foot-long Brachiosaurus skeleton model on loan from the Field Museum. You can't miss it if you head to the upper level of Terminal 1 in Concourse B.

Go into Town

The average cab fare to downtown Chicago costs between $25 and $30. The ride can take anywhere from 30 minutes to an hour, depending on traffic. Shared shuttle vans make the trip for $17. For a faster and cheaper ride into town, take public transportation: the CTA (Chicago Transit Authority) Blue Line train provides 24-hour service between downtown Chicago and O'Hare International Airport. Follow the lower-level pedestrian passageways inside the airport terminals to the CTA station. The fare to downtown is $1.50, and the ride takes about 45 minutes.

Other Information

Call the folks at the Customer Service Hotline (800-832-6352) if you need to know anything about Chicago O'Hare International Airport before you arrive.

Cincinnati/Northern Kentucky International Airport

Cincinnati, Ohio
Airport Code: CVG
Web Address: http://www.cvgairport.com

Located 13 miles south of Cincinnati, the northern Kentucky airfield now known as the Cincinnati/Northern Kentucky International Airport (CVG) served until the early 1940s as a training field for military pilots. Nearby Lunken Airport initially served the region, but after it earned the nickname "Sunken Lunken" in a 1937 flood, officials decided to replace the valley airport with the current one—which is on a plateau.

Get Oriented

- Luggage carts rent for $1. You'll get a $.25 "reward" when you replace a cart in the rack.
- Lockers are located in each terminal.

CVG has three main terminals (1, 2, and 3). Terminal 1 needs some TLC, but the newer Terminals 2 and 3 are bright and airy, with high ceilings, lots of glass, and oblong rotundas that both reflect the shape of riverboats and pay homage to the history of the Ohio River.

Terminals 1 and 2 are laid out in a straightforward manner and linked together by an easy-to-traverse corridor. Terminal 1 hosts flights from Northwest, Skyway, and US Airways, while gates in Terminal 2 serve American, Continental, TWA, United, and several other airlines. The newer Terminal 3 has three concourses (A, B, and C) which serve flights for Delta, Comair, Swissair, and others. Passengers can walk to Concourses A and B or shorten the trip by hopping on the underground tram or the moving walkways. To get to Concourse C, travelers walk or ride to Concourse B and must then board a shuttle bus.

If you're making a connection through CVG, this might be the trip to consider packing light or checking your baggage: it took me more than 15 minutes to hike from Terminal 1 out to the farthest gate of Terminal 3's Concourse B.

Take Care of Yourself

► Eat

If you're looking for a snack or a meal, head for the food court and the gate areas of Concourse B in Terminal 3. In the center area of Concourse B you'll find the Great Steak & Potato Company, Mrs. Fields Cookies, TCBY frozen yogurt, Cheers (restaurant and bar), and other food-court staples. Wander a bit beyond and your choices expand: Lefty's Bar & Grille is at Gate B17, Au Bon Pain is at Gate B21, the Thoroughbred Grill is at Gate B24, and Big Sky Bread, a bakery and sandwich shop that offers boxed lunches suitable for travel, is at Gate B8.

Elsewhere in the airport you'll find Gold Star Chili and Pizza Perfecto in Concourse A (Terminal 3) and the '50s-style River City Diner, which serves Gold Star Chili, burgers, fries, hot dogs, and ice cream, in the Terminal 2 ticket lobby. The Oldenberg Brewery, an offshoot of a local microbrewery, is located in Concourse C.

Best Healthful Nosh

Baked granola or fresh bagels from Big Sky Bread in Concourse B (Gate 8)

Best Sinful Snack

Candy (by the piece or by the pound) from the Country Store, located in Concourse A at Gate 4, Concourse B at Gate 14, and in the Concourse C lobby.

► Relax and Refresh

There are several areas at CVG that can provide shelter from the hustle and bustle. In Terminal 2, just before the security checkpoint and behind the ticket counters, you'll find two comfortable seating sections. Or you might head for the seating areas at the center area of Terminal 3 (at the top of the escalator) and in

Concourse B. These are also good spots to sit a spell if you'd like to spend some time people watching. For a truly quiet spot, stop at the chapel located in the baggage claim area of Terminal 3, where the east prayer wall is clearly marked for those of the Islamic faith.

If you need to freshen up, try the restrooms out at the ends of each concourse, or head over to the Radisson Hotel (on-site, across from Terminal 1), which has a pool and a workout room and offers a day rate (606-371-6166).

For more professional help, visit the barbershop in the Terminal 1 ticket lobby. It's open Monday–Friday, 9 AM–5 PM.

You can also take in a movie: InMotion Pictures, in Concourse B, rents portable DVD players with movies for use on-site or for return at a variety of other airports.

Take Care of Business

- Phones throughout the airport are equipped with fax and data ports.

There are four business centers at CVG: in the ticket lobbies of Terminals 1 and 2, at Gate 20 in Concourse B of Terminal 3, and in the lobby of the Comair terminal (Terminal 3, Concourse C).

ATMs are plentiful at this airport, but there's also a full-service branch of the Fifth Third Bank at Gate 12 in Concourse B. It's open seven days a week from 8 AM to 8 PM.

Explore the Airport

►Shop

If you have time to browse, head for Concourse B in Terminal 3. Stop first at the Country Store, located at Gate B14. This popular spot carries reasonably priced toys, John Deere memorabilia, marbles by the scoop, sarsaparilla, jellies, pickles, penny candy, and a variety of made-in-Kentucky gifts. The big seller here seems to be large bags of fresh-popped popcorn and bottles of Country Store Popcorn Popping Oil. Smaller branches of the

Country Store are located in Concourse A at Gate 4 and in the center area of Concourse C.

Sports fans will enjoy SportsWorld (next to the Country Store at B14), which carries autographed baseballs, caps, helmets, and other sports memorabilia, including clothing emblazoned with the insignias of the Cincinnati Reds, the Bearcats, the Buckeyes, and other area teams. Elsewhere in Concourse B you'll find the Body Shop (at Gate 18), the Disney Store (at Gate 9), and Waterstone's Booksellers and LensCrafters (in the center mall area). A Book Corner with a great newsstand is located in the Comair terminal (Concourse C, Terminal 3) and a Pro Shop is tucked into the Terminal 3 ticket lobby.

►Sightsee

Fourteen priceless 20-by-20-foot mosaic art deco murals, each depicting an industrial scene from Cincinnati's past, are scattered throughout the airport. The murals were created during the Great Depression by German-born artist Winold Reiss for the walls of Cincinnati's Union Terminal Railway Station and moved to the airport in the mid-1970s. Each mural depicts workers in action at an important local enterprise: look for images of men cutting long soap blocks into bars at Procter & Gamble, pouring molten metal into molds at the American Rolling Mill, and coating tablets in large rotary drums at the William Merrell pharmaceutical company.

Three of the 14 murals are located in the Terminal 1 baggage claim area; 4 murals are tucked behind the ticket counters in Terminal 2; 2 others are in the Terminal 2 baggage claim area; the rest are housed the Terminal 3 baggage claim area. For more details about the history of these murals and a map of their locations, look for the bright orange brochure titled "The Cincinnati Murals" at one of the airport information booths.

Besides these charming murals, look for the "Freedom Shrines" located on the right-hand wall just past the security checkpoint in Terminal 3 and in the Terminal 1 baggage claim area. Each display features more than two dozen replicas of important historical documents: everything from the Declaration of Independence to the first draft of George Washington's Farewell Address and the US Constitution.

Over in the connecting corridor between Terminals 1 and 2, look for the large bell salvaged from the second *Island Queen,* a riverboat that sailed the Ohio River from 1920 to 1947 before being destroyed by fire. Look for the vintage prints and models of Cincinnati riverboats that are mounted on the walls nearby.

You'll find good airfield viewing spots at either end of the central area in Concourse B, in Terminal 2 just behind the ticketing area, and behind the escalators in the main ticketing area of Terminal 3.

► **Play Around**

Kids will certainly enjoy (and—don't tell them—learn something from) the mosaic murals scattered throughout the airport and the historic documents featured in the Freedom Shrines in Terminals 1 and 3. Younger kids should be entertained by a visit to the Disney Store or the Country Store in Concourse B or a ride on the underground tram that runs between the main area of Terminal 3 and Concourses A and B.

Go into Town

You'll find a taxi desk near the exit in each terminal. The fare for the 13-mile ride from the airport to downtown Cincinnati or to the northern Kentucky riverfront runs about $22. You can get more information by calling 606-767-3260.

Jet'Port Express shuttle buses to downtown Cincinnati and to the Kentucky side of the river run every half hour, seven days a week, from 6 AM to 10 PM. If you leave and return to the airport on the same day, the fare is a bargain at $5. Jet'Port Express is located inside the baggage claim area of Terminals 1, 2, and 3. More information is available at the transportation desks in the baggage claim areas of each terminal or by calling 606-767-3702.

TANK bus service runs from the airport to downtown and back seven days a week. Look for buses outside near the Delta

Dash area (near Terminal 3) and between Terminal 1 and the departure area of Terminal 2. The ride takes about 45 minutes from the airport to downtown Cincinnati and costs $.75 each way. For route and schedule information call 606-331-8265.

Other Information

To help you find your way, the airport has a team of 170 Goodwill Ambassadors stationed at information booths and elsewhere throughout the terminals. If you have a layover of 4 hours or more, be sure to ask one of the Ambassadors for a copy of CVG's handy brochure titled "Cincinnati Layover—What to Do?" The brochure lists dining, sightseeing, sports, shopping, and cultural activities in Cincinnati and northern Kentucky and offers useful tips on getting into town and back.

To get information about the airport before you arrive, call 606-767-3151.

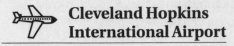 **Cleveland Hopkins International Airport**

Cleveland, Ohio
Airport Code: CLE
Web Address (unofficial):
http://www.cwru.edu/cleve/hopkins/hopkins.html

In operation since 1926, Cleveland Hopkins International Airport (CLE) is the oldest municipally owned airport in the country. Over the years, the city has tried to renovate, upgrade, and expand the facility, but travelers must still contend with narrow, low-ceilinged corridors and long walks down and between most concourses.

A few recent improvements, however, offer hope: In the store-lined connector between Concourses A, B, and C, visitors can snag souvenirs from the Cleveland Art Museum Store and from Cleveland's Rock and Roll Hall of Fame and Museum. Also, the architecture of Continental's new bright, airy Concourse D brings at least a bit of modernity to a facility not slated for overhaul any time soon.

Get Oriented

- Luggage carts rent for $1.50 and are located throughout the airport. Most machines take credit cards and make change, and return racks offer a $.25 refund.

Cleveland Hopkins International Airport has a main terminal with a small atrium area leading to four concourses (A, B, C, and D). Continental, which has a hub here, uses Concourse D for its Continental Express shuttle service and shares Concourse C with Northwest Airlines. All the other airlines divvy up the gates on Concourses A and B.

To get to Concourse C (Northwest and Continental flights), you can either walk through a store-lined corridor or take the connector corridor directly from the ticketing lobby. Either way, you'll need to make your way halfway down Concourse C before you can get access to the underground tunnel that takes you to Continental's new Concourse D.

Take Care of Yourself

► **Eat**

Food choices at Cleveland Hopkins International Airport are plentiful but not awfully exciting. For sit-down meals, try the Cheers Bar & Restaurant (main terminal atrium), the Great Lakes Brewery (Concourse A), Max & Erma's (Concourse B), or the Home Turf Restaurant & Bar (Concourse D). You'll also find a food court in the main terminal (featuring Burger King, Cinnabon, and Great American Bagel) and a variety of familiar fast-food options throughout the airport.

Best Healthful Nosh

Fresh fruit or fruit salad from the Fruit and Nut kiosk in the mall area just before the security checkpoint in Concourse C.

Best Sinful Snack

Chocolates—by the piece or by the pound—from the London Chocolatier, just a few steps away from the Fruit and Nut kiosk located just before the Concourse C security checkpoint.

► **Relax and Refresh**

To get out of the hustle and bustle, grab a seat in the atrium of the main terminal, near the entrances to Concourses A and B. On a quiet Sunday morning, I spied several folks snoozing comfortably over their morning papers. During peak travel times, however, this area no doubt gets noisy and turns into a better spot for people watching.

To grab a nap, read a book, or get some fresh air, head to the Spectator Deck at the end of Concourse B, just before the gate area for Southwest Airlines. Take the elevator up to a lovely glassed-in area with benches and plants, and if the weather is nice, be sure to go outside. If the observation deck is too noisy, head for the chapel, located at the entrance to Concourse B.

There are no on-site health clubs, beauty salons, or barbers, but there is a Sheraton Hotel on airport property with an indoor pool, health spa, and exercise facilities. Their day rate runs from $75 to $90 (216-267-1500).

Sorry, smokers: Cleveland is a no-smoking airport, so you'll need to head outside to light up.

Take Care of Business

- Phones with data ports are scattered throughout the airport, and each phone bank has a least one data port phone. The best spot to get work done is at the entrance to Concourse A, where a whole section of phones have seats, shelves, and electrical outlets for your laptop.

There's a small business center located just off the main lobby atrium at the entrance to Concourse B. You can plug in to their computer data port, print copies, send faxes, or rent a work-station. The center also provides luggage and garment storage, currency exchange, and will arrange to ship a package for you via FedEx.

Explore the Airport

► Shop

You'll find a veritable mini-mall in the corridor linking Con-courses A and B to Concourses C and D.

Cleveland Sports Scene serves up souvenirs from local sports teams and one special condiment: Stadium Mustard sells for $9.99 a gallon, but smaller containers are also available. Next door to the sports store you can watch videos, listen to music, and stock up on key chains, T-shirts, and other memorabilia from Cleveland's Rock and Roll Hall of Fame and Museum.

Elsewhere along the mall corridor you'll find the Cleveland Art Museum shop, Wilsons Leather, the Bath & Body Shop, Victo-ria's Secret, a newsstand, and the London Chocolatier, a shop filled with chocolates and other candies you might buy for gifts but end up opening before you get on the plane. On your way to Concourses C and D you'll find AltiTunes (CDs and small electronics), where you can put on headphones and sample current CDs.

►Sightsee

On the bridge connecting the ticketing area with Concourse A, there's a wonderful photography exhibit featuring black-and-white portraits of Clevelanders at work. The photos are changed several times throughout the year, so head here even if you've seen them before.

For more fanciful art, head over to Concourse D, where giant folded "paper" (aluminum, actually) airplanes by Andy Yoder hang from the ceiling at either end of the underground connecting corridor. Along the walkway, keep an eye out for whimsical wall panels by Cleveland artist Mark Howard which feature metal cutouts of propellers, planes, and airline attendants at work.

You can get good views of the airfield from the Spectator Deck at the end of Concourse B, from the connecting corridor between the ticketing lobby and Concourse A, and from pretty much anywhere in Concourse D.

►Play Around

Very young kids (and their parents) will enjoy the small play areas located in each concourse, but note that the play area at the entrance to Concourse A is located right next to a cookie store! Kids will also enjoy the observation deck and the giant "paper" airplanes hanging over the corridor that leads out to Concourse D. If the kids are full of energy, take them all the way out to Concourse D and let them work it off in the wide, well-lit corridor.

Go into Town

A taxi ride from the airport to downtown will take 15–30 minutes and cost about $22. Shuttle vans (Hopkins Airport Limousine) can get you downtown for $9.

If you don't have much baggage, consider public transportation: RTA trains leave the airport every 12 minutes and cost just $1.50. After 10 PM, the trains stop, but you can catch a bus for downtown from the ticketing level.

Other Information

"Don't jump to conclusions," a custodial staff member warned me when I asked about the needle disposal boxes posted in every airport bathroom. "Cleveland doesn't have a huge number of drug addicts, but we do have diabetics. We didn't want them to put their insulin needles in the garbage cans. It's just a sign of the times." Just so you know.

If you want general information about the airport, call 404-265-6030.

 # Port Columbus
International Airport

Columbus, Ohio
Airport Code: CMH
Web Address: http://www.port-columbus.com

When it was dedicated, on July 8, 1929, Port Columbus Airport was the eastern link on the country's first rail/air transcontinental service. For $338.10, which included Pullman lower berths and meals, passengers could travel by train from New York City to the Columbus airport and then fly to Los Angeles or San Francisco. The coast-to-coast trip, promoted as "A Miracle of Modern Transportation," took "just" 48 hours. These days a cross-country trip can sometimes take just as long, but travelers will still find a miracle of modern transportation at Port Columbus International Airport (CMH)—a 24-hour espresso stand.

Get Oriented

- Luggage carts are located on the baggage claim level and on the departure level. They rent for $1.50 and refund $.25 when a cart is returned to the rack.
- Lockers are located in Concourse C.

Port Columbus has one terminal with three concourses (A, B, and C) serving 22 airlines. Concourse A serves Midway, US Airways, and Continental. In Concourse B you'll find gates for American, Midwest Express, Northwest, TWA, United, and America West, which has a small hub here. Delta, Comair, and Southwest Airlines use Concourse C.

The concourses are laid out in a Y configuration off the bright central ticketing and service atrium. It should take you no longer than 5 minutes to get from the main terminal out to the end of any concourse.

Take Care of Yourself

►**Eat**

Max & Erma's, a full-service restaurant and bar in the main terminal Gateway Plaza, serves salads, burgers, and other straightforward dishes. Mulligan's Bar & Grill, upstairs near the end of Concourse C, is a golf-themed full-service restaurant with a great view of the north runway.

For good coffee, line up at the aptly named Cup O' Joe (in the Gateway Plaza, next to the TWA ticket counter), which also offers fruit smoothies, desserts, and quiches. It's open 24 hours—a rarity!

In the main terminal food court your choices include Charley's Steakery, Freshëns Yogurt, Godfather's Pizza, Jump Asian Cuisine, and Wendy's hamburgers. Out at the gates you'll find Damon's in Concourse A, Columbus Brewing Company & Right Stuff in Concourse B, and the fast-food version of Mulligan's ("At the Turn") in Concourse C.

Best Healthful Nosh

Salads or black-bean roll-ups from Max & Erma's in the main terminal Gateway Plaza or a fruit smoothie from Cup O' Joe, by the TWA ticket counter.

Best Sinful Snack

Hand-dipped chocolates or ice cream from Nutcracker's Suite, located on the ticketing level across from the Delta counters.

►**Relax and Refresh**

- Traveling with a pet? CMH has a landscaped pet "relieving" area, complete with cleanup tools, just outside the southernmost door of the baggage claim area.

If you're looking for a quiet spot to relax and read a book, head down to the end of Concourse A. For people watching, grab a seat on the "patio" at Max & Erma's Restaurant in the main terminal Gateway Plaza or stop at the bench by the "Brushstrokes in

Flight" sculpture near the food court at the entrance to Concourse B. There are also clusters of comfortable seats in the ticket counter corridor.

There are no massage bars, barbershops, or hair salons at CMH, but several hotels, including Comfort Suites, Hampton Inn, and the Concourse Hotel, are located right by the airport and offer day rates. Of special note: $8 buys a day pass to the athletic club at the Concourse Hotel, which features an indoor/outdoor pool, fitness club, sauna/steam room, and shower facilities with amenities.

Smokers can light up in the smoking sections of Max & Erma's and Damon's.

Take Care of Business

• The airport is replacing all pay phones with models that include data ports.

You'll find a staffed business center near the entrance of Concourse C. The center is open Monday–Friday from 7:30 AM to 5:00 PM and, refreshingly, on Saturdays from 10 AM to 3 PM. Stop here for notary, fax, and copier services, computer suites with Internet access, and overnight mail drop boxes (614-237-9224). There's also a self-service postal center in the main terminal Gateway Plaza area.

Explore the Airport

►Shop

In addition to newsstands and gift shops located in each concourse, you'll find Broad & High Emporium (news and gifts), PGA Tour Shop, Heritage Booksellers, Bath & Body Works, and Brooks Brothers in the Gateway Plaza just before the entrance to Concourse B. This area also sports the Big Ten Conference Shop, which offers a wide variety of team-related paraphernalia, including Buckeye jigsaw puzzles, socks, games, and clothing.

If you're traveling with kids or just looking for a gift to bring home, head to Kidz Club USA, near the entrance of Concourse C.

This shop offers children's books, toys, clothing, and stuffed animals. Fun gifts (and chocolate) are also featured at Nutcracker's Suite, in the main lobby area, just north of the north entryway in the ticket lobby area.

► **Sightsee**

The airport's showpiece artwork, Roy Lichtenstein's "Brushstrokes in Flight," hit the news in the mid-1980s when the city's mayor announced his intention to give the sculpture to the city of Genoa, Italy, as a thank-you for that city's gift to Columbus: a statue of Christopher Columbus. To the relief of local art fans, it turned out that the mayor didn't actually have the authority to make that gift and the artwork stayed at the airport. To see what all the fuss was about, head for the Gateway Plaza area, just before the entrance to Concourse B.

For a historical perspective on the role the Port Columbus Airport played in aviation history, spend some time looking at the vintage photographs in the pictorial timeline on display above the food court area. (There's an elevator just to the left of the food court entrance.) There's also a bright yellow vintage airplane hanging in the ticket lobby, just before the entrance to Concourse A.

For the best views of the Columbus skyline and airfield activity, head to the top level of the short-term parking garage. You can also get good views of airfield activities from the windows at Damon's (in Concourse A) and from Mulligan's Bar & Grill (in Concourse C).

► **Play Around**

Southwest Airlines has a small play area for young kids in Concourse C. There's also a well-stocked aquarium just before the entrance to Concourse C, right across from the Kidz Club USA toy store. Kids might also enjoy taking a gander at the bright yellow vintage airplane hanging from the ceiling in the ticket lobby, just before the entrance to Concourse A.

Go into Town

A taxi ride to downtown Columbus will take about 10 minutes and cost between $16 and $19. Shuttle van rides cost between $10 and $15. Or try the bus: it will cost $1.10 to ride COTA (Central Ohio Transit Authority) and you'll need to transfer at least once to reach downtown Columbus.

Other Information

For more information about Port Columbus International Airport, call 614-239-4000. Phones are staffed Monday–Friday, 8 AM–5 PM.

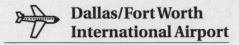 **Dallas/Fort Worth International Airport**

Dallas, Texas
Airport Code: DFW
Web Address: http://www.dfwairport.com

For years, a long-running rivalry between Dallas and Fort Worth meant each city built and maintained its own airport. However, in 1964, in response to the urging of the Civil Aeronautics Board (CAB) and its refusal to pay for two separate airports, Texas-sized differences were graciously set aside, and a plot of land 17 miles from both cities was chosen for Dallas/Fort Worth Airport (DFW).

Get Oriented

- Luggage carts rent for $1.50. You'll receive a $.25 refund when you return a cart to the rack.
- Lockers are located in each terminal, postsecurity.

DFW has four main terminals (A,B,C, and E) which are linked by walkways and two automated train systems. The all-purpose airport train runs throughout the airport and can get you from Terminal B to Terminals A, C, or E. The American Airlines TRAAIN, however, is a dedicated system serving the American Airlines gates in Terminals A, B, and C.

American Airlines, which has its hub here, is the predominant airline at DFW and uses all the Terminal C gates as well as many of the gates in Terminals A and B. Delta, which uses DFW as a domestic hub, pulls up at gates in Terminal E. To get your bearings, consult one of the large maps posted throughout the facility or stop to chat with an Ambassador Volunteer at one of the information kiosks in the baggage claim areas near Gates A29, B21, C4, and E14.

Take Care of Yourself

►Eat

La Bodega Winery (Terminal A) features highly rated Texas wines and is reputed to be the country's only wine-tasting room and licensed winery based in an airport. Other spots to chow down include T.G.I. Friday's at Gate A22, Dickey's BBQ at Gates A16, C6, and E12, Chili's Too at Gate C15, and Harlon's BBQ Grill & Bar at Gates B25 and B34. If these eateries don't tempt your taste-buds, don't worry: there are more than 80 other food and beverage concessions at DFW. Look for Au Bon Pain in Terminal A; the Texas Stadium Bar & Grill and Sbarro's Italian Eatery in Terminal B; Manchu Wok and Wendy's in Terminal C; and Mr. Gatti's Pizza in Terminal E.

Best Healthful Nosh

A smoothie or nonfat yogurt from either Frullati or Freshëns Yogurt, which are scattered throughout the airport.

Best Sinful Snack

Häagen-Dazs ice cream (Gates C17 and E15) or candy from Candy Headquarters (Gate A22).

►Relax and Refresh

DFW is busy most all the time, but if you check the schedules you should be able to find a quiet spot to relax in a gate area that's not going to be used for a while. You can grab a seat in one of the café areas in the Benjamin Bookstores located in Terminals A and E. Or stop in at one of the three airport chapels, located in Terminals B, C, and E. For plush seating, head on over to Terminal C and take a 3-minute walk out through the parking garage to the on-site Hyatt Regency Hotel, where there's a large lobby area with an espresso stand and comfortable seating.

Barbershops/salons are located in Terminals B, C, and E. While there are no massage stands or fitness rooms at DFW, you can get a great workout by passing up the moving walkways between terminals and taking the 5- to 10-minute walk between terminals along the elevated skywalks. If you have more time, take a 3-minute walk over to the Hyatt Regency Hotel and check in at their day rate (which fluctuates according to occupancy), which will give you access to the hotel's health club facilities and jogging track.

Or play a round of golf: the Hyatt Regency DFW is not only one of the world's largest airport hotels, it's also home to the Hyatt Bear Creek Golf Club, which features two championship 18-hole golf courses, a driving range, and putting greens (972-453-1234).

There is no smoking allowed at DFW.

Take Care of Business

• There are Internet kiosks in each concourse and data phones, ATMs, and currency exchange booths scattered throughout the terminal.

You'll find a business center, which rents fully equipped mini-offices by the minute, in Terminal A, between Gates 38 and 39. There's also a business center at the Hyatt Regency DFW (open Monday–Friday, 7 AM–11 PM), a computer and cell phone accessories store at Gate A37, and public fax/copy machines scattered throughout Terminal E.

Explore the Airport

► Shop

Football fans can snag some souvenirs at the Official Dallas Cowboys Pro Shop in Terminal A (Gate 24) and Terminal E (Gate 13). Other shopping highlights include Sharper Image (in the retail court in Terminal E), two PGA Tour Shops (Gates A29 and E17), a Beanie Baby stand at Gate A36, and a pair of Magnet Stores at Gates A21 and E 17. Benjamin Bookstores are located in Terminal A by Gate 16, in Terminal C by Gate 24, and in Terminal E by Gate 14. Best of all, throughout the airport you'll find well-stocked stores offering tempting western wear and other cowboy and cowgirl paraphernalia you can bring along on your next trip to the dude ranch. For a colorful souvenir from south of the border, head for Mercado Gifts at Gates A17 and C6.

►Sightsee

Surprisingly, there is little, if any, artwork or historical displays at DFW, but those western-themed shops are mighty entertaining.

You can get some interesting views of the airport facilities by taking a 10- to 15-minute ride around the airport on the train that links the terminals and the long-term parking lots. Stroll the skywalks between terminals for views of runway and gate activity or grab one of the seats at the top of the escalators leading to the train station in Terminal B.

►Play Around

DFW has no special area just for kids, but kids (and many adults) find both riding and watching the trains that run between terminals quite entertaining and sort of Disneyland-esque. Trains run every 2 minutes and a full-circuit trip around the airport might fill 10–20 minutes. Kids might also enjoy testing the accuracy of the signs estimating how long it should take to cross the skywalk to Terminal B. If nothing else, the 6- to 10-minute walk will give everyone some exercise and maybe tire some kids out enough so everyone can get some shut-eye on the plane.

Go into Town

DFW is 15 miles from Dallas and 18 miles from Fort Worth. Travel time to the downtown areas of each city is between 30 and 45 minutes, depending on traffic. Average taxi fares to downtown Dallas run about $28; to downtown Fort Worth, about $32. Information about other transportation options, including public transportation and shuttle buses, is available in all baggage claim areas or by calling 972-574-2227.

Other Information

If you find yourself at DFW with a problem or question that can't get answered, stop by the Airport Assistance Center, located in Terminal B near the Gate 30 baggage claim area. Mostly these folks are on hand to provide travel-related crisis counseling and intervention, but the office is staffed every day and the entryway is stocked with brochures for a wide variety of area attractions. If you need information about the airport before you arrive, call them at 972-574-4420.

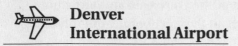 # Denver
International Airport

Denver, Colorado
Airport Code: DEN
Web Address: http://www.flydenver.com

Viewed from the outside, the Jeppesen Terminal building at Denver International Airport (DEN) is reminiscent of a circus tent or a field of whipped marshmallows, but the architects insist that the structure was inspired by the snowcapped peaks of the Rocky Mountains.

From inside the atrium, the billowing roof looks as if it might collapse under the first good winter snowfall, but airport officials promise that the Teflon-coated fiberglass structure is far safer than it first appears.

Get Oriented

- Luggage carts can be rented in the main terminal and in the parking structures for $1.50.
- Storage lockers are located on each concourse, postsecurity.

DEN consists of the main Jeppesen Terminal (with its Great Hall or atrium) and three concourses (A, B, and C) all connected by a train system that runs every 2 minutes. Passengers must take the train to reach Concourses B and C, but it's easier to walk from Jeppesen Terminal to Concourse A. From the farthest concourse (Concourse C), it should take no more than 5 or 10 minutes to get to Jeppesen Terminal.

The mile-long Concourse B primarily serves United Air Lines (which also uses some gates in Concourse A). Concourse A also serves Continental, Frontier, and other carriers. Concourse C houses American, America West, US Airways, Midwest Express, Delta, Northwest, and several other airlines.

To get your bearings, ask for a terminal map at one of the information booths located in Jeppesen Terminal and in each of the concourses. Or hail one of the DEN Ambassadors—trained volunteers stationed throughout the facility who are easily recognizable by their white cowboy hats, denim vests, and bolo ties.

Take Care of Yourself

► Eat

Head to Concourse B for the most choices: Wolfgang Puck Express (on the upper level), Lefty's Mile High Grille, Pour la France! Café & Bar, Itza Wrap/Itza Bowl, and plenty of spots in the center food court to grab coffee, ice cream, and a wide variety of fast food.

Back in the main terminal, you'll find Pour la France! Café & Bar, and Red Rocks Bar. In Concourse A, look for Lefty's Colorado Trails Bar & Grill, the MarketPlace Bar Deli & Espresso Caffe, or Panda Express. In Concourse C, Lefty's place is called the Front Range Grille.

Best Healthful Nosh

Veggie wraps from Itza Wrap/Itza Bowl in the center of Concourse B.

Best Sinful Snack

Chocolates from Stephany's Chocolates in the main terminal and in Concourse A.

► Relax and Refresh

If you enjoy people watching, try the food court on level 6 of Jeppesen Terminal or the center of Concourse B. Quiet spots suitable for reading or catching a nap are found on the upper levels of each concourse. These upper levels are also where you'll find the least-used bathrooms.

Weary travelers can get a massage in the Jeppesen Terminal (level 6 west) at A Massage Inc. from 7:30 AM to 9:30 PM. Sleepy travelers can grab a nap on the nice Italian couches near the Jeppesen exhibit in the west end of Jeppesen Terminal (level 5), or in the quieter upper-level areas of Concourses A, B, and C. For a truly tranquil refuge, visit the chapel on the upper level (level 6 south) of Jeppesen Terminal. It's open daily, 8 AM–5 PM, and there's an Islamic prayer hall right next door.

Film buffs can rent a DVD player and a movie from the InMotion Pictures booth located in the center court of Concourse B. If you're heading to another airport with an InMotion kiosk, you can take the player along and return it at your destination (www.inmotionpictures.com).

Smokers can light up—if they make a purchase—at the Aviator's Lounge. There's one in the main terminal, on level 6, and another at the center of Concourse B, up on the mezzanine level.

Take Care of Business

• Most every phone in the airport is equipped with a data port.

You'll find a business center, which rents fully equipped offices by the minute, on level 6 in the main terminal. There are also a pair of business centers located on the mezzanine level of Concourse B (303-317-0988). These centers are open around the clock, but only staffed from 8 AM to 6 PM, Sunday–Friday.

Kiosks offering free Internet access are scattered throughout the airport, at the ends of many phone banks. You can also surf the Web at one of the tabletop Internet hookups located at www.Cowboy Bar in the center court area of Concourse A (303-342-3377).

Explore the Airport

►Shop

Each concourse has a bookstore and a shop (or three) offering western wear, western jewelry, and western-themed souvenirs such as turquoise jewelry and buffalo sausage.

Concourse B offers the most shopping options, ranging from a bookstore and travel-accessories shop to branches of the Discovery Channel Store, the Body Shop, and American Motorcycle

Works. You'll also find Time Zone (watches), kids' clothing and toy stores, and more than eight apparel, sports, and accessory shops, including Susan Vale Sweaters, which offers handmade, one-of-a-kind creations.

Concourse A, a short walk from Jeppesen Terminal, has a bookstore, a sportswear store, several other apparel and accessory shops for men and women, a toy store, and many of the same western gift shops located in the other concourses.

Concourse C has a bookstore, a Body Shop, and fewer gift shops than the other concourses, but the Family Fun Center is located here, so if you have kids in tow, they can play here while you shop nearby.

There are also plenty of shops in Jeppesen Terminal, including purveyors of holograms, nature photos, and sports items.

► Sightsee

DEN has millions of dollars' worth of art scattered throughout Jeppesen Terminal and the various concourses. Works by 39 artists are integrated into the airport's design, and revolving exhibitions along the pedestrian walkway to Concourse A present folk art, crafts, and other works by regional artists. To make sure you don't miss anything, ask for a DEN art map at one of the information booths.

Notable artworks include the 140 floating steel "paper" airplanes created by Denver artist Patty Orvitz, on display in Jeppesen Terminal, which is also home to two large maps by Gary Sweeney titled "America, Why I Love Her." Each map highlights the more bizarre tourist haunts around the country, including strange museums and sites where mysterious happenings allegedly occurred.

After you've seen the art, take in some local history. The main terminal building is officially named the Elrey Jeppesen Terminal in honor of the aviation pioneer whose "Jepp" navigational maps and charts are standard equipment in most every airline cockpit. There's a bronze statue of Jeppesen in the terminal that bears his name, plus several display cases filled with Jeppesen memorabilia. Look for his single-slice "Bachelor Toaster" and the glasses his mom used to read telegrams and letters about her son's aeronautical activities.

One of the best viewing spots at the airport is the bridge between Jeppesen Terminal and Concourse A. Looking westward on a clear day, you can see a majestic 100-mile expanse of the Front Range of the Rocky Mountains. The Great Plains extend into the distance to the east, and since the bridge spans a taxiway, you can watch airplanes pass right underneath you. Other good spots to watch airfield activity are at either end of Concourse B.

►Play Around

Kids will definitely enjoy the more whimsical artwork at DEN, especially the gargoyles in the baggage claim area and the Sweeney maps in Jeppesen Terminal. If that doesn't keep your kids entertained, head for one of the Family Fun Center video arcades near the food court on level 6 of Jeppesen Terminal or in Concourse C.

Go into Town

DEN is located 23 miles northeast of downtown Denver. A taxi ride costs a shocking $45–$55 and takes 40 minutes to an hour. More reasonably priced door-to-door shuttles cost about $20. City buses leave for downtown 15 minutes before every hour from 4:50 AM until 12:45 AM and cost $6. Stop by the ground transportation information booth in Jeppesen Terminal for more information.

Other Information

To get information before you arrive, call 303-342-2000.

Detroit Metropolitan Wayne County Airport

Detroit, Michigan
Airport Code: DTW
Web Address: http://www.metroairport.com

In January 1999, a severe snowstorm so crippled operations at Detroit Metropolitan Wayne County Airport (DTW) that hundreds of passengers were forced to spend excruciating hours stuck in airplanes out on the tarmac. The experience of 198 passengers trapped on just one plane was detailed in a *Wall Street Journal* article and I suspect a made-for-TV movie is in the works. Had these travelers been stuck *inside* the terminal instead, they could have spent their time shopping for golf clubs and sports memorabilia, eating sushi, or happily drinking margaritas at the country's first airport Tequilería.

Get Oriented

- Luggage carts can be found throughout the airport and can be rented for $1.50. You'll get $.25 refund when you return a cart to the rack.
- Lockers are located at the top of each concourse, postsecurity.

Wayne County's Detroit Metropolitan Airport has three passenger terminals: Smith Terminal (south), Davey Terminal (north), and Berry International Terminal, which is accessible from the north and south terminals via a free shuttle bus.

Concourses C, D, E, F, and G in Davey Terminal are used predominantly by Northwest Airlines, which makes DTW its major hub. All other domestic airline flights use Concourses A and B in the older Smith Terminal. It's about a 10-minute walk from Concourse A to Concourse G, but you can cut the time and avoid the crowded hallways by hopping on the moving walkways or riding the free airport shuttle bus that runs between terminals.

Airport officials will be the first to point out that DTW, in its current configuration, is crowded and confusing. A new midfield terminal for Northwest Airlines will help solve the problem, but that's not scheduled to be completed until the end of 2001. In the meantime, there are colorful maps scattered throughout the terminal and green-vested customer service agents roaming the corridors eager to help you find your way around.

Every day between 9 AM and 9 PM you can also stop for directions at Airport Central between Concourses D and E, near the entrance to the Marriott Hotel. You'll find those cheery green-vested customer service agents and an Internet kiosk with links to the airport's Web site, airline Web sites, and local attractions such as the Henry Ford Museum, repository of Thomas Edison's last breath and thousands of other historical artifacts.

Take Care of Yourself

► Eat

In Smith Terminal (near the entrance to Concourses A and B), you'll find the "world's first" Jose Cuervo Tequilería, a full-service Mexican theme restaurant and bar featuring premium tequilas, tequila samplers, and a wide variety of margaritas. If you're not up for a "mini-fiesta" before your flight, head instead for the food court in Concourse F, where you'll find Jody Maroni's (gourmet sausages), Tampopo's Noodle & Sushi, and Cinnabon.

In the Davey Terminal connecting corridor you'll find the Cheers Bar, the Home Turf Sports Bar & Grill, the Ruby Moon Coffee Shop, and several fast-food outlets. For sit-down dining, the Marriott Hotel has the more formal Innkeeper restaurant.

Over in Smith Terminal, in the corridor behind the ticket counters, look for Big Apple Bagels, Mike & Pat's Deli/Lounge, and the Express Gourmet Cafeteria, which has great views of the airfield.

Best Healthful Nosh

Bagels from Big Apple Bagels in Smith Terminal or sushi from Tampopo's Noodle & Sushi in Concourse F.

Best Sinful Snack

Cookies from Mrs. Fields in Concourse E or candy from the Specialty Candy Shop in Concourse F.

►Relax and Refresh

Until the new midfield terminal is complete, you'll find very few quiet spots at DTW. Your best choice for comfortable, out-of-the-way seating will be the large open area in the ticket lobby in Smith Terminal. If you want to keep an eye on the hustle and bustle, grab a seat in the food court in the Davey Terminal corridor, just behind the security checkpoint.

There are no massage services at DTW, but you'll find Laurie's Hair Ways (barbershop/beauty salon) in both Smith Terminal (in the corridor behind the ticket counters) and in the connecting corridor of Davey Terminal (next to the game room). Hours are 8 AM–9 PM on weekdays, 8 AM–2 PM on Saturdays, and 11 AM–9 PM on Sundays.

If you need a nap, a shower, or a workout, head for the Detroit Metro Airport Marriott Hotel (734-941-9400), located between Concourses D and E (between Smith Terminal and Davey Terminal). The hotel's day rate includes access to the health club and complimentary breakfast and snacks in the hotel lounge.

Smoking is not allowed anywhere in the airport.

If the weather is nice and you've got an hour or more, take a 12-mile cab ride over to Crosswinds Marsh, one of the largest man-made wetlands in the country. Built to replace wetlands that were paved over to expand the airport, Crosswinds Marsh has boardwalks over open water, hiking trails, horse trails, and spots for canoeing.

Take Care of Business

- Phones with data ports are scattered throughout terminals.

If you need a private spot to check e-mail or get some work done, stop by the business center, located in the Smith Terminal lobby, across from the United Air Lines ticket counter, which rents fully equipped mini-offices by the minute.

If you need to send a fax or make some copies, Teleticket (in Smith Terminal) offers fax and copying services, a FedEx drop box, and currency exchange. You'll find it near the entrance to Concourses A and B, near the Southwest ticket counter. There's also a post office in the Smith Terminal corridor behind the ticket counters.

Explore the Airport

►Shop

Once, air passengers could shop for a new car at DTW's "Motor Mall," so if you were "stuck at the airport" you could, technically, escape in your own vehicle. Now, however, just one or two of the latest models are displayed in the Smith Terminal lobby as advertisements for a local dealer.

Everything is for sale, however, at the PGA Tour Shop, the Nautica store, and the Sharper Image outlet in the Smith Terminal "mini-mall" in the ticket lobby. If you're a sports fan (or know one) be sure to stop at Time Out, just beyond the mini-mall, which offers clothing and souvenirs emblazoned with logos for the Detroit Redwings, the Detroit Tigers, and other Michigan teams. And if you have a Beanie Baby fan in your family, on Concourse F you'll find an entire store filled with the colorful critters.

►Sightsee

In Smith Terminal, look for the pristine green-and-cream-colored 1929 Hupmobile Cabriolet, courtesy of the Henry Ford Museum in nearby Dearborn. Or stop at Laurie's Hair Ways in the Davey Terminal corridor and see how many world currencies you can identify on the six-foot-tall display in the window. A small game room (more of a game "alcove") is next door. Otherwise, there's not much art and entertainment at DTW.

For a bit of fresh air, go outside in front of the Airport Marriott

Hotel. For good views of the airfield, head to the end of any concourse. If you have a bit more time, take the pedestrian walkway over to the airport parking structure and take the elevator to the roof. From here you can get a good overview of the airport and a look at the downtown Detroit skyline.

►Play Around

There's no formal kids' play area at DTW, but kids might enjoy riding the moving walkways, visiting the Beanie Baby shop and the Time Out sports store, or inspecting the global paper currency displayed in the window of the barbershop in Davey Terminal. Next door to the barbershop there's a small game room. And, if your kids aren't too shy to ask, most every green-vested customer service agent keeps a pocketful of Detroit Metro Airport pilot wings.

Go into Town

The cab ride to downtown Detroit will take anywhere from 30 to 45 minutes and run about $30. Shuttle vans (Commuter Express) will take you downtown for about $19. If you want to try public transportation, look for the SMART bus in front of Smith Terminal, on the lower-level curb front.

Other Information

If you'd like some information before you arrive, call 734-247-7678.

✈ Fort Lauderdale Hollywood International Airport

Fort Lauderdale, Florida
Airport Code: FLL
Web Address: http://www.fll.net

Fort Lauderdale Hollywood International Airport (FLL) first opened for business in 1929 on the site of an abandoned nine-hole golf course. Back then, it was called Merle Fogg Field, in honor of a pioneer Fort Lauderdale aviator. Now called "Gateway to the Gold Coast," the airport serves more than 14 million passengers each year, perhaps because it's located just 20 miles north of Miami, 40 miles south of Palm Beach, and a few miles down the road from Port Everglades, the second-largest cruise-ship port in the world.

Get Oriented

- Luggage carts rent for $1.50.
- Lockers are located on the concourses. The business center in Terminal 2 will also store baggage for $2–$5 per day.

The airport has an easy-access, U-shaped layout and it's an easy 5-minute walk between any of the terminals. However, since FLL is undergoing major renovation and expansion, be prepared to encounter unfinished projects and perhaps some detours along the way. For now, though, look for Continental, America West, Northwest, and TWA in Terminal 1 and Delta, Comair, and Midway Airlines in Terminal 2. Terminal 3 (Concourses E and F) hosts MetroJet, US Airways, American, Southwest, and United. In Terminal 4 (Concourse H) you'll find Air Canada, JetBlue, and various other airlines.

Don't be shy about asking any airport employee for a map or directions. FLL employees were the first in the state to attend

"Airport Ambassador" classes, and are eager to assist travelers. The training has certainly paid off: a visitor once dropped a wallet containing $5,000 in cash that was returned by an ambassador with the contents intact.

Take Care of Yourself

► **Eat**

New restaurants (Chili's Too, T.J. Cinnamon, Spinaci's, and Jake's Coffee House) are located in Terminal 1. You can also have a sit-down meal at the Marketplace Restaurant in the middle of Terminal 3, behind the ticket counters. For pizza, try Sbarro in Terminals 2 and 4, or Americo's in Terminal 3 (Concourse C). For a wide variety of sandwiches, head for the Deli Bar in Terminal 2. For a real treat, though, try a Caribbean-style ice cream from Willie's, part of an ice-cream chain from Tobago, West Indies. It's located in Terminals 2 and 3 and features exotic flavors including "Jamaican Grate Nut" and "Chocolate Creole."

Best Healthful Nosh

The salad bar at the Marketplace Restaurant in Terminal 2.

Best Sinful Snack

Ice cream with a Caribbean twist from Willie's Tropical Ice-Cream Shop, in Terminals 2 and 3.

► **Relax and Refresh**

If you spent the last night of your vacation dancing instead of sleeping, the best place to nap at FLL is in the comfortable, cushioned seats in Terminal 3. At the south end of Terminal 3 across from the Northwest Airlines ticket counter, you'll find the meditation room—ask a guard at the security checkpoint to unlock it for you. If sunshine is what you're after, head for the benches outside Terminal 4.

Smokers can light up outside or in any of the airport bars.

Take Care of Business

• Business center services include ATM, fax, copy, and postage machines.

Business centers are located in all three terminals. The main center is located at the east end of Terminal 2, next to the bookstore. Self-service facilities are located behind the ticket counter in Terminal 3 and at the east end of Terminal 4.

Explore the Airport

►**Shop**

Golf is big in Florida and big at the airport as well. The upscale PGA Tour Shop in Terminal 3 (at the entrance to Concourse F) offers videos, books, golfing attire, and all manner of golfing accoutrements, and whenever there's a pro tournament in town, big-name golfers stop by for book signings and celebrity appearances.

If golfing isn't your bag, you can grab something to read at bookstores located in Terminals 2 and 3, or snag a Florida Marlins baseball cap or earrings made by a member of Florida's Seminole Indian tribe at any of the airport's gift shops. Kids Corner, in Terminal 2, carries stuffed animals, toys, T-shirts, Disney souvenirs, and other fun stuff.

►**Sightsee**

Although the airport owns an all-too-real-looking Duane Hansen sculpture, several large-format paintings, and a collection of Native American art and artifacts, it's all packed away until several construction projects are completed and the dust, literally, settles. In the meantime, don't be shy about heading over to the airport's administrative offices on the second floor of Terminal 4 and taking a tour through their small aviation history museum. It's open Monday–Friday, 8 AM–5 PM.

From the sidewalk that connects Terminals 3 and 4 you can look out onto an active taxiway and across to the airport's award-winning mile-long jogging trail featuring a wide variety of exotic plants. The rooftop of the new seven-story parking garage has benches and a formal viewing area offering glimpses of the airport, the city, and the nearby beaches.

►Play Around

Kids might enjoy stretching their legs in the grassy area between the two parking garages or browsing for toys and souvenirs at Kids Corner in Terminal 2.

Go into Town

To get a cab or shared shuttle ride into town, check in at the transportation podium on the lower level of each terminal. Rate-comparison charts are posted at each podium, but a ride to Port Everglades (cruise-ship central), for example, is $6. If you want to take public transportation, Broward County Transit (BCT) bus stops are located at the east end of Terminal 2, between Terminals 3 and 4, and at the east end of Terminal 2. Tri-Rail feeder buses and BCT mass transit both operate daily schedules.

Other Information

If you need information about the airport before you arrive, call 954-359-6100.

✈ Bradley International Airport

Hartford/Springfield, Connecticut (Windsor Locks, CT)
Airport Code: BDL
Web Address: http://www.bradleyairport.com

Located in Connecticut's Hartford/Springfield area and equidistant between Boston and the New York City metro areas, low-key Bradley International Airport (BDL) advertises itself as the "Just Plane Easy" alternative to the congested "big-city" airports.

Get Oriented

- Luggage carts rent for $1.50. The machines offer a $.25 refund when you return a cart to the rack.
- There are no storage lockers.

The airport has two passenger terminals, three concourses, an international arrivals building, and 28 gates. Both terminals have a State Tourism Welcome Center staffed by friendly folks who are happy to give directions and ideas for staying busy while you're "stuck at the airport."

It should take you no longer than 5 minutes to go between terminals. Continental, United, US Airways, and MetroJet operate out of Terminal A, and American, Delta, Comair, Midway, Northwest, Shuttle America, and TWA operate out of Terminal B.

Take Care of Yourself

► Eat

There are several snack bars, cocktail lounges, and restaurants in the terminals, but if you're stuck here in the morning, try lingering over the breakfast buffet at the Concorde Restaurant in the Sheraton Bradley Hotel. Later in the morning, the Sam Adams Brewhouse in Terminal B is your best bet. For coffee drinkers, the best bet is the Dunkin' Donuts coffee stand by the TWA and Northwest departure gates.

Best Healthful Nosh

Salads at the Concorde Restaurant in the Sheraton Bradley Hotel, located in the corridor between Terminals A and B.

Best Sinful Snack

Desserts from the Concorde Restaurant or a chocolate-covered banana from Munson's Chocolates, which has an outlet in both terminals.

►Relax and Refresh

There's a fairly comfortable seating area along the corridor connecting Terminals A and B, close to the Terminal B side, and spots in both Terminals A and B where it's possible to sit and relax. For more serious relaxation, there's a full-service Sheraton Hotel, the Sheraton Bradley, located right in the terminal, with an entrance in the lobby connecting the terminals. You might hang out in the seating areas in the lobby or watch the big-screen TV in the lobby bar. If you want to take a dip in the hotel pool or use the health club facilities, however, you'll have to negotiate a day rate (860-627-5933).

Smokers must either go outside the terminals to light up, or visit one of the airport cocktail lounges.

Take Care of Business

• Internet kiosks are located in both terminals and in the concourses.

American Audio Visual, a business center tucked into the lobby of the Sheraton Bradley Hotel, has copiers, a fax machine, computer workstations with printers, and FedEx, UPS, and USPO pickup boxes. Hours: Monday–Friday, 7 AM–5 PM; 860-623-5381. The business center is accessible from the connecting corridor between Terminals A and B.

Explore the Airport

►Shop

You can pick up a wide variety of New England–made products and souvenirs such as candles, gift food items, and UConn Huskies and Yale sports paraphernalia in the Paradies Shops located throughout the terminals. Candy and chocolate fans will want to visit Munson's Chocolates, even if you're just window-shopping.

►Sightsee

There's artwork by local artists in the exhibit cases in Terminal A, across from the US Airways and United ticket counters. Halfway down the connecting corridor between Terminals A and B, look for four display cases filled with items promoting area history and tourist attractions in the Hartford and Springfield areas.

For something truly unusual, look for the three large color photos hanging on the wall in the corridor connecting Terminals A and B. Next to the photos are three patch-sized embroidered scenes created by Raymond Materson to honor the 1995 Special Olympics. Materson, who was in prison when he took up embroidery, unraveled his socks to get the colored thread used in his artwork. Materson is now a free man whose embroidery is featured in top museums and art galleries.

You can keep an eye on the ramp area between the two terminals from the connecting corridor and from the restaurant in the Sheraton Hotel. There are also good views of the airfield from the end of the concourse in Terminal A (the US Airways gate area) and at the end of Concourse A in Terminal B (the American Airlines gate area).

While there are no sidewalks or park areas outside the terminal, there are interesting spots just beyond the airport that can keep a traveler occupied for hours. Just across from parking lot 3, for example, there's a "teletheater" that simulcasts live racing action from horse tracks around the country. Or take the free shuttle for a 3-minute ride over to the New England Air Museum, which features the second-largest indoor display of vintage and historic aircraft in the Northeast, dating from 1909 to the present.

►Play Around

Kids might enjoy a walk along the corridor connecting the two terminals and stopping to inspect the display cases of vintage items promoting area history and tourist attractions. If you've got 2 hours or more, head for the off-site New England Air Museum, which is full of vintage and historic aircraft. Or show the kids the embroidered patches Raymond Materson made with thread he got by unraveling his prison-issued socks. Although Materson's work is now included in museum collections, the patch display provides a good opportunity to have that heart-to-heart talk about why crime doesn't pay.

Go into Town

The 12-mile cab ride to downtown Hartford will take between 15 and 30 minutes and cost $28, flat rate. There are also shuttle and van services that make the trip for about $13. Connecticut Transit has regularly scheduled public bus service to Hartford and the surrounding area. For schedules, check with the folks at the ground transportation center on the lower level of each terminal.

Other Information

For more information about Bradley International Airport before you arrive, call 860-292-2000.

✈ Honolulu International Airport

Honolulu, Hawaii
Airport Code: HNL
Web Address: http://www.state.hi.us/dot/airports/oahu

Ranked as the 37th busiest airport in the world, the open-air Honolulu International Airport (NHL) is just 3 miles from downtown Honolulu and 9 miles from Waikiki Beach. Step off the airplane here and you know right away you're in a tropical land: everyone's in shorts, lots of folks are wearing necklaces made of bright-colored flowers, and the air smells sweet—a combination of flowers and all that pineapple heading out to the mainland.

Get Oriented

- Luggage carts rent for $2 and are located throughout the airport.
- Coin-operated lockers are located opposite Gates 12, 13, 14, 23, and 24 in the main terminal. A staffed baggage storage center is located on the ground level of the parking structure opposite the main terminal.

Honolulu International Airport has three terminals: Overseas (the main terminal), Interisland, and Commuter, which are connected via a free shuttle bus endearingly called the WikiWiki bus. If you choose to walk between terminals, be forewarned that it's a 10- to 15-minute walk from the main terminal to Interisland Terminal and up to a 30-minute walk over to Commuter Terminal.

Most services and activities are clustered in the main terminal, which is officially named John Rodgers Terminal, in honor of the pilot who first tried to fly from the mainland to Hawaii back in 1925. The main terminal has open-air breezeways and three concourses: Diamond, Central, and Ewa (which refer to which side of the island you're facing). Diamond Concourse serves United,

Northwest, and Continental, and Central Concourse serves Continental, American, and Delta. Most international flights come and go from gates in Ewa Concourse.

It takes about 15 minutes to walk from one end of the main terminal to the other, but since the corridors are open-air and there's plenty of seating, you won't mind that a bit. If you need directions or information along the way, you'll find information booths located in the baggage claim areas, near Gate 22, and on both ends of the lobby.

Take Care of Yourself

► **Eat**

Stinger Ray's, in the center court of the main terminal, is a sit-down Polynesian-themed restaurant serving pork sandwiches, salads, pupu platters, burgers, and fries. A nearby food court offers noodle soups, sandwiches, baked goods, and other straightforward fare. Elsewhere you'll find noodle shops, pizza and burger stands, and snack bars. Lappert's ice cream, a local favorite, is dished up near Gates 12 and 13 and in Interisland Terminal.

Best Healthful Nosh

Fruitasia (fresh fruit with sherbet and shredded coconut) from Stinger Ray's in the center court of the main terminal.

Best Sinful Snack

Ice cream from Lappert's, near Gates 12 and 13 and in Interisland Terminal.

► **Relax and Refresh**

There are three lovely and tranquil cultural gardens—Japanese, Chinese, and Hawaiian—located on the lower level of the main terminal (postsecurity). Linked seamlessly by a series of pathways and bridges, the gardens feature native plants, lily ponds, a contemplative pagoda, and pools filled with giant carp. Sorry, no fishing allowed.

Just across from Stinger Ray's Restaurant, on the second level of the main lobby, you'll find a hair salon with a licensed bilingual (English and Japanese) masseuse offering services that range from 5-minute neck and foot rubs to hour-long full-body massages. Hours: 6 AM–4 PM, Monday–Saturday; 808-833-6484.

If you need to freshen up, drop by the 17-room Honolulu Airport Hotel, located opposite the main terminal's center stage (808-836-3044). You can take a shower here for $8.50 (the rate includes towels, soap, shampoo, and shaving equipment) or rent a room for a 2-hour shower and nap for $20. For $35, you can rent a single room for up to 8 hours.

Feeling ill? Don't fret: the airport's Queen's Airport Medical facility is open 24 hours and a registered nurse is always on duty. It's located near the Japanese Gardens.

Smoking is permitted in several outdoor areas around the airport.

Take Care of Business

Most major airlines have clubrooms here, but nonmembers can still take care of business at the business center located in the central lobby of the main terminal. It's open 8:30 AM–4:30 PM weekdays (808-834-0058), and includes faxing, copying, and postal services, and workstation rentals.

Explore the Airport

► Shop

Go ahead, buy some pineapples and other tropical fruit. Just be sure you get the packages that are USDA-inspected and packaged for "export." Other popular Hawaiian souvenirs, such as Kona coffee, colorful flower leis, and chocolate-covered macadamia nuts, are plentiful here as well. You'll also have no trouble finding those other classics: aloha wear, T-shirts, and a wide variety of hula-girl emblazoned items.

Shops in the Galleria portion of the main terminal offer a variety of more unusual items ranging from sculpture and ceramics to food items and jewelry. Surf's Up Hawaii carries beachwear,

Hawaiian Isle Memories stocks handmade quilts and a wide variety of Pacific Islands craft items, and the Hawaiian Market offers foodstuffs that include dolphin-shaped pasta, chocolate seashells, and strips of sugar cane.

The Pacific Aerospace Museum in the center lobby of the main terminal (see "Sightsee") has a large shop chock-full of toys, books, models, and other aviation-related gift items.

►Sightsee

If you're at the airport on a Wednesday or Friday morning between 10:30 and 12:00 noon, head over to the stage area just outside Stinger Ray's in the main terminal. If there's a hula troupe or a live band scheduled to perform that day, that's where—and when—you'll find them.

Even if there's no live entertainment, there's plenty to do. The central lobby of the main terminal is the home of the Pacific Aerospace Museum (admission $3). It's open daily, with varying hours. This is a hands-on place, complete with a flight simulator, a full-scale mock-up of a space shuttle flight deck, films, and aviation exhibits ranging from the tale of the flight of the demigod Maui to the Apollo moon landings. No admission is charged to enter the gift shop, which is full of toys, books, and aviation-related souvenirs.

Also, the corridors of the both the main terminal and Inter-island Terminal are dotted with display cases filled with children's art and artifacts such as instruments, tools, cookware, and other items reflecting the local ethnic cultures. And don't forget, there are three cultural gardens in the center of the main terminal, on the lower level.

Most any gate waiting area or breezeway in the airport offers a good view of the airfield.

►Play Around

Kids will enjoy the Pacific Aerospace Museum, rides on the Wiki Wiki bus, or a walk through the gardens, where they'll be able to get up close to the giant carp. On Wednesday and Friday mornings there are often hula troupes, artists, or musicians performing on the stage in the center of the main terminal, by the museum. There's also an arcade located near the entrance to Gates 6–11.

Go into Town

Outside of rush hour, it's about a 20-minute cab ride from the airport to Waikiki. During rush hour, it can take much, much longer. The fare will run between $20 and $25. The Airport Waikiki Express shuttle bus from the airport to any Waikiki hotel is $8. Or try public transportation: City "The Bus" Service routes 19 and 20 go to downtown Waikiki and other points for $1.

Other Information

For more information about Honolulu International Airport, call 808-836-6413.

George Bush Intercontinental Airport

Houston, Texas
Airport Code: IAH
Web Address: http://www.ci.houston.tx.us/has/iah.html

Built on the site of a former dairy farm and located 22 miles north of downtown Houston, the George Bush Intercontinental Airport (IAH) is named for the former US president and ranks 13th among the nation's busiest commercial airports. Nearby Hobby Airport also serves the Houston market, but IAH is the more heavily used and is bursting at the seams and in the midst of a major renovation and expansion project.

Get Oriented

- Luggage carts rent for $2. You'll receive a $.25 refund when you return a cart to the rack.
- Lockers are located in each terminal, postsecurity.

The IAH layout is straightforward: there are four terminals (A, B, C, and D). IAH is a Continental Airlines hub and the airline uses most all the gates in Terminal C. Continental Express, Northwest, and America West operate out of Terminal B, and flights for American, United, Delta, and most other airlines cluster in Terminal A. International flights come and go from Terminal D, the Mickey Leland International Airlines Building.

A low-lit, mile-long underground tunnel connects the four terminals. If you're up for a workout, walk it. Many airport staffers use it for their personal jogging track. The corridor is flat and carpeted, but unfortunately, there's nothing on the walls to break up the monotony of the trek.

If you're toting luggage or in a hurry, skip the hike and hop on the interterminal train, which runs alongside the underground walkway. Three-car trains stop at the terminals and at the on-site

Marriott Hotel every 3–5 minutes and make the run from Terminal A out to Terminal D in 9 minutes. To ease the load on the underground train, a new aboveground monorail service (TerminaLink) runs between Terminals B and C, which serve most Continental flights. Plans call for TerminaLink to connect all terminals sometime in the future.

To get your bearings, ask for a terminal map from any visitor/airport information booth located on the baggage claim level of Terminals A, B, and C, and outside of US Customs in Terminal D.

Take Care of Yourself

► Eat

Your best bet for a snack or a full sit-down meal will be found in either end of Terminal C. The north and south concourses feature Bubba's Seafood Grill, which offers dishes such as Cajun catfish, po'boy sandwiches, and other seafood specialties. Both ends of the terminal also feature food courts offering Harlon's BBQ and other fast-food fare.

You'll find Chili's restaurants in Terminals A and B, and over in Terminal D, you'll find Lefty's Lone Star Bar & Grille, which serves Texas-style chili and "peel & eat" shrimp. Rigger's Pipeline Tavern, in Terminal A, is decorated with oil-company memorabilia and a mural depicting the oil fields of east Texas. There's also a food court in the atrium around the green tree in the south concourse of Terminal A. Look for Chili's, Pizzaria Uno, Camacho's Cantina, Little Kim Son, and a Popcorn Shop. You'll also find Dreyer's Ice Cream in the north and south concourses of Terminal C and in Terminal D.

If you have a bit more time and want to give yourself a special treat, take the interterminal train over to the airport Marriott and take the elevator up to CK's, the revolving restaurant on the top floor.

Best Healthful Nosh

Grilled tuna steak or marinated salmon from Bubba's Seafood in both the north and south concourses of Terminal C.

Best Sinful Snack

Harlon's BBQ ribs, in the north and south concourses of Terminal C, or fresh pecan pralines from the Grove in Terminal A.

► **Relax and Refresh**

A great way to get out of the airport's hustle and bustle is to head for one of the big comfortable chairs in the lobby of Houston Airport Marriott, located between Terminals B and C. If it's late morning or past 6 PM, the central seating area of Terminal D is nice and quiet as well. Or pop into the interfaith chapel in the Terminal C south concourse, by Gate 31. The atrium in the Terminal A south concourse also has a nice seating area around the tall green tree.

If you need to freshen up or get a workout, the Houston Airport Marriott (between Terminals B and C) offers a day rate that includes access to the hotel health club, swimming pool, and Jacuzzi (281-443-2310).

Take Care of Business

There are no formal business centers at IAH, so this is one of those airports where membership in an airline club will be helpful. However, you will find data ports in the majority of pay phones at IAH and public fax machines in each terminal. In addition, you can send faxes and make copies at the American Express currency exchange kiosks in the north and south concourses of Terminal C. At the Terminal D business center/currency exchange kiosk you can send faxes, make copies, or rent a computer workstation with Internet access.

Explore the Airport

► **Shop**

In Terminal D, look for the three-foot-tall cowboy boot outside the Montana Western Wear shop by Gate 7. This is the place to go if you need a pair of python or ostrich boots, a genuine cowboy shirt, or a brass armadillo for your pardners back at the office.

Terminal D also has a luggage store and, at the top of the escalator leading to the gate area, a nice jewelry shop.

Sweeter souvenirs can be found in the Candy Shop (branches in Terminal D and in the Terminal C south concourse) where they stock Longhorns (chocolate-covered pecans and caramel), Texas Chewies, and pecan pralines. In the Terminal C north concourse you'll find the Tie Rack, the Body Shop, a Watch Station, Wilsons Leather, and the Museum Company.

►Sightsee

One of the newest pieces of art at IAH is titled "Countree Music." This tall, bare, green tree is "planted" at the center of a terrazzo floor that contains a Houston-centric map of the earth. Look for the tree in the atrium of the south concourse of Terminal A and listen for the soundtrack, which features the work of local musicians. Elsewhere, you'll find a statue of the late Congressman Mickey Leland in Terminal D and, in the connecting corridor between Terminals C and D, a photo series by local photographers titled "Windows on Houston."

IAH has no formal observation deck, but you'll get great views of the airfield from CK's, the revolving restaurant at the Houston Airport Marriott and from the rooftop parking areas by Terminals A, B, and C.

If you'd rather stay inside, head to Terminal C (the busiest terminal), where most every gate offers a good view of airfield activity and, from Gates C14 and C15, a view of the impressive Terminal D.

►Play Around

While Continental Airlines provides a small play area (a PlaySkool table or playhouse) by most gates in Terminal C, there's little else strictly for kids at IAH. However, kids might enjoy a ride on the new monorail linking Terminals B and C or on the underground interterminal train, which lurches roller-coaster-like on a 2-mile loop between all four terminals. If you need to work off some extra energy, take the family on a mile-long hike on the underground walkway that runs alongside the train tracks.

Go into Town

Public buses, taxis, and shuttle services are all located on the south side of Terminals A, B, and C, and at the west end of Terminal D. A shuttle bus to downtown will cost about $16, while Metro bus service costs $1.50. If you want to take a taxi downtown, the fare will run about $33. The ride can take up to 45 minutes during morning rush hour, 6:00–9:30.

Other Information

If you need more information about the airport before you arrive, call 281-230-3000.

Indianapolis International Airport

Indianapolis, Indiana
Airport Code: IND
Web Address: http://www.indianapolisairport.com

In 1931, Indianapolis Airport was one of the first refueling stops along the "astonishingly fast" 48-hour cross-country "Airway Limited" route: travelers rode by train from New York City to Columbus, Ohio, and then boarded a plane for the balance of the trip west. In 1944, the facility was renamed Weir Cook Municipal Airport, in honor of a local military flying ace, but was re-christened Indianapolis International Airport (IND) in 1976.

Get Oriented

- Luggage carts rent for $1.50 and provide a $.25 refund when a cart is returned to the rack.
- Storage lockers are located postsecurity, in Concourse A and Concourse C.

Indianapolis International Airport has one terminal with four concourses: A, B, C, and D. Concourse A serves Northwest, TWA, Skyway, and Southwest Airlines; Delta, Delta Express, America West, American, and ProAir use Concourse B. Gates for United, United Express, ATA, Midway, and Continental are in Concourse C, and Concourse D services US Airways and US Airways Express.

It should take you no longer than 5–10 minutes to get from one end of the terminal to the other; that is, if you avoid stopping at one of the "Sky Shops" in the main corridor.

Take Care of Yourself

▶ Eat

The airport's main food court has a game room, a nice view of the airfield, and a good variety of offerings, including Asian Chao,

Charley's Steakery, the Salsalito Bar & Grill, Long John Silver's, and several other fast-food staples. In the ticketing corridor you'll encounter California Pizza Kitchen, T.G.I. Friday's, Ben & Jerry's, and a Starbucks that serves sandwiches and light snacks. Subway and Jody Maroni's Sausage Kingdom are located in Concourse A, and Concourse D sports a branch of Dick Clark's American Bandstand restaurant.

Best Healthful Nosh

Baja fish or shrimp tacos from the Salsalito Bar & Grill, in the main terminal, just outside the food court.

Best Sinful Snack

Chocolates from Godiva Chocolatier or candy by the pound from the Sweet Factory, both in the Sky Shop corridor.

►Relax and Refresh

You'll find some out-of-the-way seating in an alcove off the ticket hall on the way to Concourse A and at the tables in the back of the food court, by the windows overlooking the airfield. Other quiet spots include the observation deck (enter by the door near the Concourse B security checkpoint) and the chapel, located next to the United ticket counter.

There are no on-site health clubs or massage bars, but there's a barbershop in the ticket lobby on the way to Concourse A that's open Monday–Saturday. The nearby Holiday Inn offers travelers a day rate that includes access to their health club.

Smokers can light up in the smoking lounge next to the United Club Rooms and in the Cigarettes Cheaper shop in Concourse A.

Take Care of Business

- There are no Internet kiosks at IND, but data ports have been added to most all pay phones. Many of these phones also have fax capability.

You'll find a copy machine by the centrally located information desk and a self-serve postal center down in the baggage claim area. The Travelex kiosk offers currency exchange services, but not much else, making this airport the type of facility where an airline club membership will come in handy for folks trying to take care of business.

Explore the Airport

▶ **Shop**

Indianapolis is home to the Indianapolis 500, the Brickyard 400, and a slew of other racing events. You'll find fans of the sport gathered at the airport branch of Brickyard Authentics, which carries everything from low-cost lighters and stickers to high-end car models and clothing.

For the rest of us, there's a PGA Tour Shop, AltiTunes (CDs and small electronics), Bath & Body Works, Brookstone, Hat World, Perfumania, Waterstone's Booksellers, and the Hoosier Country Store, which sells souvenirs, candy, toys, and an interesting pamphlet titled "Who's a Hoosier?"

▶ **Sightsee**

IND is one of the increasingly rare airports with a still-intact observation deck. You'll find it at the end of the ticket lobby, just to the left of the entrance to the Sweet Shop in Concourse B.

Sports fans can get up close to a real Indy car at the Brickyard Authentics shop in the shopping corridor. History buffs might enjoy the small airport history display in the baggage claim area that includes a piece of the decorative lamp that once "lit the way for early flyers such as Lindbergh, Post, Rickenbacker, Earhart & Doolittle." Upstairs, along the corridor leading to Concourse A, you'll find a shiny silver propeller mounted Excalibur-like in a piece of concrete. It commemorates the inaugural flight of the "Airway Limited," which delivered travelers from the East Coast to the West Coast in "just" 48 hours.

You can get good views of airfield activity from the observation deck, from the food court, and from many spots along the concourses.

► Play Around

There are no children's play areas, but kids of all ages will enjoy a view from the observation deck or a look at the Indy car displayed at the Brickyard Authentics store. Video-game rooms are located out by the gates and in the food court.

Go into Town

A taxi ride to downtown Indianapolis can take from 15 to 25 minutes and cost between $20 and $22. A shared shuttle van makes the trip for $8–$10. City bus service (Indy Go) to downtown Indianapolis costs $1.

Other Information

For more information about Indianapolis International Airport, call 317-487-7243.

McCarran International Airport

Las Vegas, Nevada
Airport Code: LAS
Web Address: http://mccarran.com

Named for Patrick A. McCarran, a popular Nevada senator, Mc-Carran International Airport (LAS) ranks among the top 10 busiest airports in North America and the top 15 in the world. If you're a gambler, getting stuck here could cost (or net!) you a bundle: there are 1,200 slot machines scattered throughout the terminal, and it's not unusual to see travelers torn between getting on their planes and playing just two—or three—more rolls of quarters.

Get Oriented

- Luggage carts rent for $1.50. They are not available in the D Gates concourse.
- Storage lockers are located just past the security checkpoints in the A, B, and C Gates concourses, and near the children's play area on the second level.

Domestic flights on America West, Alaska Airlines, Continental, and US Airways operate out of Terminal 1 (A Gates and B Gates), and most international and charter flights are served by Terminal 2, just north of Terminal 1. All Southwest Airlines flights operate out of the C Gates concourse. The shiny new D Gates concourse serves American, Northwest, TWA, United, Delta, and Las Vegas–based National Airlines, as well as several other carriers.

You can walk, ride the moving sidewalk, or take a short 30-second tram ride to the C Gates concourse. The only way out to the D Gates concourse is via the tram, but once you're aboard, it's only a 90-second ride.

To get your bearings, ask for a terminal map at an information booth, located in the baggage claim area in Terminal 1, and in the D Gates concourse.

Take Care of Yourself

► Eat

If you haven't already eaten too much at the buffets in town, enjoy a sit-down Southwestern meal at Don Alejandro, or lighter fare in the new Las Vegas Raceway Cafe in Terminal 1. In the D Gates concourse you'll find the Prickly Pear restaurant and the 1940s-style Ruby's Dinette—complete with jukebox music and model airplanes hanging from the ceiling—serving hamburgers and classic diner fare.

Just past the security checkpoint for the A Gates and B Gates, you can get fresh bagels at Big Apple Deli or have a beer at Cheers Bar & Grill. Or get a box of chocolate from Ethel M. Chocolates, a locally made favorite available in Terminal 1 and out in the C Gates and D Gates areas.

Best Healthful Nosh

Salads from Big Apple Deli, near the A Gates and B Gates.

Best Sinful Snack

Chocolates from Ethel M. Chocolates in Terminal 1 and out in the C Gates and D Gates areas.

► Relax and Refresh

Finding a quiet place to rest, nap, or read a book is difficult, given the noisy slot machines, talking billboards, and chatty moving walkways. (Between Terminal 1 and the C Gates concourse, and in the D Gates concourse, recorded messages by celebrities such as Bill Cosby, Bette Midler, Dick Clark, and B. B. King remind you to "watch your step," or "stand on the right.") However, there are a few out-of-the-way couches in a slot-machine-free area above baggage claim, next to the Cannon Aviation Museum.

McCarran sports a 24-hour fitness center with a colorful neon entry on level 2, above baggage claim. This branch of the 24-Hour Fitness chain is open to members and to travelers who pay a per-visit fee. If you forgot your workout clothes you can purchase a "workout package," which includes a T-shirt, shorts, and socks (yours to keep!) and athletic shoe rental. The fitness center also offers massage, steam and sauna rooms, personal training, and to-go "snack-packs" that include nutritional supplements.

Smokers will find smoking lounges in Terminal 1 in the A Gates, B Gates, C Gates, and D Gates areas and in Terminal 2.

Take Care of Business

• Data ports are available at various points throughout the airport.

You can send a fax or make copies at Travelex, between the America West and Delta Air Lines ticket counters. While negotiations are currently under way to establish at least three self-service business centers at this airport, for now you need a membership pass to an airline club lounge if you want to conduct any serious business.

Explore the Airport

►Shop

Leaving Las Vegas with cash in your pockets? You can easily empty them at the airport's slot machines or shops. Bellagio, Treasure Island, the Mirage, New York, New York, and virtually all the big Las Vegas hotels have shops here, offering you one more chance to purchase a T-shirt, jacket, or some other logo-emblazoned item. You can also buy boxer shorts, cigars, puppets, and Harley-Davidson apparel, as well as chocolate casino chips, dice, and other gambling-related items you can use to stay in practice back home.

Without a doubt, the most unusual and "out of this world" spot to check for souvenirs is a shop called Area 51 in the D Gates concourse. The name refers to the high-security area outside Las Vegas that some folks believe is a government holding area for aliens and their spacecraft. Whether you buy that or not, it's fun to scour this shop for alien-related souvenirs and memorabilia.

► Sightsee

Airport officials claim that, because of the highly regulated nature of the gambling industry, you're just as likely to strike it rich playing one of the airport's more than 1,200 slot machines as you are playing anywhere else in town. Proceeds from the terminal slot machines exceed $25 million a year, but rest assured that, at least once in a while, jackpots are paid out: in November 1999 a lucky traveler waiting for his flight back to Alaska won $1.5 million.

For free entertainment, visit the top-notch Cannon Aviation Museum on level 2 of Terminal 1. The museum is home to a bright red 1956 Ford Thunderbird convertible and exhibits honoring Amelia Earhart, Hollywood stunt flyer Jack Frye, and eccentric billionaire Howard Hughes. An original Hacienda Cessna aircraft used for a world-record, nonstop "endurance" flight in 1959 hangs above baggage claim as an "advertisement" for the museum upstairs.

Before the D Gates concourse was built, the best viewing spot was out in the parking garage. Nowadays it's at the "Great Hall" by the D Gates, where a 45-foot-high south-facing window provides views of the airfield and the desert beyond. Cross over to any window on the north side to catch a peek of the glittering Las Vegas strip.

► Play Around

Older kids will enjoy the exhibits in the Aviation Heritage Museum and the alien-related items for sale in Area 51 in the D Gates concourse. Take younger kids to the children's play area on level 2 of the D Gates concourse, where they'll be entertained by an interactive mini control tower, a mock jet engine, telescopes, and great view of the airfield.

Go into Town

It's just 9 miles and a 15-minute cab ride from the airport to the end of the Las Vegas strip; downtown is only 12 miles away. A taxi ride downtown will cost about $21 and about $16 to the strip. Shuttle vans make the trip for no more than $4.50. You can also ride the bus: Citizens Area Transit routes 108 and 109 serve the airport for a fare of $1.25.

Other Information

To get information about the airport before you arrive, call 702-261-5733.

 **Gatwick Airport**

London, England
Airport Code: LGW
Web Address: http://www.gatwick.co.uk

Located 28 miles south of London in West Sussex, Gatwick Airport (LGW) was once the site of a horse-racing track and headquarters for a small flying club. In 1958, when Gatwick officially opened for business as an alternative to Heathrow Airport, none other than Her Majesty the queen was on hand for the festivities. Today, Gatwick Airport is the second busiest airport in the United Kingdom, serving more than 30 million passengers a year.

Get Oriented

- Luggage carts (called "baggage trolleys" here) are free and available throughout the terminal.
- No self-service lockers here. Store gear at Left Baggage in the North Terminal departure area next to Zone F check-in and in the South Terminal Arrivals Concourse at the customs exit. "Skis and polo mallets are fine," the attendant told me, "but please, no more suitcases filled with dried fish."

Gatwick has a north and south terminal, connected via a free shuttle train accessible from the arrivals area of each terminal. Trains leave about every 3 minutes and the trip back and forth takes just about 2 minutes. If you're connecting "airside" to an international flight, there's an interterminal bus that leaves every 10–15 minutes from the Flight Connections area in each terminal. That ride will take about 5 minutes.

In the North Terminal you'll find flights for Air France, British Airways, Delta Air Lines, and other international airlines. The

South Terminal serves Continental, Northwest, TWA, US Airways, Virgin Atlantic, and others.

Take Care of Yourself

► **Eat**

Gatwick boasts the only Planet Hollywood restaurant (and gift shop) located at an airport. You'll find it in the Gatwick Village shopping area in the South Terminal, decorated with film memorabilia that includes a mean-looking bat from the 1989 Batman movie and a pile of gold bars (painted, I'm sure) from the 1995 film *Die Hard With a Vengeance,* starring Bruce Willis.

Landside in the South Terminal, try Garfunkel's restaurant or the Village Inn for table service, and La Brioche Dorée in the food court for quiches and salads. Past security, try the Shakespeare Ale House or the Metro Café. In the North Terminal, you'll find the Dickens Inn before security, and the Seafood & Oyster Bar and The Red Lion pub postsecurity.

Best Healthful Nosh

The daily soup special from the New Covent Garden Soup Company or fresh oysters and seafood from the Seafood & Oyster Bar in the North Terminal, after security.

Best Sinful Snack

Chocolates from Thorntons or the Cadbury Shop in the South Terminal shopping area.

► **Relax and Refresh**

The Spectators Gallery on the top floor of the South Terminal is a lovely place to relax and get out of the hustle and bustle. If you'd rather stay inside, you'll find out-of-the-way seating areas near the Gatwick Village shopping area and additional seating beyond security, in the departure area of each terminal.

For a change of scenery, head for the quiet lobby of either the Gatwick Hilton (accessible from the South Terminal) or Le Meridien London Gatwick (attached to the North Terminal). If it's complete solitude you need, both terminals sport chapels. The chapel in the North Terminal is in the arrivals concourse, and in the South Terminal you'll find the chapel on the shopping level.

Need to freshen up? Gatwick offers free shower facilities on the departure level of the North Terminal and on the Gatwick Village level of the South Terminal. If you'd like soap and a towel, simply pick up the courtesy phone by the shower room door and someone will bring them over. There's a small charge for the soap (£1, about US$1.45) and you'll be asked to leave a deposit for the towel.

Gatwick has no on-site health clubs, but both on-site hotels, the Gatwick Hilton Hotel and Le Meridien, offer access to their pool, shower, and health club facilities for a reasonable fee of about £5, or about US$7.25. Both hotels also have hair salons and offer a day rate for rooms.

Need to smoke? Gatwick has designated smoking areas throughout the terminal.

Take Care of Business

- The Internet Exchange operates three locations at Gatwick: on the first floor of the South Terminal (in Gatwick Village) and postsecurity in both the North and South Terminals. In addition to computer and Internet access, you can print documents and send faxes. Tip: Get reduced rates by becoming a member—it's free—and log on before noon to get the cheapest rates all afternoon.

British Airways, Delta, American, US Airways, Continental, and Virgin Atlantic are among the airlines offering business lounges for their club members at Gatwick. Some clubs offer showers and other special amenities.

Non–club members who need to get work done might head for the business centers located at the Hilton Hotel in the South Terminal or the Le Meridien Hotel in the North Terminal, where they provide faxing and copying services and a variety of secretarial support services (Hilton: 44-1293-518-080; Le Meridien: 44-1293-567-070).

Twenty-four-hour currency exchange bureaus are located in

both Gatwick terminals, before and after passport control. There are ATMs and stamp machines in both terminals and a full-service post office in the South Terminal shopping village which also operates a shop selling stationery and packing materials along with postal souvenirs and other philatelic items. The post shop has a copy machine for black-and-white copies only. Many public phones have data ports and allow you to send faxes.

Explore the Airport

▶ Shop

You can spend hours shopping—or just browsing—at Gatwick, where the offerings range from socks and soccer souvenirs to watches and whiskies. Shopping areas are located before and after security in both terminals, so don't rush toward the departure lounge if you don't have to.

Highlights in the South Terminal Gatwick Village shopping area (before security) include a Warner Bros. store, Monsoon (clothing for women and kids), a post office shop (collectible stamps and postal souvenirs), the Cadbury store (chocolates!), and Manchester United, where soccer fans can get souvenir shirts, balls, and other items emblazoned with the logo of this popular team. Shops past security include a Disney Store, the Chocolate Box, a wide variety of tax- and duty-free shops, a Nike store, and a branch of Harrods.

Over in the North Terminal you'll find Nine West (shoes), Virgin Records, the Body Shop, Glorious Britain, and the Sock Shop before security. Postsecurity, you'll encounter the Caviar House, Harrods, the Pen Shop, Past Times (gifts representing various decades and centuries), the Scotch House (clothing and gifts), and the World of Whiskies.

▶ Sightsee

On the deck of the Spectators Gallery, on the top floor of the South Terminal, you can inspect the cockpit of a De Havilland Comet 2R, the world's first jetliner, and take a walk through the fuselage of a Super Dart Herald 200 series airplane.

The outdoor Spectators Viewing Area, located on the upper floor of the South Terminal, offers great views of the airfield. There's a small fee to go out there.

►Play Around

- Gatwick provides several specially equipped baby-care rooms for feeding and changing babies. These rooms are noted by a "bottle" sign or a baby-care symbol. You'll also finding changing facilities in bathrooms throughout the airport and fold-down tables in many men's and women's bathrooms.

Kids will enjoy a visit to the outdoor Spectators Gallery (top floor, South Terminal), where they can watch the planes take off and land, inspect the cockpit of a De Havilland Comet 2R, or board an airplane filled with educational exhibits. For even more fun, head for Skyview Gatwick, located in the Gatwick Village shopping area in the South Terminal. Billed as an "aviation experience," Skyview includes a multimedia show portraying a day in the life of Gatwick and a variety of "action-packed" simulator rides. Admission is charged for access to the viewing area and also for the Skyview rides.

There are video games and coin-operated kiddie rides sprinkled throughout the airport and full-fledged game rooms (Game Grid and Serendipity Entertainment Center) before and after security in both terminals.

Kids 2–6 years old will enjoy the (free) play areas located in the North Terminal departure lounge and in the South Terminal village area on the third floor.

Go into Town

A taxi ride into London will take about an hour and cost more than £50, or about US$72. You'll do better—and get there faster—if you take a train. Two trains (Connex South Central and the Gatwick Express) travel from Gatwick (South Terminal) to London's Victoria Coach Station in just about a half hour. Connex costs £8.20 one way, or about US$12, while Gatwick Express tickets cost £9.50, or about US$14. Day return tickets on both lines are just a bit more than one-way.

Buses to London's Victoria Coach Station (Jetlink 777) leave every hour or two from the ground floor of the South Terminal and make the journey into town in about 90 minutes. For more details, check with an information desk in either terminal.

Other Information

To get more information about the airport before you arrive, check the Web site or call 44-1293-535-353.

 # Heathrow Airport

London, England
Airport Code: LHR
Web Address: http://www.baa.co.uk
or http://www.heathrow.co.uk

When Heathrow Airport (LHR) first began operation as London's principal commercial airport, back in 1946, its facilities consisted of a tented village bordered by a row of red telephone boxes and a post office. Concrete prefab army-surplus buildings replaced the tents, and now Heathrow, the world's busiest international airport, has four modern terminal buildings to serve an average of 60 million passengers each year.

Get Oriented

- Free luggage carts (called "baggage trolleys" here) are available throughout the terminals and parking areas.
- Baggage can be stored at the "left luggage" shops located in each terminal. The Excess Baggage Company operates in Terminals 2 and 3, while Burns International Facility Services are located in Terminals 1 and 4.

Heathrow Airport has four terminals (1, 2, 3, 4; a fifth is on the drawing board) serving more than 90 airlines, so if you're departing from Heathrow, ask your airline which terminal to head for. If you're touring the airport, you'll find that the walk is shortest (about 5 minutes) between Terminals 1 and 2, but that Terminal 4 is not within walking distance of Terminals 1, 2, and 3. To get around, grab one of the free shuttle buses that stop at all terminals or hop on the Heathrow Express train, which is free for passengers going between Terminal 4 and Terminal 1, 2, or 3.

Take Care of Yourself

►**Eat**

You'll find both sit-down and fast-food restaurants in each terminal along with plenty of good coffee shops and snack bars. For "real meals" in Terminal 1, check Garfunkel's restaurant (before and after security), and over in Terminal 2 try the pub food offered by the Shakespeare Ale House and Wetherspoons. The "Food Village" in Terminal 3 (before security) has a salad bar and a highly rated Indian restaurant called Noon. Postsecurity in Terminal 3 you'll find both Garfunkel's restaurant and the Shakespeare Ale House. Terminal 4 sports a Wetherspoon's pub both before and after security as well as another branch of Garfunkel's restaurant and a good selection of coffee bars.

Best Healthful Nosh

Quiches and salads from La Brioche Dorée (postsecurity in Terminal 1 and before security in Terminal 2) or fresh shellfish and seafood at the Seafood & Oyster Bar (postsecurity in Terminals 1, 2, 3, and 4).

Best Sinful Snack

Ice cream from Thorntons in Terminal 3 or fish and chips from Harry Ramsden's in Terminal 1 and 3 (before security).

►**Relax and Refresh**

- Golfers rejoice: At the Golf Studio in Terminal 1 (postsecurity) you can play virtual-reality golf, enter the weekly competition for the longest drive, or get a lesson from a golf pro.

Grab a seat near any food court if you want to sit back and watch other travelers rush by. Or head "airside," for the departure lounges, if you're looking for more comfortable seating, including some areas that feature "sleeper chairs" for the extremely weary.

If a little pampering perks you up, visit The Beauty Centre in Terminal 1 (postsecurity), where several types of facials and manicures are complimentary with the purchase of varying amounts of cosmetic and body-care products.

If lighting up a cigarette is your form of refreshment, look for the glass-enclosed smoking boxes and other designated smoking areas throughout the terminals.

For more serious freshening-up, head for the free shower facilities located in Terminals 1, 3, and 4. In Terminal 1, they're located before security; in Terminal 3 the showers are next to the check-in areas and after security; and in Terminal 4 you'll find showers before and after security. A towel and some soap will cost £1, or about US$1.45.

The Business Centre (located in the Queens Building, between Terminals 1 and 2) also has shower facilities, but you'll need to pay the center's day rate of £10 (about US$15) for the privilege. For that same amount you can shower, swim, and get a workout over at the London Heathrow Airport Hilton, accessible via a covered walkway from Terminal 4. The Hilton's bright lobby and restaurant area also offer a relaxing refuge from the bustling airport activities. Rumpled travelers who must look presentable after a long flight can also use Heathrow's newest passenger amenity, "The Island." Located in Terminal 3, this lounge features 29 shower suites with towels and toiletries, shoe cleaning, and clothes valet service. They'll even steam-clean your suit! A visit to The Island will set you back £25, or about US$36.

The Hilton, as well as most any of the hotels that ring the airport, offers rooms at day rates for travelers on long layovers. The folks at the Hotel Reservation desks, located in the arrivals area of each terminal, can help you choose a place that fits your budget. Just remember they charge a booking fee.

Take Care of Business

All major airlines have club member lounges at Heathrow, and Internet café service is offered at the Internet Exchange in the Terminal 3 arrivals area and at Webpoint, in Terminal 4, past the security checkpoint. You can get copies and faxes sent at most

Travelex kiosks and there are wall-mounted pay fax machines located near some banks of pay phones in each terminal.

Non–club members who need to get serious business taken care of might consider paying the £20 day rate (about US$29) at The Business Centre, located in the Queens Building, between Terminals 1 and 2. They offer access to computer workstations and faxing, photocopying, and Internet services. The Business Centre is open Monday–Friday only (44-181-759-2434).

Explore the Airport

►Shop

You can shop for everything from jams and jellies to fine jewels at Heathrow, so be sure to leave some time—and money—for this pastime. For a complete list of shops and their terminal locations, pick up a current "Heathrow Flight & Travel Information Guide" at any information desk. And don't worry if one of the duty-free shops you want to shop at isn't in the terminal you'll be departing from: Heathrow has a free "personal shopping service" that provides escorts to take you between terminals so you can shop in whatever store strikes your fancy.

Some highlights presecurity: Virgin Music Store (Terminal 1), the Sock Shop (Terminal 2), Glorious Britain (Terminal 3), and the Body Shop (Terminal 4). Postsecurity, you'll find branches of Harrods, the Caviar House, the Chocolate Box, and the World of Whiskies in each terminal. Terminal 1 has the Golf Studio; Terminal 2 sports the Pen Shop and the Perfume Gallery; Terminal 3 has a Crabtree & Evelyn shop; and Terminal 4 features a branch of the British Museum Store.

►Sightsee

If you've got 2 hours or more to spend touring, ask the folks at an information desk for directions to the Heathrow Airport Visitor Centre, which features a series of interactive exhibits covering the airport's past, present, and future. The center is a free 10-minute bus ride from the main terminals, but it's an entertaining and educational endeavor that includes a great view of one of the airport's three runways.

For great views of airfield activities, head for the free Spectators Viewing Gallery on the roof of Terminal 2. This observation area also features a cafeteria, an aviation-oriented gift shop, and an outdoor garden area.

► Play Around

Kids of all ages will enjoy watching airplanes take off and land from the outdoor Spectators Viewing Gallery on the Terminal 2 rooftop, and they'll have a ball over at the visitor center, located on the edge of the airport property, just a free 10-minute bus ride away.

The visitor center features a wide variety of informational and interactive exhibits that explain airport operations—everything from what happens when passengers check in and go through security checkpoints to just how pilots know where to park the planes. Kids can take home souvenir brass rubbings from airplane plaques and use the center's upper level to watch planes take off and land.

Go into Town

A taxi ride from Heathrow to central London will take about an hour and cost about £40, or about US$58. A faster and much less expensive way to get into town is via the Heathrow Express train to London's Paddington station, which takes just 15–20 minutes. Fares are £10 (or about US$14.50) per person. (First-class seats cost double.) The London Underground (Piccadilly Line) also runs into town from the airport, with one station serving Terminals 1, 2, and 3 and a separate stop for Terminal 4. The trip into town will take about 50 minutes and costs £3.30, or about US$4.80. The Airbus makes a run from the airport into town 4 times an hour, making pickups outside each terminal. Fares are £6, or about US$8.70. There are two routes (A1 and A2), which make 23 stops throughout the city, including many major hotels. For more information about schedules, fares, and other methods transportation methods—including bus routes and bicycle paths to and from Heathrow—stop at one of the information desks located in each terminal.

Other Information

While you're at the airport, consider this:

The Heathrow Lost Property Office keeps busy with more than 200 phone calls per day from passengers who have misplaced things. Among the more intriguing items left or "misplaced" by passengers are a glass eye, a suitcase full of dead fish, a false leg, and the entire front end of a Ford Escort car.

If you lose your suitcase or the front of end of your car, or need any information about Heathrow, call 44-181-759-4321.

Los Angeles International Airport

Los Angeles, California
Airport Code: LAX
Web Address: http://www.lawa.org/lax/welcome.htm

Known simply as Mines Field when it first opened in 1928, Los Angeles International Airport (LAX) was a military facility during World War II that converted to commercial service in 1946. At one point the LA County Board of Supervisors proposed renaming the airport Jimmy Stewart International Airport, in honor of the late, lanky actor who earned a Distinguished Flying Cross while serving in the US Air Force, but the city council nixed the idea.

Get Oriented

- Luggage carts rent for $1.50.
- Storage lockers are located in all terminals.

The airport's nine terminals are laid out in a large horseshoe pattern with Tom Bradley International Terminal at the top. Terminal 1 serves mostly America West, US Airways, and Southwest Airlines. Terminal 2 hosts Air Canada, Northwest, Hawaiian Airline, Virgin Atlantic, and others. Alaska Airlines, Trans World Airlines, Midwest Express, Horizon, and American Airlines work out of Terminal 3, and Terminal 4 primarily serves American Airlines and American Eagle flights. Delta flights come and go at Terminal 5; Continental and Lufthansa at Terminal 6; and United and United Shuttle at Terminals 7 and 8. Tom Bradley International Terminal serves more than 35 different airlines.

To get your bearings, stop at a Travelers Aid booth in any terminal and grab an airport map. Then hop on a shuttle bus—A circles the nine terminals, B and C stop at each terminal but then go to the parking lots—and cruise around the airport.

Take Care of Yourself

► **Eat**

LAX has a bit of everything: Wolfgang Puck restaurants in Terminals 2 and 7, California Pizza Kitchen in Terminals 1 and 8, and espresso bars, wine bars, or pubs in just about every terminal. If that's not enough, you'll find El Paseo (Mexican food) in Terminal 1 and in Tom Bradley International Terminal, Malibu Al's in Terminal 5, Sushi Boy and the Daily Grill in Tom Bradley International Terminal, and the 1940s-style Ruby's Dinette in Terminal 6.

If you're not in a big hurry and crave something a bit different, take a 5-minute walk over to the landmark Theme Building in the center of the airport and ride the elevator up to the Encounter Restaurant. The folks from Disney added a Hollywood touch to the place, with everything from a theme tune in the elevator to silvery spaceship-inspired uniforms for the serving staff. Martinis at the lava lamp–filled bar have names like "Cosmos" or "Jet Set."

Best Healthful Nosh

Salads from Wolfgang Puck's in Terminals 2 and 7.

Best Sinful Snack

Candy from the See's Candy carts in Terminals 1, 3, and 4.

► **Relax and Refresh**

A great place to relax is the mezzanine level of Tom Bradley International Terminal, where you'll find comfortable chairs, places to eat, interesting bars, and lots of traffic (people and airplanes) to watch. Or rent a workstation cubicle at The Gate Escape (Terminals 7, 8, and the Tom Bradley International Terminal) and watch TV or a DVD, play computer games, or simply listen to music.

On a warm day, head for the observation deck on the roof of the Theme Building. Grab lunch, bring a book, or just relax and take in the view. It's open 8:30 AM–5:00 PM.

If you're stuck at LAX for a while, there's a 24-hour fitness center at the nearby Los Angeles Airport Hilton where for $10 you can work out, take a sauna or a shower, and get rejuvenated. In true LA fashion, the health club is open 24 hours a day (310-410-4000). Golfers can jump in a cab and head for the nearby Westchester Golf Course. For greens fees and availability of rental clubs, call 310-649-9167.

Smokers can light up in one of two outdoor mini-garden/ smoking lounges located in Terminals 3 and 6.

Take Care of Business

The Gate Escape offers business centers with cubicle-style workstations in Terminals 7 and 8 (postsecurity) and on the departure level of the Tom Bradley International Terminal. In addition to fax and copy services, these centers feature workstations with flat screen monitors, Internet access, DirecTV, on- and off-line games, and DVD players. Additional sites are planned for Terminals 1, 3, and 4 as well.

Explore the Airport

►Shop

In case you passed over the souvenirs at Disneyland, Universal Studios, or other Los Angeles tourist magnets, you'll have a second chance at the airport. In addition to the basics, there are four branches of Waterstone's Booksellers (in Terminals 1, 3, and 6, and in Tom Bradley International Terminal); a branch of Alti-Tunes and the Warner Bros. store in Tom Bradley International Terminal; and a shop called I Love LA in Terminal 4. And for your sweetie back home there are See's Candy carts in Terminals 1, 3, and 4.

►Sightsee

• Two hundred acres of sand dunes at the west end of the
LAX runways are set aside to protect the endangered El
Segundo blue butterfly and 90 other species of plants
and animals who make the dunes their home.

The largest and most intriguing piece of art at the airport is the space-age structure smack in the middle of the airport itself. This is the airport's Theme Building, constructed in 1961 as part of a $50 million construction project. Designated a city cultural and historical landmark in 1992, the building boasts 135-foot-high parabolic arches and houses the airport's observation deck, the Encounter Restaurant, and, on the first floor, the City Deli.

Great views of airfield activity and the surrounding cityscape can be had from the observation deck on top of the Theme Building. In Tom Bradley International Terminal you'll find comfortable seating near the food court, close to a large window that overlooks the main taxiway connecting the north and south runways.

► **Play Around**

Even if your kids have never seen the *Jetsons* cartoon, they'll still enjoy the space-age Theme Building, where they can watch planes from the rooftop observation deck.

Go into Town

Taxi fares to downtown Los Angeles are about $30. Travel time, of course, depends on the notorious LA traffic. Shared vans are also available. Or you can always try public transportation: free shuttle service is provided to the Metropolitan Transit Authority—Metro Green Line Light Rail's Aviation Station. (Pickup is on the arrivals level under the "LAX Shuttle" sign.) You can also get Los Angeles–area city bus information by telephone at the information display board in the baggage claim area in each terminal.

Other Information

For general information about LAX before you arrive, call 310-646-5252.

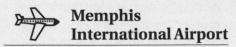

Memphis International Airport

Memphis, Tennessee
Airport Code: MEM
Web Address: http://www.mscaa.com

Built on Ward Farm, a 200-acre tract of land 7.5 miles from downtown, Memphis Municipal Airport had just three hangars and a sod field runway when it was dedicated on June 15, 1929. A year later, the airport had a lighted runway and was proudly serving more than 15 passengers a day.

In the 1960s Memphis dedicated an award-winning terminal described as a "self-contained jet-age city." To go along with the jet-age image, the airport adopted a jet-age name: Memphis International Airport (MEM). Today, if you think you see Elvis out on the tarmac, don't fret. Just remember: Elvis's Graceland mansion is just a few miles from the airport.

Get Oriented

- Luggage carts rent for $2. You'll get a $.25 refund when you return a cart to the rack.
- Lockers are located in all three gate concourses just beyond the security checkpoint.

The upper ticketing level of the main terminal at Memphis International Airport is divided into three lobby areas that correspond to the airport's three concourses (A, B, and C). Northwest Airlines, the predominant air carrier here, uses most all of the gates on Concourse B. Concourse A serves Delta Air Lines and Northwest Airlink, and Concourse C gates are used by United, American, US Airways, and other airlines.

It can take 10–15 minutes to walk from one end of the terminal to another (longer if you stop for souvenirs at Elvis Presley's

Graceland Gift Shop) and just as long to get from the security checkpoint at Concourse B out to the end of the B gates area.

Take Care of Yourself

►Eat

Besides Graceland and blues music, folks flock to Memphis for barbecue. Luckily, you needn't leave Concourse B to get a sampling from two of the city's better-known rib joints: the Interstate BBQ Restaurant is located at Gate B14 (by the Tennessee Tavern), and over at Gate B36 Da Blues Memphis restaurant features Corky's Ribs & BBQ. Both spots have takeout windows, and during the weekday lunch and dinner rush hours, Da Blues Memphis offers live blues music as well.

Not up for barbecue? A large, full-service Cheer's pub and restaurant is located just before Gate B27, and Perkins Express & Bakery, a Memphis-based, family-style restaurant that serves bread-bowl salads, sandwiches, and breakfast all day, is located in the main terminal lobby.

Or head to the Concourse B Paddleboat Food Court, just past Gate 8, where you'll find McDonald's, Baskin-Robbins Ice Cream, Kentucky Fried Chicken Express, Healthy De-Lite Sandwiches, Pizza Hut Express, and a Cinnabon kiosk.

Best Healthful Nosh

Veggie sandwiches from Healthy De-Lite Sandwiches in the Paddleboat Food Court in Concourse B.

Best Sinful Snack

Tennessee-made Goo Goo Clusters and Moon Pies (in a variety of flavors) are available in most gift shops throughout the airport. You can buy them individually—or by the box.

►Relax and Refresh

There are seating areas with fairly comfortable chairs scattered around the A, B, and C areas of the main ticket lobby level. The main terminal also features several quiet mezzanine areas with floor-to-ceiling windows, but limited seating. If you can find a chair (or don't mind sitting on the floor) this would be your best bet if you're looking for a spot to read a book, take a nap, or otherwise get out of the hustle and bustle.

If you'd rather stretch out in a real bed, take a shower, or maybe watch a movie on your layover, consider the airport's own Skyport Inn, located inside the terminal, next to security in Terminal A. "The Little Hotel in the Airport" has no pool or health club, but has an ultrareasonable $40 day rate (901-345-3220).

If you'd rather not stay smack dab inside the terminal, try the Radisson Hotel (901-332-2370), located on airport property, just a short shuttle ride away. They've got an outdoor heated pool, tennis courts, and an exercise room, and offer a reasonable day rate.

For on-site freshening up, head for the Hairport, on the ticket level of the main terminal between Ticket Lobbies B and C. Services include haircuts, facials, braiding, and scalp massage. Hours: Monday–Friday, 8 AM–5 PM.

If you want to smoke, you'll need to go outside, where signs instruct you to stand at least 20 feet away from the public entrances.

Take Care of Business

- Self-service Internet/fax machines are located at Gate A15, in Concourse B tucked behind Starbucks at Gate 8, and in the lobby area just before the security checkpoint at Concourse C.

This is another airport where (currently) you must be a member of an airline's "club" to get access to a business center with workstations and such. However, International Business Services/Travelex, in Ticket Lobby B, provides currency exchange, faxing, and copying services. Hours: daily, 7:00 AM–8:30 PM; 901-922-8090. There's another kiosk on Concourse B near the international arrivals/departures area at Gate 43, but it's only open from 6 PM to 8 PM daily.

First American Bank has a branch inside the airport in the

passenger connector between Concourses A and B that's staffed 8:00 AM–3:30 PM, Monday–Friday.

Explore the Airport

►Shop

Elvis fan or not, you won't want to pass up the chance to visit Elvis Presley's Graceland Gift Shop, located in Ticket Lobby B. In addition to all the cute, corny, and collectible Elvis memorabilia (trading cards, key rings, cookie jars, etc.), this shop carries a nice selection of souvenirs from Sun Studios, which is also located in Memphis. Vintage Elvis movies run continuously on the huge video screen at the front of the store, enticing you to stay—and shop—longer.

If you can swivel your way out of the Elvis gift shop with your wallet intact, you'll find charming Tennessee souvenirs elsewhere in the airport. Each newsstand/gift shop in the main terminal lobby and out in the concourses carries a wide variety of barbecue sauces and hot salsas, blues music, items displaying the Jack Daniel's sour mash whiskey insignia, and of course, more Elvis memorabilia. Several shops also sell Tennessee-made Goo Goo Clusters and Moon Pies by the piece or by the box. Books and Blues (near Gate B8) has the airport's best book selection and World Gear (between Ticket Lobbies B and C) carries airplane models and other merchandise emblazoned with (mostly) the Northwest/KLM company logo. Concourse B also has a PGA Golf Shop and a branch of AltiTunes.

►Sightsee

Like the blues? Da Blues Memphis, the barbecue restaurant by Gate B36, features live blues music weekdays during the lunch and dinner "pushes" (12 noon–2 PM and 6 PM–8 PM).

In the corner of Ticket Lobby B (just beyond the bank of ATM machines) you'll find the airport's Aviation Historical Room. Model airplanes hover in the center of the room and each wall is filled with plaques and photos documenting everything from early exhibition air shows to the dedication of the current "jet-age" facility. Most intriguing are the trophies and photos from the Flying Omlies—Phoebe and Vernon. She won the 1st Women's National Air Derby in 1929, he trained pilots and flew commercially. The room is dedicated to their memory.

Browsing at Elvis Presley's Graceland Gift Shop (in the main terminal, Ticket Lobby B) can fill an hour, but if you have several hours to spend, remember that the airport is just a few miles from the Graceland mansion on Elvis Presley Boulevard.

You'll find the best airfield viewing spots on the mezzanine level in the terminal ticket lobby, where the windows run floor to ceiling.

► Play Around

Look for a game room filled with electronic and video games between Ticket Lobbies A and B, across from Perkins Express & Bakery. Kids will also enjoy comparing and trying to identify the airplane models suspended in the Aviation Historical Room (Ticket Lobby B) and the airplane souvenirs in the World Gear shop (between Ticket Lobbies B and C).

Go into Town

You'll find taxi stands in front of the terminal in between the baggage claims areas of Terminals A and B and Terminals B and C. The 15-mile ride to downtown should take about 20 minutes and cost about $22. A taxi ride to Graceland, just 5 miles away, costs less than $10.

Unfortunately, there are no shared shuttle services that run downtown. MATA (the Memphis Area Transit Authority) does run bus service out to the airport, but you'll need to transfer once or twice to get to either Graceland or downtown (901-274-6282).

Other Information

For more information about the airport before you arrive, call 901-922-8000.

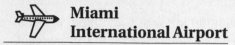

Miami International Airport

Miami, Florida
Airport Code: MIA
Web Address: http://www.miami-airport.com

Miami International Airport (MIA) boldly calls itself the "Hub of the Americas." In operation since 1928, when it was called Pan American Field, it's now the ninth-busiest passenger airport in the world. MIA is also the primary connecting point for air travel between North America and the Caribbean, and is a major gateway to Europe.

Get Oriented

- Luggage carts rent for $2 and are available throughout the terminal.
- Self-service lockers are located on the concourses, postsecurity.

The airport is laid out in a horseshoe shape, with one terminal building and eight concourses (A–H). To get your bearings, stop by the main information booth in Concourse E (just across from the hotel lobby) to get an airport map, then head for the third floor, where you can ride a series of moving walkways from one end of MIA to the other. Concourse A is on the right, or north, side of the terminal; Concourse E and the Miami International Airport Hotel are in the center; and the moving walkway wraps around the inside of the terminal on the third floor. Most concourses serve a variety of airlines, with gates serving American in Concourses C, D, and E; United in Concourse F; Northwest, TWA, and Continental in Concourse G; and US Airways and Delta in Concourse H. Concourses A and B serve international flights.

Take Care of Yourself

►Eat

There's a sushi bar in the hotel lobby at Concourse E, but if you want a nice sit-down meal and great views of the airfield and the Miami skyline, take a seat at the Top of the Port Restaurant on the seventh floor of the Miami International Airport Hotel. It's open 7 AM–11 PM. If you simply want a snack with that view, head for the Poolside Snack Bar on the hotel's eighth floor, open 11 AM–6 PM.

For Cuban food and high-octane Cuban coffee, head to La Carretta Restaurant in Concourse D, which also offers 24-hour window service. For more choices, stop at the Concourse E food court, where you'll find Casa Bacardi, a sit-down restaurant featuring Caribbean-inspired meals and décor that includes an antique still used for making rum. The Concourse E food court also houses Juice Works, Cinnabon, California Pizza Kitchen, and a Burger King restaurant, a fact MIA is especially proud of because Miami is the home of the very first Burger King.

Best Healthful Nosh

Fruit bowls from Juice Works in Concourse E, or sushi from the sushi bar in the hotel lobby.

Best Sinful Snack

Ice cream, from the shop in Concourse E, near the hotel, and elsewhere in the airport.

►Relax and Refresh

MIA is a busy place, so quiet corners for napping are hard to come by. Try the benches in the park outside Concourse E (by the hotel) or the chapel in the terminal area near Concourse B. Better yet, pamper yourself a bit and ask for the day rate at the Miami International Airport Hotel, located inside the terminal at Concourse E (305-871-4100). You don't even need to check in to use the hotel's pool and health club facilities: for an $8 fee, you can get a day pass that gives you full run of the roof pool, health club, steam bath, sauna, showers, whirlpool bath, racquetball courts, and jogging track. (The airport's Web site says use of the pool and Jacuzzi is free!) Hours: 6 AM–10 PM daily.

You can also relax by riding the moving walkways that go from one end of the airport to the other on the third floor. The corridor alongside is usually pretty empty, so it's a good place to take a brisk walk or perhaps a gentle jog. For a little professional freshening up, you'll find a barbershop and hair salon in the main terminal (at Concourse E) offering facial massages, manicures, and pedicures.

Smokers can light up in the airport hotel or outside the airport.

Take Care of Business

• There's a US Post Office on level 4 of Concourse B.

If you need to take care of business, head for the business center on the second floor of the airport hotel, where you can send faxes, make copies, or rent a workstation. Hours: weekdays, 8 AM–5 PM. Two Passenger Service Centers with data port phones are located on level 2, between Concourses B and C and between Concourses G and H. There's also a full-service Barnett Bank on level 4 at Concourse B.

Explore the Airport

►Shop

You can get cartons of oranges or stone crabs shipped or packed for travel at any of the Fruit Tree Cafés in Concourses C, D, and G. Numerous gift shops offer seashell-encrusted boxes, chocolate-covered coconut patties, sunglasses, and beach toys. For kids' toys and souvenir T-shirts, browse through the shops in the terminal area between Concourses F and G.

►Sightsee

Too bad MIA doesn't hand out up-to-date maps of the artwork scattered around the airport. Highlights include 19 digital photo-collages by Lawrence Gartel near the arrivals area at Concourse F. Titled "Miami and the Millennium," the collages feature scenes of South Beach, Parrot Jungle, Coral Gables, and other quintessential Florida spots. Concourse A boasts Christopher Janney's "Harmonic Runway," a sound-and-light sculpture that gives off a multicolored glow and emits environmental sounds and musical tones in response to passersby. While in Concourse A, check out the floor: embedded in the black terrazzo are more than a thousand cast-bronze plants, shells, and marine organisms. Titled "A Walk on the Beach," the artwork was created by Michele Oka Doner and is designed to evoke the ecology of Florida's beaches and tidal pools. As long as you're focused on the floor, head to Concourse H to see Robert Calvo's "Flight Patterns," which includes poetry on the stairs and a floor design that incorporates maps and astrological references.

Don't forget to look up. You'll avoid bumping into people, and you'll get to see the changing art exhibitions both along the walls leading to Concourse E and in the MIA Gallery behind the security checkpoint at Concourse E.

The best place to get a view of the airfield and surrounding area is from the eighth floor of the hotel, at poolside.

▶ Play Around

There's no special kids' play area at the airport, but your brood might enjoy riding the moving walkway that runs from one end of the terminal to the other or searching for the images of more than a thousand sea creatures embedded in the terrazzo floor in Terminal A. If you've got an hour or more, get a day pass for the Miami International Airport Hotel's health club facilities and take the kids to the rooftop pool for a swim.

Go into Town

- General ground transportation information is available on the automated airport information line: 305-876-7000.

A 20-minute cab ride to downtown Miami costs about $17, while a shared van will take you there for $9. If you're heading to

Miami Beach, the cab ride costs about $22, a shared van about $14.

For $1.25 you might also try Miami's Metrobus service, but you'll need to take two buses to get downtown. Rates for all forms of ground transportation are listed on kiosks at the airport baggage claim areas. If you're going into town for just a few hours, you can leave your bags in one of the baggage checkrooms in Concourse B (upper level) and Concourses G and H (lower level).

Other Information

For more airport information and directions, stop by the 24-hour Tourist Information Center located at Concourse E (across from the airport hotel), or call 305-876-7000.

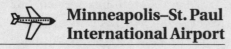 **Minneapolis–St. Paul International Airport**

Minneapolis, Minnesota
Airport Code: MSP
Web Address: http://www.mspairport.com

When it first opened back in 1923, on the site of a defunct auto speedway, the Minneapolis–St. Paul Airport (MSP) was known as the Twin Cities Airports–Wold Chamberlain Field, in honor of Ernest Wold and Cyrus Chamberlain, two Minnesota aviators killed in World War I. Renamed Minneapolis–St. Paul Airport in 1948, MSP now serves more than 30 million passengers a year.

Get Oriented

- Luggage carts at MSP cost $1.50 and are available throughout the airport. The machines will refund $.25 when a cart is returned to the rack.
- Lockers are located throughout the airport, postsecurity.

MSP consists of two terminals: the three-gate Humphrey Terminal (used predominantly for charter flights) and Lindbergh Terminal, which consists of a main building and five concourses (C, D, E, F, and G; A and B are being built). These letter codes recently replaced the airport's concourse/color system. For long-time MSP travelers, here's the code: Green Concourse is now C and D; Blue is now E, Red is F, and Gold is G.

Northstar Crossing, a concession area filled with 65 shops and restaurants, is located in the center of Lindbergh Terminal and features several Minnesota-themed shops along with nationally known retailers such as the first airport-based Lands' End.

Northwest Airlines, Mesaba Airlines, Champion Air, and Sun Country Airlines are all headquartered at MSP, and Northwest Airlines uses MSP as its main hub airport. Northwest uses all the gates in Concourse G and shares Concourse F with TWA. Concourse E is used by Northwest, US Airways, Continental, Delta, and American, and Concourses C and D host flights from Northwest, America West, Mesaba, and United.

It can take up to 25 minutes to walk the length of Lindbergh Terminal. To cut down on travel time and airport congestion, MSP plans to build a skyway to connect Concourses C and G, but in the meantime the only way to reduce your steps is to hop on the moving walkways in each concourse. If you're starting from the center retail corridor (Northstar Crossing), just past security, plan on no less than 10 minutes to get to the end of either Concourse G or D. The trip to the end of Concourses E and F will take only about 5 minutes, since these are MSP's shorter concourses.

Take Care of Yourself

▬ Eat

If you're hungry, you'll find plenty to choose from at the 250-seat food court at Northstar Crossing, the concession area in the center of Lindbergh Terminal. Highlights here include Wok & Roll/Kyoto (Chinese and Japanese), Sbarro Pizza, Wetzel's Pretzels, Cinnabon, and Cool Planet, which is a dessert and ice-cream store created by the folks from Planet Hollywood. Just outside the food court you'll find the gourmet deli D'Amico & Sons and the Split Rock Bar & Grill, a Minnesota-themed restaurant complete with historical information about scenic sites such as the famous Split Rock Lighthouse near Duluth, Minnesota.

There are also some highlights out in the concourses: Northwest's Concourse G features Minnesota-based Caribou Coffee, Big Apple Bagel, and MSP Brewhouse. Concourse F sports a California Pizza Kitchen, the Lake Line Restaurant, and the Sola Squeeze Juice Bar. In Concourse E you'll find a food court and Jody Maroni's Sausage Kingdom. Over in Concourse D you'll find sit-down service at Malibu Al's.

Best Healthful Nosh

Sola Squeeze (Concourse F) offers juices and smoothies; D'Amico & Sons (Northstar Crossing) offers salad samplers and mixed fruit plates.

Best Sinful Snack

D'Amico & Sons (Northstar Crossing) offers crème brûlée, cheesecake, and chocolate torte. Cool Planet, in the Northstar Crossing food court, offers sinful desserts and ice cream.

► **Relax and Refresh**

• There is no smoking allowed at MSP.

To get out of the hustle and bustle, head for the mezzanine level above the ticketing counters, near the entrance to the skyways that lead to the parking ramps. There's also a chapel on the mezzanine level, in room 335A. For people watching, take a seat on a bench in Northstar Crossing (in the Lindbergh Terminal main corridor) or pull up a chair in the bustling food court.

MSP is one of the few US airports with an official observation deck, and if you climb up there (it's three short flights) when there's not a crowd, this is a lovely spot to catch a nap or just watch the comings and goings on the airfield. You'll find MSP's observation deck in Concourse D.

There are no on-site health clubs or hotels, but several nearby hotels offer day rates that include access to their health clubs. For example, the Minneapolis Airport Hilton (612-854-2100) offers a reasonable day rate that hovers around $70.

If you need to freshen up on-site, you can stop at the Airport Barber and Stylist, near the entrance to Concourses C and D. Their services include hair styling, manicures, massages, shaves, facials, waxing, and tweezing.

If you've got an hour or more, why not relax with a movie? In the Northstar Crossing concession area, InMotion Pictures rents "personal movie theaters" consisting of a DVD player, headset, and a movie. You can watch the movie at the airport or, if you're heading to Portland, Seattle, or one of the other cities with an airport InMotion Pictures kiosk, you can take the entire "theater" with you on the plane.

For pets, there's an outdoor fenced area on the baggage claim level at exit door 6.

Take Care of Business

• All phones at MSP are equipped with data ports.

If you've got business to attend to, you have several options at MSP. The Airport Business Center/Teleticket (between doors 5 and 6 on the ticketing level) offers photocopy, fax, courier, currency exchange, and a variety of computer services. They're open Sunday–Friday, 5:30 AM–9:00 PM, and Saturday, 5:30 AM–6:00 PM (612-726-5184).

Another option is the Pierson M. Grieve Conference Center on the mezzanine level above the Chili's Too restaurant (near the entrance to Concourses F and G). The conference center has meeting rooms, four individual workstations, computer connections, and notary, fax, and copy machine services. They're open Monday–Friday, 8 AM–5 PM (612-794-4500).

There are also several self-service business centers that offer e-mail, fax, and photocopy services, travel insurance, and Internet connections. These work areas have data ports, ATMs, FedEx drop boxes, postage machines, change machines, and lockers and are located in the Northstar Crossing concessions area, in the Airport Business Center/Teleticket (between doors 5 and 6), and in Concourse G at Gate 9. You'll also find a self-service center in Concourse F at Gate 3, in Concourse E at Gate 1, and in Concourse C at Gate 2.

Explore the Airport

►Shop

You'll find a nice variety of shops at Northstar Crossing, the center corridor of Lindbergh Terminal. Standouts include the only airport-based branch of Lands' End and Bow Wow Meow, a store full of gifts for the cat, dog, or other pet you've left behind. Other shopping highlights include AltiTunes, the Discovery Channel Store, the Museum Company store, Liz Claiborne, Simply Books (also in Concourse C), and Bath & Body Works. For last-minute Minnesota souvenirs, head for the Minnesota! shop, where you'll find elk sausage, "Minnesalsa," and several sizes of stuffed moose toys, or pick up a gourmet food basket ($16–$250) from Minneapolis-based D'Amico & Sons.

►Sightsee

A Natural Wonders art display (on the mezzanine level above the ticket counters) is "hosted" by the Minneapolis Institute of Art and features work by Minnesota artists. And a wide variety of Minnesota-based businesses exhibit samples of their products in glass cases scattered along the concourses and in the ground transportation center.

►Play Around

While there are no specific children's play areas, kids might enjoy the bird's-eye view of the airfield from the observation deck (in Concourse C) or a visit to the small game arcades located in Concourses C and G. The Concourse G arcade is a short distance from the entrance to the concourse; the arcade in Concourse C is closer to the end.

Go into Town

Taxis, rental cars, city buses, limos, and shuttle vans can take you to Minneapolis, St. Paul, and the nearby Mall of America.

You'll find cabs on the lower level of Lindbergh Terminal. It will take 15–20 minutes (during off-peak times) and cost about $25 to take a cab the 16 miles to downtown Minneapolis. The 12-mile ride to downtown St. Paul will cost about $14.

City buses pick up and drop off on the upper-level roadway (east side) of Lindbergh Terminal. Buses travel throughout the Twin Cities area for $1.50 during rush hours and $1 during off-peak times.

If your layover is 3 hours or more, consider a visit to the nearby Mall of America. Take the 12-minute bus ride (Metro Transit) there and, if you've done some shopping, splurge for a cab back. Pick up a bus schedule from any Travelers Assistance or information kiosk and wait for a bus outside the green tower at the east upper level of the terminal.

Other Information

To get information about the airport before you arrive, call 612-726-5500.

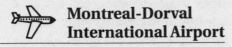

Montreal-Dorval International Airport

Montreal, Quebec, Canada
Airport Code: YUL
Web Address: http://www.admtl.com

In the early 1940s, it became apparent that Montreal would soon outgrow the Saint-Hubert Airport, which had been serving the city since 1927. Luckily, the minister of transport solved the problem by heading out to the Dorval Race Track, 14 miles west of the city. Not to bet (well, we don't know that for sure) but to buy: Montreal-Dorval Airport (YUL) opened for business on the site in 1941. Renamed Aéroport International de Montréal-Dorval (Montreal-Dorval International Airport) in 1960, the facility now serves almost 9 million passengers a year.

Get Oriented

- There is no charge for use of the airport's baggage carts, which are plentiful and scattered throughout the airport.
- There are no self-service lockers at Dorval; luggage storage service is available at the cloakroom/lost and found counter in the international arrivals area.

Montreal-Dorval has a single terminal with three concourses or "fingers," serving domestic, international, and transborder flights. The airport has a welcoming glass atrium, a nice variety of cafés and shops, and a dedicated kids' play area with a view of the airfield. A new annex that will serve international flights is currently under construction and is due to open in 2003.

Take Care of Yourself

► **Eat**

A food court and several restaurants are clustered in the main terminal along rue Montréal, which has the feel of a café-lined Parisian street, complete with umbrella-topped tables, plenty of greenery, and lots of light. Eggspectation, which serves steak, sandwiches, crepes, and salads, is the more popular spot here, but other choices include the Montréal Bread Company and Les Légendes du Jazz, which is decorated with a nice collection of jazz photos and features a wide variety of (recorded) jazz music. Elsewhere in the airport, look for Moe's Deli & Bar in the domestic concourse and the Cheers bar in the transborder concourse.

Best Healthful Nosh

Salads or crepes from Eggspectation on rue Montréal in the main terminal.

Best Sinful Snack:

Candy, by the ounce or the pound, from the Sweet Factory in the shopping corridor in the main terminal.

► **Relax and Refresh**

To relax and unwind, head for the lounge area upstairs from the food corridor in the main terminal. This nonsmoking area has comfortable seating and a great view of the airfield. Just one word of warning: a well-appointed kids' play area is also located by the lounge, so if you need total peace and quiet, dart into the chapel, which is located nearby and open 24 hours a day. Downstairs, the umbrella-topped café tables along the windows on rue Montréal (the food street) provide good perches for people watching.

Dorval has no beauty salon or massage bar, but you can get a makeup makeover at the Body Shop in the shopping corridor and take care of last-minute dry cleaning in the international arrivals area.

If you need more serious refresh-and-relax services, try the nearby Hilton Montreal Airport (514-631-2411). They offer a day rate of Can$105 (about US$68) which includes access to the hotel's health club and pool.

Smokers are welcome in the smoking sections of the airport bars and restaurants.

Take Care of Business

- Internet kiosks, labeled "Zone Interactive," are located on rue Montréal (the food street) and in the concourses.

If you're not a member of one of the airline clubs, you'll find that except for phones with data ports and Internet kiosks (located in the main terminal and out in the concourses), there are no business services on-site. However, the nearby Hilton Montreal Airport does have a business center open to the public and a complimentary shuttle service from the airport. Posted hours are Tuesday–Saturday, 7 AM–4 PM, but it's a good idea to call ahead to make sure they're open (514-631-2411).

Explore the Airport

►Shop

In addition to a good-sized bookstore, there is nice variety of shops and boutiques clustered in the main terminal between the ticket lobby and the entrance to the gates. Boutique du Terroir, for example, carries Quebec-made handicrafts, artwork, stationery, maple syrup, and a variety of decorative items. La Tour Eiffel has leather handbags and briefcases, while Le Match features outdoor clothing, T-shirts, and accessories. Branches of the Body Shop, Tie Rack, Swatch, and Batteries Plus (CDs, electronics, and, yes, batteries) are also here.

►Sightsee

No official art or history exhibits at Dorval, but the Boutique du Terroir shop in the main terminal displays a wide variety of artwork, sculpture, and other handcrafted items made in Quebec.

The best spot for watching airplanes take off and land is from the passenger lounge area on the upper level of the main terminal.

► Play Around

In addition to offering kids great views of the airfield, the lounge area upstairs in the main terminal has a well-equipped kids' play area.

Go into Town

A cab ride to downtown Montreal will cost Can$28 (about US$18.25) and take between 20 and 45 minutes, depending on traffic. The airport shuttle bus (L'Aérobus) makes the trip downtown and to some of the major hotels for Can$11 (about US$7.15). For information about taking the public bus, check with one of the information desks.

Other Information

Helpful, multilingual staffers are stationed at information desks located on the departure level and at international arrivals. If you need information before you arrive, call 514-394-7377.

Nashville International Airport

Nashville, Tennessee
Airport Code: BNA
Web Address: http://www.nashintl.com

Constructed as a Works Progress Administration project, Nashville's airport officially opened in 1937 as Berry Field, in honor of Colonel Harry S. Berry, the state administrator of the Works Progress Administration, or WPA. Berry Field became the military base for the 4th Ferrying Command during World War II and was returned to the city when the war ended. The airport's name was officially changed to Nashville International Airport in 1988, but the original three-letter identifier, BNA, which stands for Berry Field Nashville, remains.

Get Oriented

- Luggage carts are located throughout the terminal and rent for $2. The machines give change and offer a $.25 "reward" for carts returned to the rack.
- Lockers are located on Concourses B and C.

Nashville International Airport has one main terminal with four concourses, A, B, C, and D, arranged in counterclockwise spokes. It takes no longer than 5 minutes to get from any gate area down to baggage claim, and just about 15 minutes to walk from one end of the terminal to the other.

Concourse A serves Continental, United, and TWA; and Delta, Northwest, US Airways, and Comair use Concourse B. Southwest and American use the C gates, leaving the D gates for American Eagle and corporate jets.

Take Care of Yourself

►Eat

At the Capitol Hill Grill, a table-service restaurant in the main terminal, the menu includes Tennessee pork chops, country fried steak, and catfish. Their less formal coffee shop next door offers sandwiches, soups, salads, and decadent desserts.

Other choices throughout the airport include Americo's (pizza), at the security checkpoint for Concourses A and B; fresh, prepacked, "ready to fly" fare from Air Meals at Gate B5; and Carvel ice cream, located just before the Concourses C and D security checkpoint. Miami Subs, at Gate C5, makes healthy veggie wraps, and Whitts BBQ (also at Gate C5) offers barbecue sandwiches, platters, and take-away barbecue dinners.

Best Healthful Nosh

Grilled vegetable salads from the Capitol Hill Grill, the sit-down restaurant on the ticketing level in the main terminal.

Best Sinful Snack

An ice cream "Banana Barge" from Carvel, located just outside the security checkpoint for Concourses C and D, or Goo Goo Clusters (sold by the box!) from most gift shops.

►Relax and Refresh

If you need a place to relax, read a book, or catch a nap, head for the connecting corridor between Concourses A and B and Concourses C and D. This area has comfortable chairs and good views of the airfield. An ultraquiet meditation room is located at Gate A2, but to use it you'll need to get a key from the folks at the Welcome Center, down on the baggage claim level.

If you're here midday any Friday, head for the ticketing level of the main terminal. Local musicians perform live from 12 noon–2 PM, and since Nashville is "Music City USA," be prepared to hear anything from country and classical to rhythm and blues and bluegrass.

Chair massages from the Massage Bar, just past the security checkpoint for Concourses A and B, offer yet another form of relaxation. Even better, during happy hour (11 AM–12 noon), prices are reduced by a dollar (www.massagebar.com). The Massage Bar is closed Saturdays.

While there are no on-site hotels, plenty of hotels and motels ring the airport and many offer low-cost refuge if you need to sleep, shower, or get some exercise. The Hampton Inn and Suites, for example, offers a day rate which includes use of the hotel pool and exercise room (615-885-4242). Pick up a phone at the hotel/motel call board in the baggage claim area to check rates at other nearby hotels.

Smokers will find lounges in Concourses A, B, and C.

Take Care of Business

Delta and American Airlines have club rooms here (at Gates B3 and C11, respectively), but non–club members can send a fax, make copies, or rent a workstation with Internet access at Wright Travel Business Center, just outside the security checkpoint for Concourses C and D.

A branch of SunTrust Bank is located on the ticketing level, near the security checkpoint for Concourses A and B. You'll also find ATM machines behind the escalators on the ground transportation (first) level and on the ticketing level, next to the SunTrust bank.

Drop boxes for Federal Express and UPS are located at the airport Welcome Center on the baggage claim level.

Explore the Airport

► Shop

There's a well-stocked Heritage Booksellers located at Gate B5, and the PGA Tour Shop (just past the checkpoint for Concourses C and D) features a small putting green for those who want a little extra practice.

In the gift shops outside both security checkpoints, you can stock up on barbecue sauce, Jack Daniel's coffee and horseradish mustard, and boxes of Tennessee-made Goo Goo Clusters. These shops also carry sports memorabilia for a variety of local teams.

► Sightsee

Keep your eyes open for artwork by local, regional, and national artists. In the atrium, for example, you'll encounter Dale Eldred's "Airport Sun Project," an installation of solar reflecting panels that constantly change appearance according to your vantage point and the variables of sun, weather, and season. In the ticketing lobbies, the hallways, and elsewhere in the airport, look for changing visual-arts exhibits that celebrate the Tennessee Arts and Crafts Association, Black History Month, Country Music Month, and seasonal events.

Also, be sure to visit Rhythm Shoeshine, at the top of Concourse B, where the walls are covered with celebrity photos. You'll also encounter a pristine Harley-Davidson motorcycle and a display of fishing boats next to the security checkpoint for Concourses C and D. These are actually company advertisements, but still fun to look at.

The best place to keep an eye on airfield activity and catch a glimpse of the city skyline is from the connecting corridor between Concourses A and B and C and D.

► Play Around

There's a wonderful, inviting children's play area in the connecting corridor between Concourses A and B and C and D. Even if you don't have kids, go take a look: you'll find a colorful, undulating bench, tiny airplanes, and a flying carpet, all encrusted with bright mosaic tiles perfect for perking up travelers of any age.

Go into Town

The 8-mile cab ride to downtown Nashville will take about 20 minutes and cost about $20. A shuttle van (Gray Line) to downtown hotels makes the trip in about 30 minutes and costs $9 one way. The public bus (#18) leaves the airport 14 times a day, Monday–Friday, and 4 times a day on Saturdays and Sundays. The fare is $1.40 and schedules are available at the Welcome Center on the baggage claim level.

Other Information

If you need information before you arrive, call the folks at the Airport Welcome Center: 615-275-1674. And don't be alarmed if you see a big white bird dressed in an airline captain's uniform roaming through the halls. It's probably just Captain Harmony, the Magical Mockingbird and "natural aviator" who helps out with customer service. In fact, if you visit Captain Harmony's Web site (www.nashintl.com/kidsclub.html) you can sign up to become a member of Captain Harmony's Flying Friends (Kids') club and receive a membership card and a cool button.

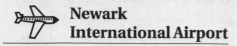 **Newark
International Airport**

Newark, New Jersey
Airport Code: EWR
Web Address: http://www.newarkairport.com

On October 1, 1928, the City of Newark opened its regional airport on 68 acres of marshland, and in short order the facility became the world's busiest commercial airport. To help things along, two of the airport's earliest customers were Amelia Earhart and Howard Hughes. In 1935 Earhart flew nonstop from Mexico City to Newark in 14 hours and 19 minutes. A year later, Howard Hughes set a west–east record and then bettered his time in 1937 when he landed in Newark 9 hours and 26 minutes after leaving Burbank, California.

Operated today by the Port Authority of New York and New Jersey, Newark International Airport (EWR) is now the 13th busiest airport in the world.

Get Oriented

- Luggage carts rent for $1.50, but are not allowed on the monorail. If you're traveling between terminals, racks at the monorail station entrance will exchange your cart for a token that lets you pick up another cart at the next station.
- There are no self-service lockers, but baggage storage services are located in the baggage claim areas of Terminal B (near carousel 4) and Terminal C (near carousel 8).

EWR is laid out in a large oval with three satellite terminals (A, B, and C). Terminal A serves predominantly American, TWA, US Airways, and United. Terminal B serves Delta, Northwest, and most international carriers. Terminal C serves Continental and America West.

It's generally a 5- to 10-minute walk between terminals, but it's much easier to take the free monorail that runs between terminals A, B, and C every 3 minutes for most of the day and every 20 minutes between 12 midnight and 5 AM. The monorail also runs to the parking lots and by late 2001 should link to northeast-corridor rail lines. To get your bearings, ask for an airport map at any of the information booths located at the ground transportation counters on the arrival levels of each terminal. You can also flag down one of the airport's "Red Coats," the customer service representatives stationed in the arrival areas, at bus stops, and on the monorail platforms.

Take Care of Yourself

►Eat

Head to Terminal C for a taste of classic New Jersey road food at the Garden State Diner (just past Gate 75). Terminal C also features Greenleaf's Grill, Sbarro, Wok & Roll, Americo's Pizza, Au Bon Pain, the Samuel Adams Brewhouse, and several other lounges and fast-food outlets.

In Terminal A, look for the two branches of T.G.I. Friday's, Dick Clark's American Bandstand Grill, Greenleaf's Grill, the Budweiser Brewhouse, and a food court. Over in Terminal B, your choices include the Sam Adams Brewhouse, Greenleaf's Grill, Charley's Steakery, Madison Avenue Deli, Asian Chao, pizza, pasta, and hamburgers.

If you have an hour or more, you might try going over to the on-site Marriott Hotel (accessible via courtesy bus from the monorail "E" station stop) which has an English-style pub (Chatfield's) and two restaurants: Allie's American Grill and Priscilla's, which serves French cuisine.

Best Healthful Nosh

Salad wraps from Greenleaf's Grill in Terminals A, B, and C.

Best Sinful Snack

Nathan's hot dogs "with the works" in Terminals A, B, and C.

► **Relax and Refresh**

At the far end of Terminal A (near the United ticket counters) the doorways create an out-of-the way V-shaped seating area. Here I spotted a gentleman deeply engrossed in a philosophy book seated across from a young couple fast asleep on a luggage cart full of baggage doing double duty as a comfortable-looking bed-on-wheels.

If you can't find a corner like this, head for the courtyard at Monorail "E" Station. There are benches outside and seats inside. From here you can also call for a shuttle bus to take you over to the 10-story on-site Marriott Hotel (973-623-0006). Day rates, if available that day, will give you access to the hotel's exercise facilities. If a little primping helps freshen you up, stop by the Departure Spa in Terminal C, near gate 92. The folks there offer haircuts, manicures, pedicures, and massage services, daily from 7 AM to 10 PM.

For a truly quiet spot, look for the meditation room in Terminal C, opposite the entrance to the monorail station.

Smokers can light up in the airport bars or outside.

Take Care of Business

• ATM machines and phones with data ports are scattered throughout the terminals.

There are a few Internet kiosks in each terminal—and more on the way. If you need to send a fax or make some copies, stop by the concierge desk in Terminal B or visit the folks at Staples (the office supply store) in Terminal C.

For more serious business, try making your way to the on-site Marriott Hotel (accessible via a courtesy bus from the monorail "E" station stop). They provide notary services and have a business center with computers, copiers, and fax machines (973-623-0006).

Explore the Airport

►Shop

For souvenirs that say "I've been to New Jersey," stop by the Explore New Jersey shop in Terminal A. For a gift that shouts "I've been to America," head over to the American Scene in Terminal B. For pretty much anything—and everything—else, make tracks for Terminal C, where you'll find Waldenbooks, Benjamin Books, the Museum Company, the Discovery Channel Store, Kenneth Cole, Speedo Authentic Fitness, Staples, Travel 2000, AltiTunes, and several other shops.

►Sightsee

Occasional art exhibits are mounted in Terminals A and B featuring local and regional artists and the work of children from the community. There's also a timeline exhibit tracing the airport's history in the Terminal B3 departures lounge.

The skybridge in Terminal A is a great spot to watch activity on the airfield, but most any terminal gate area seems to provide equally good views. If you're riding around on the free monorail you'll get good views of the airfield activities and, if the weather is good, a view of both the Newark and New York City skylines.

►Play Around

You'll find a kids' play area in Terminal C between Gates 70 and 99, but it's far more enjoyable to take the kids around (and around) on the monorail or over to the Discovery Channel Store in Terminal C.

Go into Town

A cab ride from EWR into Newark will cost about $15, while the ride to Manhattan can cost between $35 and $50 (plus tolls) and take anywhere from 30 minutes to over an hour, depending on traffic and time of day.

Shared van services to Manhattan cost between $10 and $20, and Express buses to various spots in the city cost $10. For $4 you can take a bus (Airlink/New Jersey Transit Bus #302) to Amtrak and PATH train stations.

Whatever you choose, make sure you avoid getting overcharged for your trip into town by letting the Ground Transportation Information Agents help match you, your destination, and your budget with the most appropriate mode of travel into Newark, Manhattan, or elsewhere in the region. You can also call ahead to the 24-hour ground transportation hotline at 800-AIR-RIDE (800-247-7433). This line is staffed Monday–Friday, 8 AM–6 PM.

Other Information

If you need information about the airport before you arrive, call the EWR information line: 888-EWR-INFO (888-397-4636). If you need help finding something at the airport—or in town—stop by the Concierge Center in the International Arrivals Hall in Terminal B. They can help you get theater tickets, a hotel room, any sort of traveler's aid services, and even sell you a New Jersey lottery ticket.

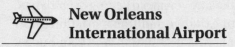

New Orleans International Airport

New Orleans, Louisiana
Airport Code: MSY
Web Address: http://www.flymsy.com

Back in the 1930s, the city of New Orleans was already outgrowing its municipal airport. So in 1940 city officials chose a site for a new airport just 10 miles from downtown and named it Moisant Field, in honor of early aviation pioneer John Moisant. The facility was officially rechristened New Orleans International Airport (MSY) in 1962, and today it serves close to 9 million passengers a year, many of them conventioneers and Mardi Gras revelers.

Get Oriented

- Luggage carts are located throughout the terminal and rent for $2. You'll get a $.25 "reward" when you return a cart.
- Lockers are located on each of the four concourses, postsecurity.

MSY has two terminals, East and West, which are in one building and connected by a long corridor of ticket counters. In the East Terminal, Concourse A serves US Airways, Northwest, and MetroJet, and Continental and Southwest stretch out in Concourse B. Over in the West Terminal, Delta uses Concourse D, and most other airlines use Concourse C. While it's easy to walk between Concourses A and B or between Concourses C and D, if check-in lines are crowded it can take 10 minutes to get from one end of the East Terminal over to the West Terminal concourses.

There are no moving walkways, and although terminal maps are displayed throughout the airport, the folks at the information booths have no printed brochures to hand out.

Take Care of Yourself

▶ **Eat**

At the cafeteria-style French Quarter Café in the East Terminal you can feast on gumbo, po'boy sandwiches, and a variety of other Southern staples. Or head for Jester's Grill in the West Terminal, which features a Louisiana sampler that includes fried shrimp, catfish, jambalaya, and red beans and rice. Jester's Express in Concourse B offers many of the same menu items.

If you missed any other New Orleans food treats, Bag-A-Beignet (in the East Terminal) offers one more chance to order up fried dough covered in confectioners' sugar and the Praline Connection (Concourse B) keeps brownies, cookies, and other sweet treats alongside those decadent buttery pralines. Another local favorite, the Lucky Dog hot dog cart, is located in each concourse.

Snack bars and ice-cream kiosks are located in each concourse, but the only place to get really good coffee is PJ's Coffee & Tea Company, in the West Terminal lobby. This New Orleans–based business also operates a shop in a downtown neighborhood.

Best Healthful Nosh

Beans and rice from Jester's Grill in the West Terminal lobby or from Jester's Express in Concourse B.

Best Sinful Snack

Pralines from the Praline Connection in Concourse B or from just about any airport shop.

▶ **Relax and Refresh**

There's a pleasant seating area in the lobby of the West Terminal and another, smaller one near the entrance to Concourse D. Both provide good spots for people watching or napping.

Smokers must either go outside to light up or visit one of the airport bars.

There are no on-site health clubs, massage bars, or hair salons, but many nearby hotels offer day rates, including the New Orleans Airport Hilton, where day rates include access to the exercise facilities club, the outdoor pool, and the hot tub (504-469-5000).

Take Care of Business

• Very few phones have data ports, but airport officials promise new phones "coming soon" will all sport hookups.

A branch of the Whitney National Bank (open weekdays only) is located in the ticket lobby, next to a branch of the US Post Office. ATM machines are located in each terminal lobby and on the lower level near the Southwest Airlines baggage claim and near the charter baggage claim areas.

A conference center is located on the mezzanine level in the West Terminal lobby above Concourse C. For reservations and information, call 504-464-3547.

Explore the Airport

►Shop

• All airport shops participate in Louisiana Tax Free Shopping, which gives refunds on the 9 percent local sales tax to non-US citizens. For more information, stop by the Tax Free Counter on the upper level of the main terminal. Hours: 7 AM–6 PM daily except Mardi Gras and Christmas.

Several of the airport's most unusual shops, Lulu White's, Rine Chapeaux, and Haitian Treasures, are in Concourse B. Lulu White's Storyville offers lingerie, sensual gifts, antique cigarette cases, and other personal gifts in a French Quarter bordello-inspired setting. Rine Chapeaux carries novelty hats and a wide variety of jewelry, including fanciful pins made by local homeless and disabled artists. (This store's outlet in the West Terminal lobby carries more hats but less jewelry.) The Haitian Treasures kiosk is chock-full of jewelry, carved boxes, statues, masks, and paintings.

Stores in the East Terminal lobby include a House of Blues shop with a CD listening station, AltiTunes (also with a listening station), Waterstone's Booksellers, and the Creole Kitchen, where you can stock up on pralines, hot sauces, coffee, and other New Orleans foods. If you need a photo, painting, poster, map, or other visual souvenir of the Big Easy, stop by Scenes of New Orleans.

The larger West Terminal lobby features the hat-heavy branch of the airport's two Rine Chapeaux stores, a bookstore, and the tempting Louisiana Market, full of pralines, beignet mixes, hot sauces, French Market and Café du Monde coffee, and other gift foods you might eat before getting home.

►Sightsee

One wall of the lobby in the West Terminal sports a huge mural with a jazz theme. See how many musicians you can pick out and then ask the folks at the information booth to help you identify the rest.

In Concourse B (Gate 7) a photographic exhibition sponsored by the Louis Armstrong Foundation features large photos of legendary New Orleans jazz bands and performers including Louis Armstrong, Sidney Bechet, and the New Orleans Rhythm Kings.

An exhibit honoring the alligator's role in the area's economy ("From Marsh to Market") is also located near Gate B7. Boots, bags, and other items made from this "renewable resource" are on display along with a wildlife diorama featuring the sounds of bull gator bellows and hatchling alligator chirps and grunts.

You can keep an eye on the airfield activity from most any concourse.

►Play Around

Play tables for small children are located on each of the four concourses and in several spots in the baggage claim area. There's also a small arcade area located in the West Terminal lobby, just before the security checkpoint for Concourse C.

Older kids might enjoy looking at the photographs of noted jazz musicians mounted on the wall by Gate 7 in Concourse B and the alligator exhibit nearby.

Go into Town

A cab ride to the French Quarter or the central business district can take more than half an hour during rush-hour traffic and will cost $24 for one person and $10 per person for three or more passengers.

Shuttle van service to hotels downtown and to the French Quarter will cost $10 per person. Purchase tickets on the lower level outside the baggage claim area.

Jefferson Transit buses leave from the airport every 15–20 minutes during the week and every 30 minutes on the weekend. The fare to the central business district is $1.50. For more information, stop by one of the airport information booths or contact the Jefferson Parish Transportation Department at 504-367-7433.

Other Information

The airport's five Visitor Information Service booths are open daily from 8 AM to 9 PM and most Visitor Information Service representatives are bilingual or multilingual. If you need more information before you arrive, call 504-464-2650.

✈ John F. Kennedy International Airport

New York, New York (Jamaica, NY)
Airport Code: JFK
Web Address: http://www.kennedyairport.com

If you feel an irresistible urge to hit some golf balls when you land at John F. Kennedy International Airport (JFK), it's probably because the airport was built on the site of Idlewild Golf Course. In fact, even though the airport was officially christened New York International Airport when it opened for business in 1948, most folks just called it Idlewild until it was officially rededicated as John F. Kennedy International Airport on December 24, 1963.

Get Oriented

- Luggage carts rent for $1.50 and are available throughout the airport.
- There are no lockers at JFK, but there are staffed baggage check services in Terminals 1 and 4.

JFK has nine terminals, arranged counterclockwise in the airport's Central Terminal Area (CTA). No terminal is entirely airline specific, but there are some general groupings: Terminal 1, the newest terminal, is operated by four international airlines (Lufthansa, Japan Airlines, Air France, and Korean Air). Terminals 2 and 3 are operated by Delta Air Lines, and Terminal 4 is the International Air Terminal. Terminal 5 is operated by Trans World Airlines, United Air Lines operates Terminal 6, and British Airways operates Terminal 7. Terminals 8 and 9 are operated by American Airlines.

A free shuttle bus between terminals runs approximately every 10 minutes and makes the trip from terminal to terminal in 10–15 minutes. In 2002, the buses will be replaced by a light-rail

"AirTrain" service that will run right through the center of Terminal 4—just like the monorail at Disney World.

To get your bearings, grab a map from an information counter or look for one of the 118 eager "Red Coats," as JFK's customer service agents are known. Don't worry if you don't speak English—most Red Coats speak 2 or 3 languages, and the team as a whole is proficient in as many as 30 languages. You can also call ahead to the 24-hour information hotline at 718-244-4444.

Take Care of Yourself

► Eat

JFK is big enough that traveling between terminals to eat may not be practical, but each terminal offers several dining options. Terminal 1 has the Brooklyn Brew Pub, the Eurasia Coffee House, the Greenwich Village Bistro, Anton's Napa Valley Wine Bar, and Wok & Roll, which is expanding its menu to include sushi and bento boxes. In Terminal 2, look for Creative Croissant, Links on Tap (a golf-themed restaurant!), and a cybercafé. If you're in Terminal 3, try Big Apple Bagel, Chili's, Manchu Wok, or the New Amsterdam Pub. In Terminal 4, hungry travelers will find Sylvia's of Harlem, Superbowls (soup), Asiana, The Grille, Zum Zum (sausages), a kosher deli, and, for sit-down service, Naples Italian Restaurant. Terminal 5 has an assortment of fast-food outlets and coffee shops, and Terminal 6 has a sausage place called World Links and a branch of Nathan's Hot Dogs. Terminal 7 has cafeterias and coffee shops, a pasta and pizza eatery, and Lattitudes, a full-service, sit-down restaurant. In Terminal 8, look for Edy's Ice Cream and Wok & Roll. Au Bon Pain bakery, Everything Yogurt, and Sbarro are in Terminals 8 and 9, and T.G.I. Friday's has a branch in Terminal 9.

Best Healthful Nosh

Salads or fruit shakes from Everything Yogurt in Terminals 8 and 9.

Best Sinful Snack

Sausages or wieners, with the works, from World Links in Terminal 6.

►Relax and Refresh

To escape the hustle and bustle, grab a seat at an unused gate or visit the chapel on the second floor of Terminal 4. The altar and stained-glass windows in this interdenominational place of worship were salvaged from three other chapels formerly located in different spots at the airport.

You can spring for a facial at Clinique in Terminal 1, or pay the day rate at the Ramada Inn (on JFK property) to use their exercise and health club facilities (718-995-9000).

Smokers can light up only outside or in an airport bar.

Take Care of Business

• A business center is planned for Terminal 4, the International Air Terminal.

JFK recently installed numerous Internet phones with touch screens in Terminal 4. These "Web phones" will appear in Terminals 1, 2, 3, 5, 6, and 8 when construction projects now under way are completed. You'll also find Internet kiosks at Gates 1, 2, and 8 in Terminal 8 and Gates 41, 45, 48, and 49 in Terminal 9. There are also two cybercafés in Terminal 4. If you're toting your own laptop, data ports are currently most plentiful in Terminals 1, 4, 7, 8, and 9.

For other business services (faxing and copying, mostly) head to Gate 7 in Terminal 1, to the departure level of Terminal 2, to the South Concourse of Terminal 3, and to Travel Express on the second floor of Terminal 4. You'll find slim pickings in Terminals 5 and 6, but there's a conference facility in Terminal 7, and a variety of self-service spots in Terminals 8 and 9.

A full-service First Union Bank is located in the retail hall of Terminal 4.

Explore the Airport

►**Shop**

The shops at JFK are getting updated along with the terminals and the landscaping. For example, Terminal 1 boasts the largest duty-free shop east of the Mississippi, a Clinique/Estée Lauder outlet, and stores selling pens, gadgets, watches, sunglasses, sportswear, ties, toys, jewelry, and electronics. Terminal 3 has a music store where you can listen to CDs on headphones for as long as you like, and every newsstand in the airport carries miniature Statue of Liberty figurines, Big Apple T-shirts, and "I Love NY" tote bags.

The new International Air Terminal (Terminal 4) offers four "blocks" of shops, including Greatest Museums of New York, the New York City Store, New York Undercover (lingerie, socks, etc.), New York Minute (watches), Broadway Backstage, Metropolis (educational toys), and several other New York–oriented stores and kiosks. Rounding out the choices, you'll find Brookstone, the Music Store, H. Stern (jewelry), and W. H. Smith Books.

In Terminal 8 you'll find AltiTunes (CDs and electronics), The Athlete's Foot (athletic shoes), Brookstone (gadgets galore), a New York souvenir shop, and a Speedo store, just in case you're going swimming anytime soon. Terminal 9 has the airport's main bookstore (Book Connection) and branches of AltiTunes, Brookstone, Fossil Watches, and the Sunglass Hut.

►**Sightsee**

JFK's most famous piece of art is Terminal 5, better known as the TWA terminal. Designed by noted architect Eero Saarinen in 1959, the building has been featured in dozens of movies and has been designated a historic landmark.

While Terminal 5 has history and tradition on its side, it's the new Terminal 1 that's getting most of the attention. Designed to invoke the spirit of flight, the terminal is bright and airy, with soaring ceilings, great views, waterfalls, and an abstract sheet-metal-and-aluminum sculpture by Alice Aycock in the central rotunda that made at least one visitor feel as if she were inside a radar screen.

And then there's Terminal 8. When the building opened in 1959, the red, white, and blue stained-glass window across the front of the building made it into the *Guinness Book of World Records* as the largest stained-glass window in the world. Terminal 8 also boasts two vintage murals by Carybe, the Brazilian artist who won the design competition sponsored by the building's original architects.

For the best views, head for Terminal 1—it's got lots of glass and was designed to let in natural light. From the mezzanine, look one way to see a wildlife refuge, look the other way to view the Manhattan skyline.

▶ Play Around

Kids will enjoy the waterfalls and the big sculpture in Terminal 1 and the Lego-sponsored play area near Gates 5 and 7. There's also a kids' play area in Terminal 6 in the JetBlue Airways gate area. Or pile everyone on the free shuttle bus to Terminal 8 to inspect the murals and see how many different historical figures you and your kids can identify.

Go into Town

- If you take a taxi to Manhattan, be sure to get one that is licensed by the city. If you end up in a "gypsy" vehicle instead, you may get charged an arm and a leg for what should be a $30 ride.

If you've exhausted all of the on-site entertainment, remember that you're just a 40-minute subway ride from Manhattan aboard the "A" train. To get to the subway, catch the free yellow-and-white airport bus. The fare is $1.50, and in town the sky really is the limit.

Of course, you can also take a taxi into the city. The New York City Taxi and Limousine Commission has established a $30 flat fare from JFK to Manhattan. Look for signs and kiosks in the baggage claim area. The ride can take anywhere from 45 minutes to 2 hours, depending on traffic.

Other Information

For more information about JFK before you arrive, call 718-244-4444.

 **LaGuardia Airport**

New York, New York (Flushing, NY)
Airport Code: LGA
Web Address: http://www.laguardiaairport.com

In 1929, the site of the Gala Amusement Park in Queens, New York, was transformed into Glenn H. Curtiss Airport. The airport was subsequently renamed North Beach Airport, New York Municipal Airport–LaGuardia Field, and finally, in 1947, LaGuardia Airport (LGA), in honor of Mayor Fiorello H. LaGuardia.

Get Oriented

- Luggage carts rent for $1.50.
- There are no lockers at LGA.

LaGuardia's Central Terminal Building (CTB) serves America West, Continental, Midwest Express, Trans World Airlines, United, and several other carriers. US Airways and the US Airways Shuttle operate out of terminals to the east of the CTB, and Delta and Northwest are headquartered at a terminal just a bit farther east. West of the Central Terminal Building are the Marine Air Terminal and the Delta Shuttle flights. The Marine Air Terminal was the original airport terminal building and was located near the bay so it could serve the "flying boats" that dominated international travel in the 1930s and 1940s.

You can walk between most terminals in less than 10 minutes, but it's much easier to take the shuttle bus that comes by approximately every 10 minutes. Don't try walking to the Delta Shuttle terminal, however, as it's about 1.5 miles from the Central Terminal Building.

To get your bearings, ask for an airport map from one of the friendly "Apple Aides" who staff the information booths on the departures level of the Central Terminal Building, or flag down a customer service representative (they're called "Red Coats") and ask to be pointed in the right direction.

Take Care of Yourself

►Eat

For the widest range of choices, head for the food court in the Central Terminal Building. Choices at the LaGuardia Marketplace (a three-story atrium between Concourses B and C that has views of the airfield) include Brooklyn National Deli, Asian Chao, Figs (a sit-down restaurant), and the decadent Godiva Chocolatier. A smaller food court in Concourse D offers branches of Sbarro, New York Coffee Station, and the Sweet Factory.

Au Bon Pain, which serves bakery items as well as hearty soups and sandwiches, has outlets in Concourses A, B, and C, and Caliente MexPress, between Concourse C and Concourse D serves Tex-Mex food. Just outside of Concourses A and D you'll also find Hangars, which offers burgers, sandwiches, salads, and full bar service.

In the US Airways Terminal, you can get table service at Anton's or browse the nearby food court, which features Sbarro's, Wok & Roll, and a yogurt shop.

Best Healthful Nosh

Fresh salads or fruit plates from Brooklyn National Deli, in the food court in the Central Terminal Building.

Best Sinful Snack

Chocolates from the Godiva Chocolatier in the LaGuardia Marketplace in the Central Terminal Building.

►Relax and Refresh

To escape the hustle and bustle, head for the center section of the Central Terminal Building, where you'll find comfortable seating areas and a nice view of the airfield. The area between the US Airways Terminal and the Central Terminal Building has pleasant landscaping and several benches. For an even nicer spot, take the airport shuttle bus over to the Marine Air Terminal, which also has a small landscaped area with benches.

Don't be shy about freshening up in the bathrooms. The folks at LaGuardia did serious research and learned that passengers rated clean bathrooms near the top of the list of desired airport amenities. As a result, the high-use restrooms in the Central Terminal Building and in the Marine Air Terminal have been upgraded and now feature better ventilation, live plants, and uniformed attendants on duty during peak travel times.

Got a toothache? LGA has a dental office on-site. You'll find it in the Central Terminal Building, upstairs behind the American Airlines ticket counter.

For more serious relaxation or exercise, several nearby hotels, including the Garden Hotel, Crown Plaza, and the LaGuardia Airport Marriott (718-565-8900) offer day rates that include access to health clubs, pools, and exercise rooms. Use the hotel phones in the baggage claim area to ask for current rates and specific facilities.

Smokers: LaGuardia Airport is a no-smoking facility, but paying customers can light up in the bar at Caliente MexPress in the Central Terminal Building.

Take Care of Business

You'll find a business center (which rents fully equipped offices by the minute) on the lower level of the Central Terminal Building. You'll also find Internet kiosks (some are free) at the top of Concourses B and C in the Central Terminal Building and in many concourses. There's a Federal Express drop box in Concourse C, and self-service business centers offering fax service, currency exchange, and ATMs in each terminal.

Explore the Airport

► Shop

- Street pricing is in effect at LaGuardia, meaning that shops can't charge more for that last-minute gift at the airport than you'd pay anywhere else in town.

At LaGuardia Marketplace in the Central Terminal Building, you'll find travel accessories at Travel 2000, perfume and cosmetics at Cosmetics Plus, vitamins and health products at the General Nutrition Center, and a wide variety of team caps at Lids.

Music Express offers CDs, batteries, and audio equipment, and Barbara's Books carries a nice selection of reading material. Discover New York carries a variety of New York–area museum gift-shop items.

The US Airways Terminal offers more CDs at AltiTunes, more books at Benjamin Books, more travel gear at Bon Voyage, and a branch of Brooks Brothers, which offers mostly menswear.

►Sightsee

If you have time, take the free 10-minute shuttle bus ride to the Marine Air Terminal and view the James Brooks mural "Flight." Completed in 1942, this is the largest mural created under the auspices of the federally funded Works Progress Administration art program. The building's rotunda houses a model of the "Flying Boat"—the Boeing 314 that Pan American World Airways operated from March 1940 through June 1945. On the wall is an exhibit detailing that airplane's layout, including the areas where pampered travelers once dined and slept.

Good views of the airfield can be had from the food and retail court located between Concourses B and C and at the end of each concourse area. There's also an area near the escalators to the parking garage that has some seating and offers a good view of the runways.

►Play Around

LaGuardia has no kid-specific play areas, but you might take the kids over to the Central Terminal Building for good views of planes taking off and landing, or hop on the shuttle bus to the Marine Air Terminal to see the mural.

Go into Town

• For more information about ground transportation options, call 800-AIR-RIDE (800-247-7433).

A taxi ride to Manhattan costs about $26 (plus tolls) and can take anywhere from 30 to 60 minutes, depending on traffic. Alternatives to taxis include the New York Airport Service Express Bus for $10 and shared door-to-door minivans for about $13. For $1.50 you can have a real New York experience: the M60 Bus (New York City Transit Authority) goes to 125th Street, where you can connect with any number of subway trains. If you're headed to Wall Street (Pier 11), you can take the Delta Water Shuttle ferry from the Marine Air Terminal/Delta Shuttle. Tickets are $15 one way.

Other Information

If you need more information about LaGuardia Airport, call 718-533-3400.

John Wayne Airport (Orange County Airport)

Orange County, California (Santa Ana, CA)
Airport Code: SNA
Web Address: http://www.ocair.com

Although rechristened in 1979 to honor the passing of actor (and neighbor) John Wayne, the Orange County Airport can claim star status on its own: the facility has served as a backdrop for scenes in many films, including *Demolition Man, Jerry Maguire, Clear and Present Danger,* and *The Out of Towners.* When not posing for the camera, John Wayne Airport (SNA) offers its "star service" to almost 8 million passengers a year.

Get Oriented

- Luggage carts rent for $2. You'll get a $.25 refund when you return a cart to the rack.
- There are no lockers at John Wayne Airport.

John Wayne Airport has one main terminal building with 14 gates divided among two concourses, referred to as Terminals A and B. Terminal A gates serve Alaska, American, Continental, Delta, and Delta Connection. Terminal B gates serve America West, Northwest, Southwest, TWA, United, United Express, and US Airways.

It will take you just a few minutes to go from one end of the A gates to the end of the B gates; the concourses are mirror images of each other and meet in a central area.

Take Care of Yourself

►Eat

Table service is available at the Orange Grill Restaurant, perched in the food court areas between the two concourses.

Their menu includes sandwiches, salads, tacos, and "express" lunches. Just down the way, by Gate 6, Creative Croissants offers sandwiches, tasty baked goods, juices, and smoothies. The Pavilion Pub (by Gate 11) has an espresso machine.

Best Healthful Nosh

Salads and sandwiches from the Orange Grill Restaurant, or smoothies and fresh orange juice from Creative Croissants (Gate 6) or Juice Works (center food court).

Best Sinful Snack

Chocolate fudge or bulk candy by the pound (or partial pound) from Catarina's Candies by Gate 9, or Häagen-Dazs ice cream from the snack bar in the connecting corridor on the ticketing level.

►Relax and Refresh

Comfortable, out-of-the-way seating areas are located at the intersection between Terminals A and B, in the lower-level atrium by the John Wayne statue, and across the corridor from several gate "holding" areas. There are also several out-of-the-way benches in the connecting corridor between Terminals A and B.

This nonsmoking airport sports no on-site health clubs, beauty services, or hotels. However, the Atrium Hotel (directly across the street from the airport) and most nearby hotels offer day rates that include use of their pools, health clubs, and exercise facilities. (Atrium Hotel: 949-833-2770.)

Take Care of Business

• Only a few phones down in the baggage claim area have data ports.

This is yet another airport where an airline club membership (American or United) is pretty much essential if you need to send a fax, make copies, or get down to serious business. In a pinch, head across the street to the Atrium or Hilton hotels and see if they can help out.

Explore the Airport

►Shop

California Kidz (by Gate 8) has great toys, Beanie Babies, and other fun stuff; Catarina's Candies (Gate 9) has "gift" candy; and each newsstand/gift shop carries Southern California souvenirs ranging from seashell-filled bottles to hockey pucks, coasters, and pennants emblazoned with the Mighty Ducks logo. True John Wayne fans can even go home with a small statue or bust of the Duke himself.

►Sightsee

Speaking of the Duke, there's a nine-foot-tall bronze statue of John Wayne by sculptor Robert Summers down in a lovely atrium section of the baggage claim level. He's appropriately dressed in his best western regalia, complete with cowboy hat, guns, and gun belt filled with bullets. And those palm trees nearby? They're real but never need watering because they're freeze-dried!

SNA mounts at least a half-dozen museum-quality exhibitions each year and hosts an annual countywide student art contest. Look for these exhibits at each end of the terminal: opposite Gates 1–4 in Terminal B and Gates 11–14 in Terminal A. Artwork is also located near each security checkpoint.

History buffs should head for the wall-mounted Freedom Shrine in the ticket-level connecting corridor. Reproductions of 29 historical documents include John F. Kennedy's Inaugural Address, the Declaration of Independence, and Ben Franklin's epitaph, which he penned in his twenties but replaced with something much simpler in his eighties.

The entire wall facing the airfield is glass, offering great views of airplane activity and nearby Southern California scenery. The best viewing spot is from the seating area at the intersection of the two concourses, near the food court.

►Play Around

Kids might enjoy monitoring the airfield activities, visiting the nine-foot-tall statue of John Wayne (in the baggage claim area), or trying to identify the documents in the Freedom Shrine (in the ticket-level corridor). Or just give in and head for the California Kidz toy shop by Gate 8.

Go into Town

Taxis, shuttles, and buses are located in the ground transportation center, located across the roadway from the terminal.

A half-hour cab ride from here to Anaheim/Disneyland will cost about $28. Shared shuttle vans make the trip for $8–$12 per person. Rides to downtown Santa Ana or Irvine will run $7–$15.

For public bus routes and other transportation options, visit the helpful folks who staff the information booths in the baggage claim level of the terminal. You can also call ahead to Orange County Transportation at 714-636-7433 or The Airport Bus (to Disneyland or LAX) at 800-772-5299.

Other Information

For more information about the airport before you arrive, call 949-252-5200.

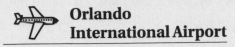 **Orlando
International Airport**

Orlando, Florida
Airport Code: MCO
Web Address: http://www.fcn.state.fl.us/goaa

Is this a mall or an airport? With 36 shops, 23 restaurants, 6 bars, a microbrewery, and a hotel all within the main terminal building, Orlando International Airport (MCO) works hard to make your trip through the airport as entertaining as the surrounding tourist destinations. For the most part, they succeed.

Get Oriented

- Luggage carts rent for $2. You'll receive a $.25 refund when you return a cart to the rack.
- Storage lockers are located postsecurity, in the concourses.

MCO has four concourse areas, referred to by their "gate cluster" and position in relation to the main terminal. Gates 1–29 and 100–129 are on the "A" side of the main terminal, while Gates 30–59 and 60–99 are located in the "B" side of the terminal. The two-sided main terminal has shop-lined corridors and a lush foliage-filled atrium complete with a fountain and plenty of comfortable seating.

If the shops don't sidetrack you, it should take no more than 15 minutes to walk through the terminal and onto one of the shuttle trams that take passengers out to the gates. Gates 1–29 serve mostly American, America West, Continental, and Trans World Airlines. Northwest, United, and US Airways use Gates 20–59, and Delta and several other carriers pull up at Gates 60–99. The new concourse containing Gates 100–129 serves Southwest, Spirit, AirTran, Sun Country, and JetBlue.

People movers shuttle passengers between the main terminal

and the gate areas, providing enticing views of lakes, waterways, and lush foliage. Airport officials call this the "Orlando Experience."

To get your bearings, pick up a terminal map, a guide to the airport's art collection, and a brochure listing all the shops and services from one of the two airport information centers located at the gate entrance areas in the main terminal building.

Take Care of Yourself

▶ **Eat**

In the main terminal you'll find the Shipyard Brewing Company, reputedly the world's first airport microbrewery. Sure, other airports have bars serving microbrews, but here they actually brew the beer and offer tours of the facility. Self-guided tours take you along six-foot-high glass windows on the brewery's perimeter. More fact-filled guided tours are offered weekdays, 11 AM–3 PM. There's also a play area with traditional pub games such as darts, chess, checkers, and backgammon. Other choices throughout the airport include Chili's (upstairs in the main terminal building near the security checkpoint for Gates 1–59) and Stinger Ray's Beach Bar & Grill, which offers barbecue sandwiches, tropical fare, and PG-rated floor shows featuring waitstaff performing song-and-dance numbers. Head out to Gates 30–59 for Miami Subs and Don Pepe's Café, a branch of a well-known local Cuban restaurant.

For a more upscale, sit-down meal, Hemisphere in the on-site Hyatt Regency Hotel offers four-star dining with a ninth-floor view of airfield activity. The restaurant faces east and is also a prime viewing spot for space-shuttle launches. The hotel also has a less formal restaurant called McCoy's.

Best Healthful Nosh

Veggie deli sandwiches from the 24-hour Big Apple Bagel Deli in the main terminal food court.

Best Sinful Snack

Candy and nuts from the Grove Sweet Shop in the Great Hall outside Gates 20–59.

►**Relax and Refresh**

Orlando International Airport is brighter and quieter than you'd expect. Head to the atrium in the on-site Hyatt Regency Hotel at the east end of the terminal and you'll find comfortable seats and fountains that will lull you to sleep in moments. If you need a more serious nap, ask about the hotel's day rate. Day guests also get access to the hotel's health club (407-825-1234).

If you need some professional freshening up, Profiles Express Salon (on the B side of the mall corridor) is a full-service unisex salon offering hair styling, pedicures, and massage therapy (407-825-6485).

Smokers may light up only in the lounge areas of restaurants.

Take Care of Business

- The business center in the Hyatt Regency Hotel offers computer workstations, Internet access, and other business services. It's open daily, but hours vary (407-825-1234).

A business center, which rents fully equipped mini-offices by the minute, is located in the hotel atrium area of the main terminal. There's also a self-serve business center located on the east side of the main terminal, adjacent to the security checkpoints for Gates 60–99. Fax, mail, copy, and Internet-access services are located here, along with several small alcoves with phones and desktops.

Telephone data ports and Internet kiosks are located throughout the airport.

Explore the Airport

►**Shop**

You might find yourself so swept away with shopping that you'll forget you're here to catch a plane.

Two corridors of shops and concessions connect the main

terminal areas, and Disney World, SeaWorld, and Universal Studios all have gift shops here. Street pricing is in effect, which means souvenirs cost no more (or less) than at the theme parks and area malls. Even if you're not buying, the shops are entertaining: at the Warner Bros. Studio store, an oversize Bugs Bunny sports tourist duds, while the SeaWorld shops boast aquariums filled with colorful tropical fish.

Highlights in the main Great Hall area include the Bunches of Books, the SeaWorld store, Bow Wow Meow (gifts for pets you left behind), Disney Magic, the Universal Studios store, and the Warner Bros. Studio store. In the North Walk (which connects the Great Hall to the Hotel Atrium on the A side of the terminal) you'll find AltiTunes (CDs), a Bon Voyage Travel store, an Electronics Boutique, a large Discovery Channel Store, Toobs Toys & Games, and numerous jewelry, perfume, souvenir, and watch shops. The South Walk (which connects the Great Hall to the hotel atrium on the B side) features the Museum Company store (with a large kids' toy section), the Body Shop, Wilsons Leather, Speedo Authentic Fitness, and a travel agency.

► Sightsee

Orlando International Airport's extensive public art collection features works from such renowned artists as Jacob Lawrence, Miriam Schapiro, and Edward Campos. Take a self-guided tour with the free art brochure from the information booth, and don't skip the parking garages, where sculptures of armadillos, pelicans, eagles, and other animals help folks remember where they parked.

The new concourse area for Gates 100–129 is decorated with impressive stained-glass windows and a mosaic floor imbedded with images of Florida's native flora and fauna.

In the main terminal, be sure to look behind the potted plants by the elevators near the security checkpoint for Gates 1–59. That's where Duane Hansen's realistic life-size bronze, "The Traveler," is stashed. Looking like a stereotypical tourist who's fallen asleep, the piece used to be out in the open, but people kept touching him. Hanson came through the airport himself one day and demanded that the work be returned to him for some "freshening up." Now the piece sits behind Plexiglas.

Also, be sure to examine the glass display cases located along the moving walkways in the mall corridor on the B side of the terminal. They're filled with items on loan from NASA's Kennedy Space Center, including a full-size moon suit and other out-of-this-world souvenirs.

For a great view of airplanes taking off and landing, head to the top floor of the terminal parking garage. From here you can see the Orlando skyline, EPCOT Center's Spaceship Earth, and the numerous nightly fireworks displays at the area theme parks. This is also a good spot to watch space-shuttle launchings.

► Play Around

- Seating areas in the main terminal feature small chairs designed to make the airport's younger "customers" feel welcome.

Kids will enjoy inspecting the space rocks and NASA souvenirs on display in the mall area. If they're lucky, they might be on time to watch a diver feed the fish in the SeaWorld store aquarium in the shop near the entrance to Gates 60–99. The theme park stores are an obvious home run, and there's a game arcade on the A side of the mall corridor.

Very small children can work off some energy in the play area located in the concourse serving Gates 60–99. The large, over-sized foam sea-creatures featured here have been so popular with families that airport officials promise there will soon be similar spots in each concourse.

Go into Town

A taxi ride to downtown Orlando takes about 30 minutes and costs approximately $27, and a taxi ride to Disney World, about 40 minutes away, costs about $40. Shuttle vans can get you downtown for $12 and to Mickey's place for about $14. You can also catch a public bus (Lynx) on the first level of the A side of the main terminal. Bus fare to the downtown (Pine Street) bus terminal, the International Drive resort area, and the popular Florida Mall is $.85. The ride can take up to 40 minutes.

Other Information

For more information about the airport before you arrive call 407-825-2353.

Roissy–Charles de Gaulle Airport

Paris, France
Airport Code: CDG
Web Address: http://www.adp.fr

When it opened in 1974, the giant, all-concrete, dark, drum-shaped Terminal 1 at the Roissy–Charles de Gaulle airport (CDG) was hailed as a space-age masterpiece of design. Now the long escalator trip through glass tubes that passengers must make to get to and from their airplanes is more tedious than entertaining. The "fun" at Roissy these days is over in Terminal 2, especially over in the new Hall F, a welcoming facility reminiscent of an old-style grand railway terminal, but full of glass and light.

Get Oriented

- Luggage carts are available free of charge throughout the airport.
- In compliance with French antiterrorist laws, there are no lockers or baggage check services at Roissy–Charles de Gaulle.

Terminals 1 and 2 at Roissy–Charles de Gaulle are used for most commercial flights. Terminal 9 serves predominantly charter flights. It will be important to know which terminal your airline uses, because it can take up to 20 minutes to get from one terminal to another via the free airport shuttle bus. US passengers flying United, British Airways, KLM, and Northwest will generally find themselves using Terminal 1; Continental, Delta, Air France, and others use Terminal 2.

Take Care of Yourself

►Eat

On the lower level of Terminal 1 you'll find hearty buffet meals at Les Palmes and a wide variety of bars, snack bars, and sandwich shops, including one called Paris Bye Bye. Postsecurity (on the 11th floor) you'll find the gourmet Terrasse de Paris.

In Terminal 2, your choice of table-service restaurants includes Hippopotamus (hamburgers) in Hall D and the more French-feeling Bistrot Fontaines des Halles, in Hall A. The food court in Hall B boasts the Salmon House, Li Weng, La Brioche Dorée, and other reasonably priced alternatives. In Hall F, look for Brasserie Flo, Flo Express, and Bar Maxim's.

If you simply can't find anything to eat at the airport, both the nearby Hilton and Sheraton hotels boast top-drawer restaurants.

Best Healthful Nosh

The Salmon House, located in the food court in Hall B (landside) offers fresh oysters and a "30-Minute Special" consisting of smoked salmon, cheese, and a glass of beer or wine for fr97 (about US$13).

Best Sinful Snack

"Gift" chocolates from the grocery in the lower level between Halls B and D in Terminal 2, or ice cream from Häagen-Dazs in the food court in Hall B (Terminal 2).

►Relax and Refresh

If you're craving light and wide-open relaxing spaces, head to the new Hall F in Terminal 2. There's lots of seating in the ticketing hall and several spots behind the shops (before security) that are out of the flow of traffic. In Terminal 1, you might head downstairs and look for a chair facing the fountain, but it's often too busy down there to truly relax. If you have some time and want to chill out in a more luxurious spot, take a bus over to the Sheraton Hotel or Hilton Hotel and plop down in the lobby. There's also a chapel on the lower level of Terminal 1, near the grocery store.

There are free showers in both terminals, but a more pleasant place to freshen up on-site is at the Cocoon Hotel on the lower level of Terminal 1. Windowless, compact (tiny), ship-cabin-like rooms are rented for either day or night use. Many folks stop here to shower and/or nap after a long flight or an arrival late in the evening to ensure that they make their early morning flights. Rates: fr250 (about US$34) for one or fr300 (about US$40) for two. Phone: 33-1-48-62-06-16.

More traditional, and more expensive, hotels nearby include the Hilton Paris Charles de Gaulle Airport, which has a pool and exercise facility (phone: 33-1-49-19-29-29), and the Sheraton Paris Airport, the ship-shaped hotel "berthed" in the center of airport property, by Terminal 2 (phone: 33-1-49-19-70-70). Even if you don't want to spring for a room, the lobby areas and restaurants of these hotels offer delightful respite.

You'll find a hairdresser on the lower level of Terminal 1, which is open Monday–Saturday. Check with the information desk in Terminal 2 to see if their barbershop/beauty salon has opened.

Roissy is a nonsmoking facility, but smoking is permitted in many bars/cafés and in designated smoking areas.

Take Care of Business

- There's a single Internet kiosk in the grocery story (Petit Casino) on the lower level of Terminal 2, between Halls B and D. Internet access is also available at business centers in the nearby Hilton or Sheraton hotels.

All major airlines have club lounges at Roissy. Nonmembers who need to get work done can visit the on-site business center, located on the lower, or boutiquaire, level of Terminal 1. From the departure level, take the down escalator near Gate 34. Hours: Monday–Friday, 8 AM–7 PM. Services range from faxing and copying to meeting space for 2–15 people.

There's a copy machine tucked in a corner next to the grocery on the lower level of Terminal 1. You can also get copies made at the post offices, located on the lower level of Terminal 1 and on the lower level of Terminal 2, between Halls A and C and Halls B and D.

Nearby hotels, including the Hilton, Sheraton, and Ibis, all have business centers as well and are accessible by courtesy buses that circle the airport frequently.

Explore the Airport

►Shop

In Terminal 1, you'll find the duty-free shopping upstairs on level 4. Highlights there include gourmet foods such as foie gras, caviar, and pâtés, perfumes and cosmetics, and a shop selling reproductions from the national museums. Shop here before you board a flight from Terminal 1, but if you have some time to browse, head over to the public areas of Hall F in Terminal 2. Many of the shops here offer the same merchandise you'll find elsewhere in the airport, but here everything looks generally more enticing and inviting. Presecurity highlights include a lingerie and swimwear shop (Koba Cabana), a toy store (Poulbo), and a tableware and gift-food shop (Richesse des régions de France). For some reason even the toothbrushes in the pharmacy here look elegant.

►Sightsee

There are no official art or history displays at CDG, but if you have time, make sure to visit the new Hall F in Terminal 2, which is being heralded as an architectural tour de force. Designed by Paul Andreu, whose architectural team also designed the darker Terminal 1 back in 1969, Hall F has soaring, wide-open spaces and bright, straightforward paths that lead passengers to and from their airplanes.

Ceiling-to-floor windows in Hall F in Terminal 2 provide good views of airfield activity, as do many of the seating areas in the cafés, the mezzanine levels, and elsewhere in Terminal 2.

►Play Around

Air France has a tiny play area in Hall A in Terminal 2. There's also a fairly good video-game arcade in the lower level of Terminal 1. Otherwise, you might take kids to Hall F, where there's a good toy store and wide corridors perfect for running around.

Go into Town

A taxi ride into town will cost between fr200 and fr300 (about US$27–US$40) and take anywhere from half an hour to quite a bit more than an hour. Other choices for getting to town include trains (RER), for fr49 (about US$6.60), and buses (Roissybus and Air France), which cost between fr45 and fr70 (US$6–US$9.50) and take about 45 minutes. For details about the best route for you, check in with the folks at the information desks.

Other Information

If your plane spends any time sitting on the runway, take a good look at the grassy areas: you'll probably see a good number of rabbits. Airport officials have nothing against these cute furry animals, but they'd like to get rid of them. Why? Rabbit droppings bring mice. Mice bring birds of prey. And sometimes, when those birds of prey swoop in for a tasty snack, they get sucked into an airplane engine. So the airport has instituted something they call "Operation Zero Rabbit," which involves seasonal hunting, ferrets, traps, but no poison.

Orly Airport

Paris, France
Airport Code: ORY
Web Address: http://www.adp.fr

Orly (ORY), located just 9 miles south of Paris, once served as an airfield for balloonists and, during World War II, as an American army base. Now this very manageable facility serves as the city's secondary airport, making do with an evening flight curfew and strict noise restrictions.

Get Oriented

- Luggage carts are available throughout the airport and are free of charge.
- In compliance with French antiterrorist laws, there are no lockers or baggage check services at Orly.

Orly's two terminals, Ouest (west) and Sud (south), are connected by a shuttle train that travels back and forth in just 2 minutes. Orly west is the smaller of the two, but it has the more interesting restaurants. Orly south is larger and sports an outdoor observation deck and more amenities. Information booths scattered throughout each terminal provide free maps and terminal guides.

Take Care of Yourself

► Eat

For a great choice of sit-down meals, start on the mezzanine level of the west terminal, where you'll find the Clifden Pub, Le Grill, Le Trèfle, and the more upscale Maxim's. Several of these restaurants also have great views of the airfield.

In the south terminal, Le Clos Saint-Germain, on the third

floor, is considered a fine gourmet restaurant, but the sandwiches, quiches, and snacks offered at less formal places such as L'escale Bleue (on the ground floor) and Le Méli-Mélo (on the third floor) are easier on the budget.

Best Healthful Nosh

Fresh seafood from the seafood bar out in front of the Clifden Pub, on the mezzanine level of the west terminal.

Best Sinful Snack

Foie gras or caviar from Chedeville Gastronomie, which has outlets in both terminals.

►Relax and Refresh

To escape the hustle and bustle of the airport, head to the mezzanine level of the west terminal or grab a seat on the second level of the south terminal, near the windows. The outdoor observation deck here is a lovely spot to get some fresh air and keep an eye on airfield activities. If you need a bit more solitude, Orly west has a chapel and Orly south offers separate rooms that serve as a chapel, a synagogue, and a mosque.

There are no on-site health clubs at Orly, and unfortunately, the airport's free shower facilities have been closed due to some sort of virus. (Ick!) "Besides," an information desk hostess told me, "there was never any hot water anyway." The showers should be fixed—"oh, someday" is all airport officials will say—but in the meantime, and just to be safe, shower up at one of the nearby hotels, such as the Mercure or the Hilton, which offer day rates at fr360 and fr580 (about US$49 and US$78), respectively. Or splash up in a bathroom and head to the lower level of the south terminal to see what the hairdresser or the dry cleaners can do to freshen up your appearance.

Orly is a nonsmoking facility, but there are several marked areas for smokers to light up. Smoking is also permitted in many of the bars.

Take Care of Business

- Orly has no Internet kiosks, but there are self-service fax machines in the telephone centers in each terminal.

There is a business center at Orly west, up on the mezzanine level, where you can rent a meeting room or a workspace and get materials faxed or copied. Both terminals have full-service post offices, where you can also get copies made. At Orly south, the post office is open from 7:00 AM to 6:15 PM, Monday–Friday; at Orly west the post office is open from 6:30 AM to 7:00 PM, Monday–Friday, from 7 AM to 12 noon on Saturday, and from 9 AM to 6 PM on Sunday. Nearby hotels, such as the Hilton, should also be able to help you out with faxes, copies, and other business services.

Explore the Airport

► Shop

Both terminals have a good assortment of shops, but in the west terminal you'll have more choices before security, while in the south terminal you'll have more fun shopping once you pass through security. Souvenir hunters should note that the pharmacies in both terminals offer lovely French shaving brushes, and the Chedeville Gastronomie food boutiques in both terminals offer caviar, salmon, foie gras, French wines and cheeses, and a wonderful cognac-filled decanter in the shape of the Eiffel Tower.

► Sightsee

Orly has two art galleries, each offering changing exhibitions of paintings, sculpture, and photography. The gallery in the south terminal is located on the upper level (fourth floor), while the west terminal display area is on the mezzanine level.

In the west corridor of the west terminal, as you're going from Halls 1 and 2 toward Halls 3 and 4, be sure to look up. The astronomical work of art is called "Astrolabe" and it moves, but very very slowly.

The Panoramic Terrace on the upper level of the south terminal is your best bet for fresh air *and* great views of the activity on the airfield. Even if you don't venture outside, the windows on the upper level offer good views.

► **Play Around**

There are no formal children's play areas at Orly, but kids might enjoy riding the shuttle back and forth between terminals and browsing in the toy shop in the landside corridor in the west terminal.

Go into Town

A cab ride to the city will cost at least fr150 (or about US$20) and take anywhere from 30 minutes to an hour, depending on time of day. Other popular choices for traveling into town include the Air France bus (fr45 or about US$6) or the train (fr57 or about US$7.70).

Other Information

Don't be surprised if you look out the window of your airplane and see an alarming number of rabbits on the grassy areas near the runways. The airport has a little "rabbit problem" and officials have tried a variety of ways to get rid of them, everything from inviting hunters onto airport property to capturing the critters in cages and taking them "to the country."

Philadelphia International Airport

Philadelphia, Pennsylvania
Airport Code: PHL
Web Address: http://www.phl.org

Opened in 1940 as Philadelphia Municipal Airport, today's Philadelphia International Airport (PHL) is the 19th busiest airport in the country and encompasses a plot of land once known as Hog Island, site of a giant World War I emergency shipbuilding yard.

Get Oriented

- Luggage carts are located throughout all five terminals and rent for $2.
- Lockers are located in each concourse, postsecurity.

To get your bearings on-site, pick up an airport map and directory from one of the information centers (operated by Rosenbluth International) located in each of the terminals. Hours: 6 AM–11 PM, daily.

US Airways, which has its major hub at this airport, occupies all the gates in Terminals B and C. Other airlines use Terminals A, D, and E. Look for American, British Airways, Midway, and US Airways in Terminal A; Air Canada, America West, Continental, United, and some overflow US Airways in Terminal D; and in Terminal E, you'll find Delta, Midwest Express, Northwest, and TWA.

It should take you no longer than 5 or 10 minutes to make your way along and between most terminals. If you're in a hurry, you can hop on an "express" moving walkway to get between Terminals B and C and between Terminals A and B. But if you're headed to Terminals D and E toting baggage, consider renting a cart or checking your baggage—it's a bit of a hike.

Take Care of Yourself

► Eat

If you're hungry, head to the Philadelphia Marketplace, located in the connecting corridor between Terminals B and C, where a spacious food court is ringed by outlets of both local and chain eateries. "Philadelphia fare" is offered at Hymie's Deli (cheese steaks), Philly's Finest (Tastykakes, Hank's soda, and Bassett's ice cream), and Barson's Seafood & Salads (crab soup). If you want table service, try T.G.I. Friday's or the Bell Brewery & Pub.

Highlights elsewhere in the airport include Edy's Gourmet Ice Cream (Concourse A), Bubba's Baked Goods (Concourse B), Philly Steak and Gyro (Concourse C), Famous King of Pizza (Concourse D), and the Philadelphia-style pretzels available from kiosks in most every concourse.

Best Healthful Nosh

Salad by the bowl from Salad Works in Concourse A or a smoothie from Frozen Fusion, the juice bar in Concourse B.

Best Sinful Snack

Pretty much anything from Godiva Chocolatier, located in the Philadelphia Marketplace, or maybe a tiny jar of caviar from Caviar Assouline, also in the Marketplace.

► Relax and Refresh

To rest your feet a bit and do some serious people watching, grab a seat in the Philadelphia Marketplace food court (the connecting corridor between Terminals B and C) or snag one of the white rocking chairs thoughtfully scattered all along the central corridor. At first glance, these rocking rest stops seem unlikely places to evade the crowds, but I spied folks using the rockers to complete both serious work and some blissful napping.

For more out-of-the-way spots, head for the lobby of the Philadelphia Airport Marriott, which is connected via a skybridge to Terminal B. You'll find a quiet, bright seating area along the skybridge but more comfortable seats in the lobby of the hotel.

Once you're in the hotel lobby, you might inquire about spending the day here. Offered from 6 AM to 6 PM, the day rate includes access to the hotel's health club and pool facilities (215-492-9000).

PHL has no hair salon on-site, but a massage kiosk (The Healing Touch) is located at the entrance to Terminal D.

Feeling sick? Mercy Careport (Fitzgerald Mercy Hospital) in the corridor of Concourse A has a doctor or paramedic on duty Monday–Friday, 8 AM–10 PM, and weekends, 9 AM–9 PM. If you need a flu shot or a last-minute travel immunization, you can also call ahead for an appointment (215-492-2196).

Need a smoke to relax? Smoking is allowed in the Jet Rock Café in Concourse B, the Aviators restaurant in Concourse C, and in the International Bar in Terminal D.

Take Care of Business

- Phones with data ports are located across from Gate A3, between Gates B3 and B5, across from Gate C16, at Gate D1, and between Gates E3 and E5.

A business center, which offers fully equipped mini-offices rented by the minute, is located in the link between Terminals A and B. You can also make copies, send faxes, and purchase office supplies at Staples (Terminal B, right after the security checkpoint) or over at the business center in the Philadelphia Airport Marriott, accessible from the airport via a skybridge near Terminal B. In addition to faxing and copying services, the Marriott's business center offers desktop printing, shipping services, Internet access, and computer workstation rentals (215-492-9000). You'll also find an Internet kiosk in the upper level of the hotel lobby.

Self-service postal centers are located in both Terminals A and C. You'll find FedEx drop boxes in Terminals A, C, and E, as well as a UPS drop box in Terminal C.

Explore the Airport

►Shop

In the Philadelphia Marketplace, located in the connecting corridor between Terminals B and C, you'll find a wide variety of familiar shops, including the Gap/Gap Kids, Wilsons Leather, Jockey International, the Discovery Channel Store, Brookstone, Godiva Chocolatier, Barbara's Booksellers, and a PGA Tour Shop. More out-of-the-ordinary shops include the Philadelphia Museums Store and Pennsylvania Market, which offers Philadelphia-area souvenirs such as miniature Liberty Bells and biographies of Ben Franklin. More tempting souvenirs can be found at Caviar Assouline, which carries caviar, chocolate, mustards, olive oil, and other gourmet gifts, while original and antique jewelry is featured at Fire & Ice.

If you know you'll have a layover and want to plan your shopping spree ahead of time, check out the Philadelphia Marketplace Web site: www.philamarketplace.com

No need to limit your shopping to the Marketplace—kiosks scattered throughout the airport offer everything from sports paraphernalia to watches, pens, and kids' clothing.

►Sightsee

PHL has an extensive art program with both permanent works and a changing exhibition program featuring everything from fine arts and photography to ceramics, whimsical sculpture, and items on loan from the Franklin Mint and area museums. For a map of the exhibit spaces and a listing of current shows, pick up an "Art and Exhibitions" brochure from one of the information kiosks located in each terminal.

The skybridge out to Concourse A offers both comfortable seating areas and nice views of airport activities. You'll also get a nice panoramic view from the rotunda at the end of Concourse A. Other good spots for keeping an eye on your airplane are over in Terminals D and E.

► Play Around

Very young kids will enjoy the kids' play area (the Please Touch Aviation Station) located in Terminal E, adjacent to Gate 4. Kids of all ages might enjoy an art treasure hunt: stop by an information booth and ask for a brochure containing a map and a listing of current exhibits in PHL's art and exhibitions program, then see how many art and history exhibits you can find. PHL's Web site also lists the current exhibitions, so your family might plan the treasure hunt ahead of time.

Go into Town

You'll find a ground transportation coordinator in each baggage claim area who can help you determine your best route out of the airport.

A cab ride to downtown Philadelphia will take from 15 to 30 minutes and cost a $20 flat fee. You can also take a shuttle van, or hop on the high-speed SEPTA R1 train, which stops at all five airport terminals every half hour from 6 AM to 12 midnight. The trip to downtown takes about 25 minutes and costs $5. For additional information, call the Ground Transportation Hotline: 215-937-6958.

Other Information

You can call ahead to get a variety of airport information at 800-PHL-GATE (800-745-4283). Live video of the PHL airfield is also available from the airport's Web site, where a camera scans aircraft and vehicle movement at the airport.

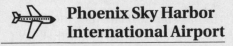

Phoenix Sky Harbor International Airport

Phoenix, Arizona
Airport Code: PHX
Web Address: http://www.phxskyharbor.com

Phoenix Sky Harbor International Airport (PHX) has had its share of quirky brushes with celebrity. The first passenger jet to land at Sky Harbor was a Boeing 707 diverted by bad weather from Los Angeles. That was back in 1959 and Marilyn Monroe was one of the passengers. John Irving set the climactic scene of his 1990 bestseller, *A Prayer for Owen Meany,* in Phoenix Sky Harbor. And PHX's newest terminal, Terminal 4, is named after a famous US senator and failed presidential candidate, Barry M. Goldwater. Celebrity or not, you should easily be able to find your way around.

Get Oriented

- Luggage carts rent for $2.
- Lockers are located behind security in each terminal.

Sky Harbor's three terminal buildings—2, 3, and 4 (there is no Terminal 1)—are served by a free on-site shuttle bus system scheduled to run every 7 minutes. Each terminal has a very different feel and you may find yourself feeling a bit like Goldilocks: Terminal 2 is a bit small, Terminal 4 is too big, but the midsize Terminal 3, with its shops and service-filled central court area, is just right.

To get your bearings, stop by an information booth (they're in each terminal) and pick up a foldout airport pocket guide. You'll find that Alaska, Sun Air, United, Trans World Airlines, Air Canada, and US Airways operate out of the smaller Terminal 2; Northwest, Delta, American, American Trans Air, and Frontier are over in Terminal 3; and the sprawling Terminal 4 serves America West (for which PHX is a major hub), Southwest, Continental, and several other airlines.

Even with the shuttle bus, it can be a 10- to 15-minute journey between terminals, and in Terminal 4 alone it can take more than 10 minutes to get from the end of one concourse to another. So if you have a long layover here, consider checking your luggage or stowing your gear in a locker.

Take Care of Yourself

►Eat

A nice selection of eateries, including Oaxaca, the Paradise Café & Bakery, Juice Works, and several fast-food staples, are located where the concourses intersect in Terminal 4. Good bets out in the Terminal 4 concourses include the Great Steak & Potato Company in Concourse A and the Oasis Deli or the Phoenix Roadhouse in Concourse B. Venues along America West's new concourse (Gates A17–A30) include the Blue Burrito Grille, California Pizza Kitchen, and a José Cuervo Tequilería.

No need to make your way over to Terminal 4, though, if you're already in Terminals 2 or 3. Terminal 2 sports Lefty's South Rim Bar & Grill and the center court in Terminal 3 offers Johnny Rockets (burgers, shakes, and fries), the Oasis Deli, and several other snack spots.

Best Healthful Nosh

Juices and fruit smoothies from Frozen Fusion (Terminal 2) or from Juice Works (Terminal 4, center and most concourses); also healthy deli sandwiches and salads from the Oasis Deli in the Terminal 3 food court.

Best Sinful Snack

Malts and shakes from Johnny Rockets in the Terminal 3 food court.

►Relax and Refresh

A great spot to sit and people-watch is the upper-level concourse "crossroads" and food court seating in Terminal 4. The center courts in Terminal 2 and 3 are smaller but also offer comfortable seating.

If you need to get out of the hustle and bustle, grab a seat by the mural in the west end of the Terminal 4 lower level, or in the center court area of Terminals 2 or 3. For a truly quiet spot head for the interfaith chapel in Terminal 4, just east of the food court area. There's also a lovely covered garden area with benches and a bubbling fountain located outside the "Operations Center" on the walkway between Terminals 2 and 3. There are no on-site health clubs, and the airport's one barbershop (located in the Terminal 2 concourse) doesn't seem to be keeping regular hours. But plenty of nearby hotels offer day rates that include use of their pools, hot tubs, and exercise facilities. Use the courtesy phones in the baggage claim area of any terminal to call nearby hotels to check rates.

PHX is a nonsmoking facility, but bars in each terminal have smoking sections. Otherwise, light up outside.

Take Care of Business

The information booths in each terminal sell stamps, make copies, and send faxes. If your business needs are more complicated, head for the business center, where fully equipped mini-offices rent by the minute. There's one branch in Terminal 2 at Gate 4, another in Terminal 3, next to Starbucks, and yet a third planned for Terminal 4.

Automated teller machines are located in each terminal, and there's a full-service bank in Terminal 4.

Explore the Airport

► Shop

The center areas of both Terminals 3 and 4 sport a nice variety of shops offering gift items with a Southwest theme. Highlights in Terminal 3 include Not Just Chilis, with a wide variety of chili food items, cookbooks, and other gift items; Curious Creatures, which offers CDs, stuffed animals, and other fun stuff; and the wonderful jewelry featured in Earth Spirits. In Terminal 4, you may be drawn to Naturally Arizona, Pueblo Spirit, and all the shops offering ceramics, jewelry, cactus-emblazoned sportswear, and other Southwest gifts. Wild Wild Best has outlets on both Concourse A and B and their prices are a tad more reasonable.

►Sightsee

Work from Sky Harbor's permanent art collection is scattered throughout the airport. Galleries and display cases in each terminal also feature changing exhibits that showcase Arizona's artistic and cultural heritage.

Highlights include Paul Coze's 16-by-75-foot historical mural, "The Phoenix," in the lobby of Terminal 2, and the Navajo rugs and the "Bizarre and Beautiful" bugs exhibit in Terminal 3. On the upper level of Terminal 4 look for Robert T. McCall's stained-glass window at the chapel entrance and the changing exhibit gallery just across the hall. Level 2 features Mark Klett's black-and-white photographs of cacti, large ceramic sculptures, and several murals.

For good views of airfield activities, the folks at the information booths always suggest the upper levels of the parking garage in Terminals 3 and 4. Otherwise, grab a spot by a window and see what flies by.

►Play Around

Kids and their families will enjoy the "Arizona Bizarre and Beautiful" bug exhibit in the Terminal 3 center court area (on the wall just past the business center), where the specimens include butterflies, a giant water bug, and other out-of-the-ordinary insects. In Terminal 4 kids might also enjoy riding the moving walkways or visiting the toy store (Awesome Atoms) in Concourse A. Or how about a "treasure hunt" to find all the artwork in each terminal?

Go into Town

A taxi ride to downtown Phoenix should take about 10 minutes and cost less than $10. Shared shuttle vans make the trip for about $7 per person. If you're up for taking public transit, the Phoenix Transit Bus Red Line and bus #13 serve the airport. For route, fare, and schedule information call 602-253-5000 or ask for a copy of the "Bus Book" at the information desk in any terminal.

Other Information

If you need information about the airport before you arrive, call 602-273-8863.

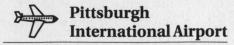 **Pittsburgh International Airport**

Pittsburgh, Pennsylvania
Airport Code: PIT
Web Address: http://www.pitairport.com

When the Greater Pittsburgh International Airport (PIT) first opened in 1952, the seven-story granite-and-glass terminal was ridiculed by critics as the "Taj Mahal" and applauded by others as a "bold step into the World of Tomorrow." Back then, the terminal had an observation deck, a movie theater, a nightclub, and an amusement arcade. But it had only 10 gates, and by 1986 PIT could no longer serve the needs of this northeast hub. Pittsburgh-trained architect Tasso Katselas was hired to design a huge new facility, which opened in 1992.

Get Oriented

- Baggage carts can be rented at various spots in the Landside Building for $1.50. You'll receive a $.25 refund for returning a cart to the rack.
- Lockers are located in each concourse, all postsecurity.

Today, the award-winning Pittsburgh International Airport is easy to navigate: there are two main buildings, "Landside" (ticketing and security) and "Airside" (where the planes are). The two buildings are linked by an efficient people-mover subway system that zips back and forth in about 70 seconds.

The Airside Building is basically a large atrium (the "Center Core") with four concourses laid out in a giant X. Concourses A and B are used by US Airways, which uses Pittsburgh as its major hub airport. Concourse C serves Air Canada, British Airways, TWA, and United; American, Continental, Delta, and Northwest Airlines use Concourse D. Commuter flights on US Airways Express come and go from Concourse E, in the Landside Terminal.

Toting luggage? Once you board the people mover, it will take you just over a minute to get from the Landside Building to the Airside Building. And once you're in the Center Core, it should take no longer than 2 or 3 minutes to make it down any one concourse, especially if you hop on one of the moving walkways.

Take Care of Yourself

►Eat

Pittsburgh International Airport has more than 40 restaurants and eateries, where prices are kept reasonable by the airport's strictly enforced rule that prices must be the same as those charged off-site. Highlights include O'Brien's Grille & Pub (Center Core) for Irish specialties, Irish beers, Irish whiskies, & Pittsburgh-style pierogies; Hotlicks Bar & Grill (Gates A18 and B41) for barbecue; Fat Tuesday (Gate B35) for New Orleans–style po'boys; and Au Bon Pain (Center Core and at the Landside Terminal security checkpoint) for fresh salads, sandwiches, and baked goods. Taste of the Tropics (across from Arby's in the Center Core) offers Jamaican-style turnovers, curry chicken, jerk chicken and pork, and healthy fruit smoothies.

Elsewhere, you'll find salads, wraps, and smoothies in Concourse A (Gate 14) at Treat Street; decadent desserts at T.G.I. Friday's (Center Core and Gates A6 and D78); and pizza at Village Pizza (Gate A14), Sbarro (Center Core and Gate B37), and Alberto's Pub & Pizza (Gate A10).

Best Healthful Nosh

Salads and smoothies from Treat Street (Concourse A, Gate 14) or fruit shakes from Taste of the Tropics in the Center Core. Café Classico offers healthy salads, spinach pesto pasta, southwestern lentils and rice, and other healthy meals at Gate B32.

Best Sinful Snack

Chocolate, by the piece or the pound, from Godiva Chocolatier in the Center Core (ask for a sample) or decadent desserts ("Pie-In-The-Sky" or "Oreo Madness") from T.G.I. Friday's in the Center Core and at Gates A6 and D78.

►**Relax and Refresh**

PIT is big and busy, but there are plenty of places to get out of traffic and refresh. In the Landside Building, there's a bank of comfortable seats tucked behind the flight schedule screens, overlooking the security checkpoint and the *Miss Pittsburgh* airplane. In the Airside Building, head to the mezzanine level where you'll find a chapel, a meditation room, and a good number of comfortable out-of-the-way chairs just outside the US Airways club.

If you're up for a massage, visit the folks at Touch & Go in Concourse C (Gate 54) for a bit of work on your hands, feet, neck, or shoulders.

If smoking relaxes you, you'll either have to go outside or patronize one of the bars (Hotlicks, Fat Tuesday, and others) with a smoking section.

If you'd like to work out, shower, or even take a sauna on your layover, you're in luck: PIT has the country's first in-airport health club, Airport Fitness, located on the lower level of the Airside Building, just below the Center Core. For just about $10 a visit, you'll have access to strength machines, aerobic machines, showers, and a sauna. If you're a frequent PIT visitor, workouts get cheaper with a 10-visit punchcard. And if you forget your workout gear, don't fret: the shop rents workout clothes and will even give you workout tips. Hours: daily, 6 AM–10 PM; 412-472-5231.

The brand-new Hyatt Hotel (724-899-1234) located adjacent to the Landside Building, and other nearby hotels, such as the Pittsburgh Airport Marriott (412-788-8800) and the Embassy Suites Hotel (412-269-9070), all offer day rates that include access to the hotels' pools and exercise facilities.

Take Care of Business

• Passenger Service Centers and phone banks located throughout the airport have phones with data ports and convenient shelves to hold papers or laptops.

PIT is the US Airways main hub airport, and their large clubroom on the mezzanine level of the Center Core is the place to get business done—if you're a member. Most everyone else will have to try to match up their needs at a variety of locations throughout the airport:

Travelex (Mutual of Omaha) has two business centers, equipped with telephones, fax machines, copiers, and currency exchange facilities. Their Landside Terminal center also offers a telephone-conferencing suite where you can plug in your laptop. A smaller, limited-service branch is located in the Airside Terminal, near international arrivals (412-472-5151).

Passenger Service Centers located throughout the airport are predominantly filled with telephones, but most have ATM machines and a few have FedEx drop boxes.

National City Bank has a branch at the security checkpoint in the Landside Building, and PNC Bank has a branch in the Airside Center Core. In a pinch they can help you out with copies.

Explore the Airport

► Shop

If you enjoy the convenience of getting some shopping done on airport layovers, thank the folks at Pittsburgh International Airport. This is the airport that introduced the airport mall concept and one of the first places to guarantee that prices cannot be higher than those outside the airport. To sweeten the pot, remember that there's no sales tax on clothing in Pennsylvania and that many stores here offer free shipping, which means you won't pay sales tax on your purchases *and* you won't have to tote yet another bag onto the plane.

So what's to buy? Lots! There are 62 shops here, each conveniently listed in the Airmall guide you can pick up at any information booth. Most shops are clustered in the Airside Center Core, but a few gems are in concourses. Head to Dogs and Cats at Gate A3 for animal-inspired treats for you and your pet or to Audrey's Attic (Gate A1) for collectible dolls, toys, and stuffed animals. Signatures, at Gate B28, has a large greeting-card selection, and

Candy Express (Gates A7 and B40) offers sweets and candy-filled gifts.

Highlights in the Center Core include Ty-riffic (a giant Beanie Baby store), Brookstone, the Discovery Channel Store, Perfumania, Electronics Boutique, the Body Shop, and Godiva Chocolatier. Other national retailers represented here include Victoria's Secret, the Gap, GNC, Nine West, Samsonite, Bon Voyage, London Fog, Wilsons Leather, and Clinique, which offers free makeup consultations. There's also a PGA Tour Shop, a Timberland shop, Waterstone's Booksellers, and Legends of the Game, which has autographed baseballs, photos, jerseys, and other collectible sports items on display—and for sale. For a complete store listing, check the Airmall Web site (www.airmall.com) before you fly.

► **Sightsee**

The main art attraction here is the huge Alexander Calder mobile that spins gently in the atrium of the Center Core. While it's delightful to look at, viewers may also be interested to learn that each "leaf" represents a piece of Pittsburgh history. According to a flyer distributed at the information booths the four large leaves represent Pittsburgh's four major steel companies (US Steel, Bethlehem Steel, Jones & Laughlin Steel, and Allegheny Ludlum Steel); the set of three large leaves represents Pittsburgh's three rivers (the Allegheny, the Monongahela, and the Ohio); the large lower leaves represent the Gateway Center and the Golden Triangle; and the smaller, lower leaves represent the first three Gateway Buildings.

Miss Pittsburgh, a restored vintage mail plane, hangs over the entrance to the security checkpoint in the Landside Building. On April 21, 1927, this Waco 9 airplane carried Pittsburgh's first commercial airmail to Cleveland under the Air Mail Act of 1925.

Pittsburgh is home to public television's Fred Rogers and his Neighborhood of Make-Believe. An exhibit about the television show featuring some of the more recognizable props is located just outside the Kidsport play area, at the top of Concourse C. (See "Play Around.")

You can get nice views of airfield activities from the seating area in the main food court in the Center Core, from T.G.I. Friday's, and from most gate areas. There's also a lovely fountain area just across from the main ticket lobby in the Landside Building.

► **Play Around**

- Ask nicely, and the folks at the information booths (412-474-5525) located in the Landside ticket lobby and in the Airside Center Core will give your kids a coloring book with an airport theme.

Young kids will enjoy the Kidsport play area, located at the beginning of Concourse C. This large play area has tiers of seating, padded floors, miniature airplanes, and pint-size ticket counters. There's even a map of the United States woven into the carpet so kids can get an idea of just where it is they're off to. Family-oriented cultural institutions, such as the Pittsburgh Children's Museum and the Carnegie Science Center, keep a display case filled with intriguing exhibits, and Pittsburgh-centric videos run pretty much continuously on an overhead monitor.

The Kidsport area also has a baby-changing station and restrooms with both child-size and adult-size toilets and sinks.

Just outside the Kidsport play area is a mini-museum honoring Fred Rogers, who taped his *Mister Rogers' Neighborhood* program at Pittsburgh's public television station, WQED. Scripts, sneakers, puppets, and one of Rogers' trademark sweaters are included in the exhibit.

Older kids (and adults) might enjoy PocketChange Amusements, at Gate A5, which has video games, pinball machines, and other games. Smaller game corners are located at Gates A15 and B33 and elsewhere in the airport.

Go into Town

A taxi ride to downtown Pittsburgh will take between 30 and 45 minutes and run between $25 and $30. Shuttle vans make the trip downtown for $11 each way. You can also take public transportation: the 28X Airport Flyer runs downtown on a 16-mile express route every 30 minutes. Fare: $1.95.

Other Information

To get more information about the airport before you arrive, call 412-472-3525.

Portland International Airport

Portland, Oregon
Airport Code: PDX
Web Address: http://www.portlandairportpdx.com

On April 1, 1936, city officials bundled up in a freak spring snowstorm for the groundbreaking of what was then called Portland-Columbia Airport. In 1948 the airport had to close down for three months because of catastrophic flooding in nearby Vanport, Oregon. For a few years during the 1990s, locals thought renovation disruptions would never end. But when construction on everything from concourses, parking structures, and a light-rail connection to downtown draws to a close, sometime in 2001, Portland International Airport (PDX) should easily regain its reputation as an easy-to-maneuver facility with great shopping and good food.

Get Oriented

- Luggage carts rent for $2.
- Lockers are located in the baggage claim area and in the concourses, past security.

The PDX terminal is shaped like an H with a ticket lobby and baggage claim level between the concourses. If you need help finding your way, look for one of the enthusiastic clipboard-equipped Volunteer Information Persons, or VIPs, stationed throughout the terminal wearing shirts with an "Ask Me" logo.

Take Care of Yourself

►Eat

For nourishment, head for the lovely food court in the Oregon Market at the center of the terminal. You'll find a variety of restaurants serving everything from hamburgers, bagels, and sandwiches to Mandarin Chinese food (Panda Express), burritos (Macheezmo Mouse), and 30 beers on tap (Red's Pizza & Brewpub).

Coffee stands and food concessions are sprinkled throughout the airport, but for a sit-down meal (and a good view of runway action) head for the Red Lion Restaurant in the main terminal, where you'll find seafood and other Pacific Northwest specialties.

Best Healthful Nosh

Healthy Mexican food from Macheezmo Mouse in the main terminal.

Best Sinful Snack

Chocolate-filled croissants and cookies from Marsee Baking in the Oregon Market food court.

►Relax and Refresh

If you enjoy people watching, grab a seat in the Oregon Market or the food court. For a quick nap or some quiet time, sit back in one of the comfortable chairs in the North Lobby. There's also a quiet room off the women's bathroom at the end of the main terminal, just before the entrance to Concourse C.

If you need to freshen up, there's a hair salon (PDX Hairlines) in the North Service Center that also offers chair massages. If you have a longer layover or delay, several nearby hotels offer day rates, including the Sheraton Portland Airport Hotel (503-281-2500) and Embassy Suites (503-460-3000).

You can also relax with a movie—PDX was one of the first airports to offer DVD movie rentals from InMotion Pictures. Watch a movie while you wait for your flight or, if you're heading for one of the increasing number of airports with an InMotion Pictures outlet, take the DVD player along and turn it in at the other end.

Take Care of Business

A business center, which rents mini-offices by the minute, is located at the end of Concourse C. The PDX Conference Center, near the clock tower in the Oregon Market, offers meeting rooms and business services ranging from copying and faxing to work-station rentals and secretarial services (503-460-4050). You can also mail packages, make copies, plug in your computer, or do similar self-service business at the Concourse D Service Center near Gate 7.

Explore the Airport

►Shop

There are three good reasons to shop at PDX: Oregon has no sales tax; many shops offer wonderful made-in-Oregon goods; and "street pricing" is enforced, which means prices are the same here as downtown. For some, the recent lifting of the 20-year ban on chewing-gum sales at the airport adds even a fourth reason to shop here with abandon.

Bundled together in the main terminal, the shops in the Oregon Market are laid out along a corridor designed to look like a downtown street, complete with a clock tower in the center. There's a Nike sporting goods store—Portland is home to the shoe giant's corporate headquarters; an Oregon Pendleton Shop featuring that company's famous clothing and blankets; and the Real Mother Goose, Norm Thompson, and Made in Oregon, which all carry handmade crafts and locally made—or caught—products. Portland's famous Powell's Books is here, too, with new and used books and a section devoted to items for young travel-ers. Long-banned gum—along with gifts, food, and travel items—is now sold at Travel Mart. Bow Wow Meow offers pres-ents for that special pet you left behind.

►Sightsee

Near the Concourse D international gates, across from the duty-free shop, you'll find "Provincial Narrative," a 26-foot-long, four-panel oil painting on wood described by the artist, Jack Port-land, as "an abstract narrative depicting the lushness and com-plexity of the Pacific Northwest." In the Oregon Market, above the

Coffee People stand, look for PDX's first piece of art, a 1960s-vintage abstract work by Louis Bunce.

On a clear day, head to the top floor of the parking garage for views of Mount Hood to the east, Mount Saint Helens to the north, and downtown Portland to the south. Good viewing spots inside the terminal include the window seats at the Red Lion Restaurant, and the North Lobby between Concourses D and E.

►Play Around

The Kids' Flight Deck, just before the gates for Concourses D and E, features a scale-model aircraft fuselage and a control tower where kids can listen to aircraft-to-tower communications and weather reports. A second play area is due to open in the South Lobby.

Go into Town

Cabs will get you to downtown Portland in 20–25 minutes for an average fare of $22–$28. The bus (Tri-Met's #12) costs $1.15 and makes the downtown run in about an hour. The Grayline Express bus makes the trip downtown in 20–45 minutes and costs $15. In the fall of 2001, however, the airport link of Portland's light-rail service (MAX) is scheduled to be completed and then the trip downtown should take no longer than 15 minutes.

Other Information

To get information about Portland International Airport before you arrive, call 877-739-4636.

Raleigh-Durham International Airport

Raleigh-Durham, North Carolina (Wake County, NC)
Airport Code: RDU
Web Address: http://www.rdu.com

When it first opened to commercial traffic in May 1943, the passenger terminal at Raleigh-Durham International Airport (RDU) was constructed with materials from four army barracks left over from the airport's days as a World War II US Army air-training facility. Today, RDU has two (somewhat) more modern terminals and plenty of plans for expansion.

Get Oriented

- Luggage carts rent for $1.50. You'll receive a $.25 refund when you return a cart to the rack.
- Lockers are located on the concourses, postsecurity at Gates C15 and A24.

RDU has two terminals: A and C. There used to be a Terminal B, but that facility was renovated and attached to Terminal A. Sneaky, eh? This new area is now referred to as the Terminal A extension.

Terminal A serves Air Canada, AirTran, Continental, Continental Express, Delta, Northwest, Southwest, TWA, United, and US Airways. Terminal C serves American, American Eagle, Midway, and Midwest Express.

It's a quarter-mile and good 10-minute walk between Terminals A and C, so if you have luggage it's best to hop on the inter-terminal shuttle bus, which stops out in front of each terminal. Terminal C is fairly compact, but treks to some parts of Terminal A can get long, especially if you're headed for the Terminal A extension (Gates 25–28) which serves Continental and Southwest.

Take Care of Yourself

► **Eat**

New food concessions will be opening at RDU during the summer and fall of 2001. In Terminal A you can look forward to finding Gelato Amare at Gate 10, Rapidos (wraps) at Gate 16 (along with Godfather's Pizza and Popeyes Chicken & Biscuits), and for sit-down meals, Greenleaf's Grill at Gate 24. Over in Terminal C look for Rapidos at Gate 6, the Triangle Cyber-Café at Gate 13, Gelato Amare at Gate 17, a deli (Jersey Mike's) at Gate 19, and the Pinehurst Microbrewery at Gate 20.

Best Healthful Nosh

Wraps from Rapidos at Gates A16 and C6.

Best Sinful Snack

Ice cream from Gelato Amare at Gates A10 and C17.

► **Relax and Refresh**

Currently, there are no hair salons or massage bars at RDU, but you might find a quiet spot to get out of the hustle and bustle in Terminal C down by the less-used Gates 20–25, or in the Terminal A extension (Gates 25–28). In off-peak hours, grab a chair in the seating area near the information desk in the baggage claim area. Last time through I spied a half-dozen folks happily napping there at 6 o'clock one weekday evening.

If you need a shower, a swim, or a few hours' nap, several close-by hotels with pools and fitness clubs offer day rates. The Hilton Garden Inn, for example, is just 1 mile from the airport and features a business center, a fitness center, and an indoor pool (919-840-8088). For information about other hotels, check the hotel information board in the baggage claim area of either terminal.

Smokers will be happy to know that special smoke-filtration systems have been installed in restaurant/lounge areas in each terminal. In Terminal A, you can light up at the Carolina Varsity Bar by Gate 17. In Terminal C puff away at Carolina Corks & Kegs at Gate 9 or at the Pinehurst Brewery by Gate 20.

Take Care of Business

- Phones with data connections are located in Terminal A at Gates 14 and 22 and in Terminal C at Gates 7, 13, and 18.

A business center, which rents mini-offices by the minute, has a branch in Terminal A by Gate 24. You'll also find a Travelex/Mutual of Omaha currency booth as well as self-service fax and photocopy machines on the baggage claim level of Terminal A, in Terminal C just before the security checkpoint, and by Gate C16.

Explore the Airport

► Shop

During the summer and fall of 2001, retail outlets at RDU will be moving, changing, and expanding. Here's what's in store:

You'll find the Book Cellar, one of the few used-book stores located at an airport, in Terminal A at Gate 15 and in Terminal C at Gate 10. This shop is so dedicated to your reading pleasure that they offer an after-hours "honor system" section so there's no excuse to board a plane empty-handed. If you need a new book, W.H. Smith bookstores are located in Terminal A at Gate 17 and in Terminal C by the security checkpoint.

Shoppers can load up on all sorts of North Carolina products at A Southern Season in Terminal A at Gate 22 and in Terminal C at Gate 14. Sports fans will want to visit the PGA Tour store in Terminal C at Gate 17 and the Atlantic Coast Conference stores located in Terminal A at Gate 14 and Terminal C at Gate 17. Terminal A has a Brooks Brothers store at Gate 17 as well.

► Sightsee

Airport officials are working on an official art program, but in the meantime you can review "Aviation Art" by area elementary school students in the corridor leading to the Terminal A extension (Gates 25–28). I especially enjoyed the crayon masterpiece that declared "Flying Is Fun Because Looking Down Is Cool!!!!"

You can get a nice view of the airfield from the upper level of Terminal A on the way to the extension, Gates 25–28.

If it's a nice day and you've got an hour or so between flights, head over to the Observation Park, located about a half mile from the terminals, across from the air traffic control tower. This is a parklike area with a playground, picnic tables, and a speaker plugged into the air traffic control radio channel. To get there, take the #2 Park and Ride shuttle bus and ask the driver to point out the park.

►Play Around

RDU has a Playport activity center located across from Gate 12 in Terminal A that features a small airplane, an air traffic control tower, a baggage belt, and a mural.

If you've got extra change, take the kids over to the "stretch-a-penny" machine at Gate 13 in Terminal C. Invest two quarters and a shiny penny and you'll go home with a flat penny that says "North Carolina—First in Flight."

Go into Town

It costs about $22 and takes between 20 and 30 minutes for the 14-mile cab ride to either downtown Raleigh or downtown Durham. A shuttle ride (R & G Shuttle, 800-840-2RDU, or 800-840-2738) will cost about $18, but the bus (Triangle Transit Authority, or TTA) will cost just $1.50. To check the schedule, call 919-549-9999.

Other Information

If you need additional information before you arrive, call the RDU information desk at 919-840-2123 from 7 AM to 11 PM daily.

Reno-Tahoe International Airport

Reno, Nevada
Airport Code: RNO
Web Address: http://www.renoairport.com
or http://www.reno-tahoeairport.com

In 1927, when Charles Lindbergh stopped at Reno's Blanchfield Airport he proclaimed that the airfield the local folks were so very proud of simply "would never do" once larger, commercial airplanes filled the skies. Taking Lindbergh's pronouncement to heart, city officials quickly established the much larger Hubbard Field, now Reno-Tahoe International Airport (RNO), and turned the old airport site into a golf course.

Get Oriented

- Luggage Carts rent for $2. The machines refund $.25 when a cart is returned to the rack.
- Lockers are located beyond the security checkpoints. Bags N Us, in baggage claim, also stores bags.

Reno International Airport has a main terminal and two concourses, north and south, and is easy to navigate. It will take you no more than 3 minutes to walk from one end of the terminal to the other, *if* you don't stop to play the slot machines.

Most all the restaurants, shops, and service facilities are located on the lower level of the terminal, just around the corner from the baggage claim area. Southwest Airlines has the most flights through Reno, but the airport is also served by Alaska Airlines, United, America West, Delta, and others.

Take Care of Yourself

► Eat

On the lower level of the terminal there's one table-service restaurant (the City Grill) and a small food court offering the standard fare from TCBY, Burger King, Pizza Hut, and Taco Express. Out by the gates, you'll find coffee stands and snack shops.

Best Healthful Nosh

Veggie burgers or salads from City Grill, the only sit-down restaurant on the lower level of the terminal.

Best Sinful Snack

Chocolates, by the piece or the pound, from Ethel M. Chocolates, also on the lower level of the terminal.

► Relax and Refresh

If you enjoy gambling, you're in luck: Reno-Tahoe International Airport has 237 slot machines scattered throughout the terminal. If you'd rather avoid the clatter of coins and the bleating of bells, there's a bank of comfortable seats in the connecting corridor between the north and south concourses where you can get out of traffic, watch the activity on the airfield, or stretch out and catch a nap.

There is no massage bar or beauty salon on-site, but if you need to freshen up, the Airport Plaza Hotel, across the street from the parking garage, offers a day rate (775-348-6370). Or take the free shuttle to the Reno Hilton (just a mile away) and pay $16 to use the hotel's health club and pool for the day (775-789-2000). The Reno Hilton also has a bowling alley and a movie theater.

Smokers can light up inside one of the slot-machine-equipped special smoking rooms located in each concourse, or go outside in front of the terminal.

Take Care of Business

There is no business center here, but Bags N Us, in baggage claim, can make copies, send your FedEx package, or sell you lift tickets and flowers. Just a few phones in the baggage claim area have seats and a small work shelf.

Explore the Airport

►Shop

On the lower level of the terminal you'll find a PGA Tour Shop, Ethel M. Chocolates, a well-stocked kids' toy and clothing store (Baby Ballooners), and Great Outdoor Gifts, which sells T-shirts, sportswear, jewelry, candles, and other gift items. The newsstand/gift shop has books, souvenir bowling pins from Reno's National Bowling Stadium, and a wide variety of gambling-related items such as teapots in the shape of slot machines and chocolate gaming chips. Two shops on the concourse level, Tahoe Cigar Company and The Boutique, also feature a variety of gift items.

►Sightsee

Several vintage cars from Reno's National Automobile Museum (the Harrah Collection) are parked in the connecting corridor (airside) between the north and south concourses.

The hallway in the connecting corridor is also where you'll find the airport's small aviation museum. Look for the smart vintage uniforms, the heavy-duty airplane control panel, and photographs of Charles Lindbergh, Amelia Earhart, and the very first "Flying Nurses," whose job it was to take tickets, serve food, and generally "reassure" passengers. Museum notes highlight some intriguing "firsts": for example, in 1929 the University of Nevada football team became the first team to travel by air. An asterisked note reveals that the team lost to the University of Southern California, 66–0.

Joseph DeLappe's mosaic "Hello/Goodbye" features digitized images of the hands of more than 2,000 Reno residents and covers the wall of the parking structure opposite the terminal. Each image also contains a message written by the "hand owner" during their photography session.

The seating area in the connecting corridor between concourses is a good spot to catch views of the airfield activity. For a view of the mountains to the west and the rolling hills to the east, head for the top of the parking structure.

► Play Around

Young kids will have fun in the toy store on the lower level. Older kids might enjoy the vintage cars on the concourse level and the photos and artifacts in the small aviation museum in the connecting corridor between the two concourses. There are also arcades located at the ends of both concourses.

If your layover is 2 or 3 hours, take the kids over to the nearby Reno Hilton on the free shuttle, where there's a bowling alley and a movie theater.

Go into Town

If you're headed for one of the major downtown hotels, look for the free hotel shuttle area just outside baggage claim. Otherwise, a 15-minute cab ride to downtown Reno costs about $15 and a shared ride in an airport minibus is $2.60. The city bus (#13) makes the trip downtown for $1.25 and leaves from outside door B in the baggage claim area.

Other Information

The volunteers at the information booth (in the lower-level baggage claim area) are enthusiastic and knowledgeable. Feel free to call ahead with questions: 775-328-6870.

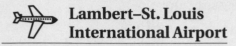 **Lambert–St. Louis International Airport**

St. Louis, Missouri
Airport Code: STL
Web Address: http://www.lambert-stlouis.com

Lambert–St. Louis International Airport (STL) is named in honor of Major Albert Bond Lambert, who took his first airplane ride with Orville Wright and was the first person in St. Louis to receive a private pilot's license. During the airport's early days, a young man named Charles Lindbergh could be found hanging around what was then known as Lambert–St. Louis Flying Field. Lindbergh served as a flight instructor and, in 1926, as the chief pilot of a St. Louis–Chicago airmail route. That job didn't last too long: on May 12, 1927, Lindbergh left St. Louis for New York to begin his historic nonstop solo flight to Paris, France.

Get Oriented

- Luggage carts rent for $1.50.
- Lockers are located in the concourses, postsecurity.

Lambert–St. Louis International Airport has two terminals, Main and East, and a total of five concourses. All A, B, C, and D gates are in the Main Terminal, while the E gates, serving mostly Southwest Airlines flights, are in the East Terminal, which is accessible from the Main Terminal via a shuttle bus or by a long trek through Concourse D.

TWA, which has its main hub here, uses most all the gates in Concourses B, C, and D; Southwest uses most E gates, and all the other airlines come and go from Concourse A. It should take you no longer than 5 minutes to get to the Main Terminal from the ends of the A, B, C, or D concourses, but a walk from Concourse E (even if you take the moving sidewalks) could take up to 15 minutes. If you're in a hurry or toting luggage, you might consider hopping on the free interterminal shuttle, which runs every 10 minutes.

Take Care of Yourself

►Eat

For St. Louis barbecue with a view, try the Rib Café in the soaring upper level of the Main Terminal. Other restaurants offering sit-down service include the Cheers Bar in Concourse D and Chili's Too in the East Terminal building. Along with the snack bars and fast-food outlets scattered throughout the airport, you'll find Juice Works, Fanny May Candies, and the 1904 World's Fair Ice Cream Parlor in the Main Terminal, and Burger King, Manchu Wok, and Gateway City Deli in Concourse D. Concourse A has a Pizza Hut; Concourse B sports the Trailhead Brewing Company; and Concourse C has a deli and the Sam Adams Brewhouse. Over in the East Terminal, snackers can choose from Burger King, California Pizza Kitchen, and the Great American Bagel.

Best Healthful Nosh

Juice Works (in the Main Terminal) offers smoothies, fruit juices, and healthy vegetable drinks.

Best Sinful Snack

Ice cream from the 1904 World's Fair Ice Cream Parlor located on the lower level of the Main Terminal.

►Relax and Refresh

You'll find a great spot to both relax and watch other travelers rush by in the seating area overlooking the security checkpoint for Concourses C, D, and E. Other out-of-the-way seating (depending on time of day) includes spots along Concourse D as you make your way to the East Terminal, the lower level of the Main Terminal by the airport director's office and the Freedom Shrine, and the outer ticket lobby of the East Terminal. For a truly quiet spot, head for the chapel located in the lower level of the Main Terminal by the baggage carousel near exit MT11. It's open 24 hours.

If you need to freshen up, you'll find the least-used bathrooms on the upper level of the Main Terminal, by the Metrolink station hallway. For more professional cleanup help, stop by First Flight Out, the hair salon in the connector between Concourses B and C, which also offers manicures, pedicures, and chair massages.

If smoking helps you relax, you'll find brightly lit smoking lounges scattered throughout the airport.

While there are no hotels right on airport property, there are many nearby. Several, including the St. Louis Airport Hilton and the St. Louis Airport Marriott, have day rates and courtesy shuttle buses.

Take Care of Business

- Telephones with data ports are clearly marked and scattered generously throughout the airport.

There's an Internet kiosk located by Gate D12 and a cashier's window in the Main Terminal, near the entrance to the A gates, that offers copy services. A post office is located in the lower level of the Main Terminal, near exit MT18, and there's a full-service bank in the Main Terminal on the lower level. Otherwise, this is another airport where an airline club membership would be useful.

Explore the Airport

►Shop

You'll find bookstores (Bookmark Books) in the lower level of the Main Terminal and in Concourses A, C, D, and E. Golfers will be delighted to learn that there are two PGA Tour Shops (one in each terminal), but note that only the one in the Main Terminal has facilities that allow you to practice your putting. Sports fans can pick up T-shirts, magnets, pins, and other souvenirs sporting the insignias of the St. Louis Cardinals, the Rams, and the St. Louis Blues in any of the Paradies News & Gift Shops throughout the airport. If it's sweets you're after, be sure to stop in the lower level of the Main Terminal, where you'll find a Fanny May Candies shop and the 1904 World's Fair Ice Cream Parlor.

►Sightsee

Spend a few hours in the lower level of the Main Terminal and you'll get a unique history lesson.

In the 1920s, Charles Lindbergh was a flight instructor at Lambert Field, and when a St. Louis–Chicago airmail route was inaugurated in 1926, Lindbergh became chief pilot. Just two years later, Lindbergh made his historic nonstop solo flight from New York to Paris in his monoplane, the *Spirit of St. Louis*. While the Smithsonian Institution now houses the legendary *Spirit of St. Louis*, STL is home to Lindbergh's personal airplane, a Ryan Monocoupe suspended from the ceiling in the Main Terminal just outside the security checkpoint for Concourses C, D, and E.

There are two extremely detailed and (don't tell the kids) educational murals located in the lower level of the Main Terminal by the baggage claim area called "Aviation—An American Triumph" and "Black Americans in Flight."

The seven-panel "Aviation—An American Triumph" was created by well-known St. Louis–based painter Siegfried Reinhard and includes images that range from the discovery of the jet stream to the launch of *Columbia*, the first space shuttle. Just around the corner from the general-aviation mural, you'll find a mural honoring African-American achievements in aviation from 1917 to the present. "Black Americans in Flight" is a large five-panel painting created by St. Louis artist Spencer Taylor featuring 75 portraits as well as 18 aircraft, 3 American bald eagles, 5 unit patches, and 1 spacecraft. Printed panels identify the dates, people, and milestones featured in each mural. If you want to remember what you've seen and learned, stop by the airport director's office (located in the lower level of the Main Terminal; Monday–Friday, 8:30 AM–5:00 PM) and ask for copies of the lovely booklets describing each mural. The volunteer-staffed information booths should have them as well.

If you have room for a bit more history, peruse the "Freedom Wall" outside the office of the airport director, near the entrance to Concourse A. The "shrine" features copies of a wide variety of important historical documents, including the Declaration of Independence and the Constitution of the United States.

There are plenty of spots throughout the airport where you can keep an eye on the airfield activities, but many folks favor the view from the Rib Café in the upper level of the Main Terminal.

► Play Around

There's a kids' play area in Concourse B and a game room with video machines in the connector between Concourses B and C in the Main Terminal.

Small kids can work off some energy riding the moving walkways through Concourse D or making the long trek on foot down the wide corridor. Older kids will definitely enjoy trying to identify the images featured in the historical murals in the lower-level baggage claim areas.

Go into Town

Well-organized information kiosks in the lower-level baggage claim areas of both the Main Terminal and the East Terminal detail your options for getting to town.

A cab ride downtown will cost about $27 and take anywhere from 20 to 30 minutes. Shuttle vans make the trip for a $10 fee. Far less expensive is the Metrolink light-rail service, which will take you from the airport to downtown for $3. If your layover is going to last a few hours, get the $4 Metrolink day pass and head downtown for some sightseeing. The Bi-State bus service also runs downtown from the airport, for a fare of $1.25.

Other Information

If you'd like more information about the airport before you arrive, call 314-426-8000.

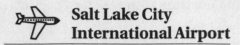

Salt Lake City International Airport

Salt Lake City, Utah
Airport Code: SLC
Web Address: http://www.ci.slc.ut.us/airport

In 1911, Basque Flats, a marshy pasture named for the local Spanish-French sheepherders, was put into service as Salt Lake City's first landing strip. Soon after, in 1920, world heavyweight boxing champion Jack Dempsey was on hand to help christen Salt Lake City's Woodward Field, in honor of local pilot John P. Woodward. By 1968 Salt Lake City Municipal Airport had become Salt Lake City International Airport (SLC), and today the facility serves more than 21 million passengers a year.

Get Oriented

- Luggage carts rent for $2. You'll get a $.25 refund when you return your cart to a stand.
- Lockers are located throughout the concourses, postsecurity. There are also ski lockers in both baggage claim areas.

Salt Lake City International Airport has a straightforward layout: there are two terminals and five concourses, A–E, with a new terminal to be completed sometime in 2003. It can take up to 15 minutes to walk from Concourse A to Concourse E, but you can shorten the trip by hopping on one of the moving walkways.

In Terminal 1, America West, American, Continental, Frontier, and Northwest use the gates in Concourse A, and Southwest, TWA, and United are clustered in Concourse B. In Terminal 2, you'll find Delta (their third-largest hub is here) dominating the gates in Concourses C and D (and a few in Concourse B), and short-haulers SkyWest and Delta Connection can be found in Concourse E.

To get your bearings, stop by the one of the airport information desks located in the Terminal 1 lobby before security or in Terminal 2 at the entrance of Concourse C and ask for a copy of the "Airport Guide."

Take Care of Yourself

► Eat

Table-service restaurants include the updated Terrace Restaurant & Lounge on the third level of Terminal 1, Dick Clark's American Bandstand Grill in the center area of Terminal 2, and the Squatters Brewpub at Concourse C. There's also a newly refurbished food court just before the Terminal 1 security checkpoint that features a branch of a local Italian deli called Granato's as well as a large Starbucks, TCBY, Pizza Hut, and Burger King.

Elsewhere in the airport you'll find Great American Bagel & Bakery and TCBY/Juice Works on Concourse B; Sbarro's near Concourse C; and, in Concourse D, California Pizza Kitchen and the Wasatch Brew Pub. Concourse E sports a kiosk filled with savory sandwiches, salads, and baked goods from Café de Normandie.

Best Healthful Nosh

Veggie wrap sandwich at the Terrace Restaurant in Terminal 1.

Best Sinful Snack

Ben & Jerry's ice cream, at the top of Concourse C, or pecan pralines from The Grove in Concourses B, C, and D.

► Relax and Refresh

If you're trying to get out of the hustle and bustle, head for the seating areas along the connecting corridor between Terminals 1 and 2. Several of the women's restrooms also have separate lounge areas with comfortable chairs.

If you need to freshen up, there's a barber/beauty shop on the second level of Terminal 2 in front of the security screening area. In addition to haircuts and trims, this shop offers manicures, pedicures, foot massages, reflexology, and mini-massages. Hours: 9 AM–6 PM, Monday–Saturday.

SLC has no on-site health club, but you can get a good workout walking the length of the terminals. For more serious exercise, pick up a courtesy phone in the baggage claim area and call the nearby Hilton Hotel. Their day rate includes access to a fitness club, pool, and hot tub.

If you need to smoke, you'll find glass-enclosed smoking rooms by Gates C8, D1, and D8, in the lower level of Concourse B, and in the lobby of Concourse E. The area at the top of the escalators in Terminal 1 is also a designated smoking area.

If you have a layover of 2 hours or more, stop by the Utah Information Center, located on the corridor connecting Concourses C and D in Terminal 2. The center is open 24 hours but staffed from 9 AM to 5 PM, Monday–Saturday. There's another information desk in the baggage claim area of Terminal 2. These folks can tell you about places to go if you have a long layover and want to leave the airport.

If you have at least 90 minutes between flights you can take a free tour of historic Temple Square, which includes the domed home of the Mormon Tabernacle Choir, the six-spired Salt Lake Temple, the Assembly Hall, and two exhibit-filled visitor centers. Tour vans leave the airport every half hour, from 9:30 AM to 7:30 PM from the bus plaza between Terminals 1 and 2. You must show your airline ticket (to prove you have at least a 90-minute layover) and store your baggage.

If temples aren't your bag, try golf: Wingpointe, an 18-hole golf course operated by the Salt Lake City Parks and Recreation Department, is located just south of the terminals. You can walk there, take a short cab ride, or ride (free) on the employee shuttle buses that stop in front of the terminals. Get off at stop "N." The clubhouse has a pro shop and a restaurant (801-575-2345). Wingpointe is open 10–11 months a year.

Take Care of Business

- Phones with data ports are located throughout the airport, near the concourses.

You'll find a business center, which rents mini-offices by the minute, in Terminal 2 between Concourses C and D. Full-service branches of the Zion First National Bank are located in the lobby of both terminals and are open 9 AM–4 PM, Monday–Thursday, and 9 AM–6 PM on Friday. The bank branch in Terminal 2 will also make copies and send faxes.

Explore the Airport

► Shop

West of Brooklyn, located in Terminal 1 just past the security checkpoint, carries children's clothing and toys, a wide variety of made-in-Utah crafts and artwork, western wear, and souvenirs relating to the 2002 Winter Olympics, which will be held in Salt Lake City. Another branch of West of Brooklyn is located just past the security checkpoint in Terminal 2.

An all-things-Olympics store filled with collectible pins, mascot-emblazoned T-shirts, and other souvenirs is located in Concourse D. More Olympics-related shops will appear as the big event gets closer. Full-fledged bookstores are located at the top of Concourse C and in the lower level of Concourse B. Each branch of News and Views also carries a selection of reading matter.

The environmentally friendly store Your Planet is located in the connecting corridor between Concourses C and D, and the connector levels of Terminals 1 and 2 feature kiosks offering everything from hand-dipped chocolates to jewelry, crafts, and gift items with a regional connection. Vistas, which has branches in Concourses B and D, is a western-themed gift shop carrying Native American jewelry, rugs, and pottery, lotions and soaps made from Montana beeswax, and a variety of other Americana-rich products.

Forget your skis? Don't fret: there are ski shops open November–April where you can rent or buy everything you need. The shops also have information about ski conditions and sell lift tickets. These shops are located just behind the baggage claim areas in both terminals.

►**Sightsee**

SLC has an extensive art collection with large murals, sculptures, photographs, stained glass, and other artwork displayed throughout the airport. You can get a brochure describing the collection at any information booth.

The photography collection, displayed along the moving walkways and in the corridors, surveys Utah's scenery in both black-and-white and color. The Utah landscape is also featured in the seven huge murals by Anton J. Rasmussen that are scattered throughout the airport. Look for "Delicate Arch" (Arches National Monument) at the top of the staircase in the east lobby of Terminal 1, "Bryce Canyon National Park" in the Terminal 1 ticket lobby, and "Lake Powell" in the Terminal 1 baggage claim area.

Elsewhere in the airport you'll find "Beyond the Clouds," an aluminum screen sculpture by Edie Roberson and Kazuo Matsubayashi, hanging over the escalators in Concourse E, and Dennis Smith's "Three Airships" suspended over the lobby of Terminal 2.

You can get a great view of the Wasatch Mountains from pretty much anywhere in the terminal, but especially in the connecting corridor between Concourses C and D and from the Terrace Restaurant in Terminal 1.

►**Play Around**

There's no official kid-oriented playspace at SLC, but kids will enjoy riding the moving walkways, looking at the photographs and artwork scattered throughout the airport, and inspecting the large world map imbedded in the center of the main lobby in Terminal 1.

There are infant-care rooms in both terminals and in Concourse E. In Terminal 1, the infant-care room is next to the restrooms just to the right of the security screening area. In Terminal 2, infant care can be found on the second level next to the restrooms to the left of the security screening area. In Concourse E, the infant-care room is next to the restrooms.

Go into Town

The airport is located 12 miles from downtown Salt Lake City. To survey your options for getting to town, stop by the Ground Transportation desk located at the far end of baggage claim in both terminals. Video monitors in each baggage claim area also display this information. To call ahead: 801-575-2477.

A taxi ride to downtown will run about $15 and take 20–25 minutes. A shared shuttle ride will cost just a bit less, about $14 each way. If you want to try public transit, pay the $1 fare and hop on the bus. The #50 (#150 at night) bus operated by UTA (Utah Transit Authority) makes the run downtown in about 30 minutes. You may want to check the schedule before you arrive (801-287-4636; www.utabus.com), because the UTA doesn't operate on most major holidays.

To get a cheap ride downtown, consider the free van service to historic Temple Square. (See "Relax and Refresh.") In order to get this free ride, however, you'll need to agree to take a guided tour of the temple.

Other Information

For more information about the airport before you arrive, call 801-575-2400.

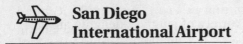 **San Diego International Airport**

San Diego, California
Airport Code: SAN
Web Address:
http://www.portofsandiego.org/sandiego_airport

In 1928, Lindbergh Field at San Diego International Airport (SAN) was named in honor of aviation legend Charles Lindbergh, who left San Diego on May 10, 1927, for the East Coast and his epic nonstop transatlantic flight just 10 days later. His plane, the *Spirit of St. Louis*, was built in San Diego by the Ryan Aircraft Company. In 1998 Lindbergh's grandson, Erik Lindbergh, was on hand to help celebrate the opening of the airport's new terminal.

Get Oriented

- Luggage carts can be rented for $1.50.
- There are no lockers.

The airport's addition, Terminal 2, serves American, America West, British Airways, Continental, Delta, Frontier, Northwest, Sun Country, and other airlines. The striking edifice features a slanted glass-and-concrete facade and stately steel overhangs, reminiscent of the flaps on an airplane. Inside, it's done up in a "sun, sand, and sea" color scheme, with natural colors mimicked in the concrete, stonework, and other building materials. Terminal 1 serves United, Southwest, US Airways, Trans World Airlines, Alaska Airlines, and AeroMexico. It's an easy 5-minute walk between terminals, but if you have baggage or small children in tow, opt for the free shuttle bus that stops at Terminals 1 and 2 and at the nearby Commuter Terminal. To get your bearings, visit one of the information booths (on the lower level of Terminal 1 or in the baggage area of Terminal 2) and request a map and an airport art brochure.

Take Care of Yourself

►Eat

Food courts offering a variety of culinary delights are scattered throughout both terminals. Highlights include the Karl Strauss Brewery Garden, Cramer's Bakery & Deli, California Pizza Kitchen, Naked Juice, La Salsa Mexican Grill, and Nathan's Hot Dogs, all in Terminal 2. Terminal 1 hosts Rubio's Baja Grill (famous for fish tacos), the Seaside Deli, Skyline Sweets, and Häagen-Dazs.

Best Healthful Nosh

Juices from Naked Juice in Terminal 2 or fish tacos from Rubio's Baja Grill in Terminal 1.

Best Sinful Snack

Sweets from Skyline Sweets in Terminal 1.

►Relax and Refresh

For a relatively quiet spot, try downstairs in Terminal 2 between the baggage claim area and the ticket counters. Also, if there isn't a flight scheduled to board at Gate 41 (at the end of the Terminal 2 concourse, by the Sports Bar), the seating area behind the bar is perfect for napping. For a bit of pampering, get a chair massage at Express Bodicare in Terminal 2 or rent a DVD player and movie at the InMotion Pictures outlet in Terminal 1. Travelers Aid volunteers often point stranded travelers to the great views and restaurants and the marina at Harbor Island, a 15-minute walk or a quick, free ride away on the Sheraton Hotel shuttle bus.

Smokers will have to go outside to light up, because San Diego International Airport is a nonsmoking facility.

Take Care of Business

- SAN has three Internet kiosks: in the east and west rotundas of Terminal 1 and in Terminal 2 at Gate 25.

Visit the Travelex America booth in Terminal 1 if you need to send a fax or make copies. It's located on the lower level, across from the United Air Lines ticket counter, and is open 6:00 AM–8:30 PM on weekdays and 7:00 AM–5:30 PM on Saturdays and Sundays.

Explore the Airport

►Shop

There's a nice Hallmark card shop and bookstore in Terminal 1, along with a branch of the San Diego Zoo store and several well-stocked newsstands and souvenir shops. Terminal 2 features Authors Bookstore, gift shops with beach clothing and souvenirs, and Express Bodicare, which offers lotions, body products, and chair massages.

►Sightsee

As part of the construction of Terminal 2, SAN purchased 14 pieces of art and scattered them throughout the terminal. Look for Joan Irving's "Wind Dance," made up of 52 etched and painted panels that span 520 feet of the building's glass face. Down in the baggage claim area, search for "At the Gate," by Gary Hughes. This whimsical sculpture of polyester resin and fiberglass features several bundled-up passengers waiting impatiently in line with their hands stuffed in their pockets and suitcases at their sides. At the entrance to each bathroom in Terminal 2 you'll find bright porcelain-and-glass-tile artwork, reminiscent of the designs you'd find on a beach towel. Each piece has a column of translucent glass squares filled with real beach sand and seashells. And on the way to the North Concourse rotunda (toward Gate 41), look for the sports trivia about legendary San Diego athletes on the advertisement placards, courtesy of the San Diego Hall of Champions Sports Museum.

You can see planes take off and land from the observation lounge in Terminal 2, across the corridor from the Marketplace Rotunda. The dome-shaped circle on the floor is titled "Cloud Experience," a work of art by Deanne Sabeck containing clouds that seem to mysteriously float through space.

▶ Play Around

Kids will enjoy "Cloud Experience" in the observation lounge. They might also enjoy climbing and sliding on the fountain at the far end of the North Concourse, near Gates 39–41.

Go into Town

The 10-minute taxi ride to downtown San Diego costs about $10. Less-expensive shared shuttle vans depart from the Transportation Plazas, across the skybridge from Terminals 1 and 2. The public transit system also operates a "flyer bus" (route 992) between the airport and downtown San Diego. The fare is $2 for the 15-minute ride.

Other Information

For more information about the airport and ground transportation, contact the information hotline at 619-231-2100.

 **San Francisco International Airport**

San Francisco, California
Airport Code: SFO
Web Address: http://www.flysfo.com

An ambitious and good-humored museum exhibition program has long made San Francisco International Airport (SFO) one of the most entertaining and enlightening airports in which to spend a layover. With the opening of a new amenity- and light-filled international terminal, complete with an aviation museum and a bevy of top-notch local eateries, the world's ninth-busiest airport is now practically a destination in its own right.

Get Oriented

SFO has four interconnected terminals—North, South, International, and Central (closed for renovation until 2003)—laid out in a circle around a two-level circular roadway system. Color-coded gate areas (A–F) run counterclockwise: in the South Terminal you'll find Air Canada, Alaska, America West, Continental, Hawaiian, Northwest, TWA, and US Airways at the B gates. Delta and Delta Connection operate from the C gates. In the North Terminal, American Airlines uses the E gates, while United/United Express/United Shuttle use most of the F gates. All international flights now come and go from gate areas A and G in the shiny new International Terminal.

It can take 15 minutes or more to trek from one end of the airport to the other. If you have the time and aren't toting heavy luggage, by all means walk. SFO's Airport Museum department keeps many of the corridors filled with cultural, educational, and just plain entertaining exhibits that you won't want to miss. If you're in a hurry, head outside the terminal and hop on an interterminal shuttle bus, which makes the trip around the airport loop in about 10 minutes.

To get your bearings, ask for a terminal map and a facilities guide at one of the information booths sprinkled throughout the airport.

Take Care of Yourself

►Eat

Sixteen much-needed new eateries, all branches of local favorites, are featured in SFO's new International Terminal, so head here first and choose carefully.

For "fine dining," consider Qi. Created by George Chen, the fellow responsible for some of the Bay Area's most popular hot spots, Qi offers Asian-influenced cuisine and a concierge to help make sure you don't bliss out and miss your flight. For sushi, udon, noodles, teriyaki, and other Japanese favorites, look for Ebisu, Osho, and Tomokazu. Chinese-food lovers can visit Fung Lum Express and Harbor Village Express, while folks seeking burgers can choose Lori's Diner or the Burger Joint, which offers hormone-free beef and free-range chicken.

There's more: Willow Street Café offers Italian fare, the Andale offers California cuisine with a Mexican influence, and a variety of delis, bistros, and cafés tempt you with soups, sandwiches, baked goods, and great coffee.

If you can't make it to the International Terminal, don't fret. There's plenty to choose from in the North and South Terminals.

In the South Terminal you'll find the North Beach Trattoria, the Bay View Restaurant and Bar, a diner-style restaurant called the Hangar, Jamba Juice, and Raving Wraps.

More choices are available in the North Terminal, near the United gates. The Crab Pot Restaurant and the Crab Pot Brew Pub are favorites among the airport staff, and the Terrace Room Restaurant (across from Gate 71) offers sit-down service as well. There's also a food court between the two United Air Lines concourses that offers everything from Japanese food to decadent desserts. Look for Jamba Juice, Noah's Bagels, and Just Desserts.

Best Healthful Nosh

Sushi from Ebisu, Osho, or Tomokazu in the International Terminal.

Best Sinful Snack

Chocolate from a See's Candy cart or a decadent (and pricey) dessert from Qi, in the International Terminal.

►Relax and Refresh

With frequent fog-induced delays, SFO can get awfully crowded. To escape the hustle and bustle, head for the wide-open spaces and comfortable seating areas throughout the new International Terminal. Most cozy: the seating area behind the ticket lobby, just beyond the Esprit Clothing shop and SFMOMA store. The hushed, multi-ethnic Reflection Center is also located in the International Terminal, in the far corner of the ticket lobby, near the entrance to Boarding Area G.

Comfortable seating is also available in the United Air Lines gate area, not far from Compass Books. If you enjoy people watching, the circular restaurant and bar between the two United concourses makes a good vantage point.

If you need to freshen up, the on-site SFO Hairport, located in the South Terminal, offers showers, neck and shoulder massages, facials, and haircuts at reasonable "hair fares" daily, 8 AM–6 PM. For less-formal cleanups, try the restrooms; SFO officials traveled to Disneyland to learn the secrets of keeping much-used facilities neat and tidy.

Feeling ill or forget your flu shot? SFO has a 24-hour medical facility located on the lower level of the Central Terminal. (The terminal is undergoing renovation, but the medical center remains open.)

If you have an hour or two to meander and get some fresh air, the Travelers Aid employees will help you locate a shuttle to one of the hotels just south of the airport where you can have lunch and take a walk along San Francisco Bay.

Sorry, smokers. You can light up only outside the terminal building.

Take Care of Business

• There are 29 kiosks with internet access scattered throughout airport.

A business center, which rents mini-offices by the minute, is located by the north end of the International Terminal, near the G-gates boarding area.

Explore the Airport

►**Shop**

The opening of the new International Terminal brought a delightful new set of shops to SFO. Highlights presecurity include the SFMOMA store, Esprit Clothing, the Discovery Channel Store, Sephora Perfumes, WH Smith Booksellers, Aviation Inc. (airplane-themed toys and models), and To Your Health, which carries juices, sundries, vitamins, babycare products, and assorted other useful travel items. In boarding area A (postsecurity), you'll find SF Golf, SF Bay Traders, SF Wine Gourmet, and an assortment of other shops. In the G boarding area, look for Wine Country Gourmet, US Sporting Style, Leather Report, Pacific Outfitters, a chocolate shop (Embarcadero Treats), and a variety of gift and souvenir shops.

In the South Terminal (presecurity), find reading matter at Simply Books, chocolates and gift foods at Simply Gourmet, and all manner of souvenirs at I Love San Francisco.

In the North Terminal, you can pick up fresh and frozen crab, smoked salmon, and other seafood specialties packed for travel at Pacific Catch & Carry, squeeze into the small BZINC shop, which carries books, tin toys, art supplies, and other unusual gift items, or visit Awesome Atoms, filled with educational toys, books, and fun stuff for kids. You'll find Simply Books between Gates 81 and 83, but don't pass by the well-known and well-stocked Compass Books, near Gate 71, which offers a great selection of new and sale-priced reading matter. Next door to the SFO Aviation Museum there's a great gift shop called Aviation Inc.

► **Sightsee**

SFO's many display cases are stocked by the airport's highly regarded Bureau of Exhibitions, Museums, and Cultural Exchange, which organizes more than 40 exhibitions each year throughout all the airport terminals. Exhibitions range from documentary photography and kitsch collectibles to significant exhibitions on loan from museums and private collections. At Gate C1 a permanent display titled "Under Water Planet" includes soothing, well-stocked aquariums portraying three aquatic communities: a coral reef, Lake Malawi, and the Amazon River.

The International Terminal features a state-of-the-art library, archive, and museum dedicated to commercial aviation and San Francisco International Airport's role as the "Gateway to the Pacific." Even if you're not a history buff, be sure to stop by the Louis A. Turpen Aviation Museum. By stepping inside you get an old world/ new world experience: the museum's 11,000-square-foot facility was designed to re-create the airport's original passenger waiting area and includes a marble tile floor, ornamental scrollwork, and other charming features that once graced 1930s-era air terminal buildings.

Seventeen new permanent works of art, ranging from large-scale architecturally integrated installations to smaller museum-quality pieces, were commissioned for the new International Terminal, so be sure to take a tour of this $7 million collection.

Look up to see James Carpenter's four boat-shaped reflectors tucked into the skylights of the departures lobby. Look down to see Lewis DeSoto's terrazzo floor in the arrivals lobby that is actually a 12,000-square-foot weather map showing statistical atmospheric pressure zones for July and August, which are the months in which most travelers take to the sky.

Highlights in the gate areas include "Salty Peanuts," Mildred Howard's two-story wall sculpture made out of 130 saxophones; Enrique Chagoya's multilingual, laminated glass work titled "Love Letters"; and "Waiting," a huge mosaic tile mural by Larry Sultan and Mike Mandel that portrays five people waiting at the airport for a loved one to arrive.

When you're not looking at art, watch the planes. Earthquake retrofitting eliminated SFO's formal observation deck, but you can still watch takeoffs and landings from the end of any concourse and get great views of the airfield and surrounding scenery from just about any gate in the International Terminal.

► Play Around

A kid-oriented play area can be found in the United Air Lines boarding area near Gate 88. It has slides, climbing toys, and an exhibit showing how a tornado forms. Kids will also enjoy the aquariums in the South Terminal and the art exhibits scattered throughout the terminals.

Go into Town

SFO hopes to have both an on-site rail transit system (ART) and its own stop on the Bay Area Rapid Transit system (BART) sometime in 2001, but the project is running late. An AirTrain system of electric-powered light-rail trains is also planned. For now, you can get to and from SFO by taxi, public transit, shuttle van, or a shuttle bus that links to the BART subway.

A 12-mile taxi ride to downtown San Francisco will cost about $30–$40 and can take about an hour, depending on traffic. The good news is that up to five people can ride for one fare. Shared vans cost $11–$14, and for $1.10 a shuttle bus will take you on a 25-minute ride to the nearest BART subway station. If you don't have much luggage, the best deal is public transportation aboard an express bus to downtown for $3.

Other Information

For additional information about San Francisco International Airport, call 800-IFLYSFO (800-435-9736).

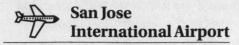 **San Jose International Airport**

San Jose, California
Airport Code: SJC
Web Address: http://www.sjc.org

The original San Jose Airport was established in 1945 on farmland that once served as California's first honeybee ranch. The original "settler" bees made the trip here from Panama in 1853 via mule, rail, and steamship, but these days, the buzz at San Jose International Airport (SJC) comes from air passengers making a beeline for Silicon Valley.

Get Oriented

- Luggage carts rent for $2 and are available in the parking garages and within each terminal.
- Lockers are located in Terminal A across from Gates 4 and 8, and in Terminal C next to Gate 7.

Located 2 miles north of downtown San Jose, San Jose International Airport has two terminals: A and C. Terminal A serves American and Southwest Airlines, and Terminal C serves all other airlines, including Alaska, United, Northwest, TWA, and Delta.

It will take you no longer than 5 minutes to walk the length of either terminal, but it's a 15-minute walk, or a 5- to 10-minute shuttle bus ride, between terminals.

Take Care of Yourself

► **Eat**

In Terminal C you'll find Togo's, serving soup and sandwiches, at the north end of the terminal and Noah's Bagels at the south end. The food court in the center of the terminal features Lappert's Ice Cream, Señor Jalapeño, Ocean Harbor Express, a bar called Martini Monkey, and—for hungry multitaskers—the very first Expedia.com Café. Tables in this Internet café are equipped with data ports and power plugs, so you can surf while snacking on meals prepared by the folks at Max's San Jose, a gourmet deli. (You'll need to bring your own laptop, but Internet access is free.)

Over in Terminal A you'll find another branch of Max's San Jose Deli—sans data ports—as well as ASAP California Pizza Kitchen, the Gordon Biersch Brewery Company, Juice Works/ TCBY, and McDonald's.

Best Healthful Nosh

Healthy deli sandwiches from Togo's Restaurant in Terminal C, by the entrance to Gates 14–16.

Best Sinful Snack

Lappert's (Hawaiian!) ice cream, in the Terminal C food court.

►Relax and Refresh

If you're looking for an out-of-the-way spot to read a book or catch a nap, head for the mezzanine level of Terminal C (there are stairs over by the Kidport) or make a beeline for the open-air observation deck, also in Terminal C.

If you'd rather relax with a movie, you'll find an InMotion Pictures kiosk in Terminal C (at Gate 2), where you can rent movies and portable DVD players. Hours: 6 AM–9 PM daily.

San Jose International Airport has no barbershop or massage kiosks, but the nearby Doubletree Hotel offers a day rate that includes access to their health-club facilities. Call them from the hotel information board in baggage claim.

Smoking is allowed only outside the terminals.

Take Care of Business

- The Expedia.com Café in Terminal C offers data ports and power plugs at each table.

In addition to the Expedia.com Café in Terminal C, you'll find data ports on some public pay phones and at kiosks scattered throughout both terminals. These kiosks also have faxing capabilities. If you just need a space to spread out your laptop and papers, you'll find a set of work desks in Terminal C, postsecurity at Gates 14–16.

Terminal A has a mailbox upstairs at the ticketing-side entrance to the skybridge and a stamp machine near Gate 8. Terminal C mailboxes are located in the main lobby near the Kidport.

Explore the Airport

►Shop

The shops at SJC are all operated by DFS Gifts & News and feature books, magazines, toys, toiletries, and souvenirs, including T-shirts, See's candies, Ghirardelli chocolates, pistachios, and other "gift foods." The shop in Terminal A has a nice wine section.

►Sightsee

You can read all about the role this site had in the birth of California's modern beekeeping industry on a plaque outside Terminal C, at door 10.

Inside Terminal C, look for the 20-by-30-foot mural on the lobby wall, up above the food court. Created by Millard Sheets, the mural depicts a thousand years of Santa Clara Valley history and is intended to be read counterclockwise, starting in the lower left-hand corner, with the group of Costanoan Indians in primitive dress. The scene moves to Spanish invaders, the old Santa Clara Mission, and Mexican ranch life in the valley. Modern life unfolds from the upper left corner where the scenes include the coming of the railroad and San Jose's famed 237-foot electric tower built in 1881 but demolished in 1915.

There are also two murals in Terminal A: Maria Alquilar's "Los Viajeros Vienan a San Jose" (The Travelers Come to San Jose) and an aerial relief map of the Santa Clara Valley, by David Middlebrook.

San Jose is one the few airports with an open-air observation deck. You'll find it in Terminal C, just to the left of the cocktail lounge across from the Kidport. You can also get great views of the airfield and downtown San Jose from the sixth floor of the parking garage in Terminal A.

►**Play Around**

- There are baby-changing tables in both the women's and men's restrooms in both terminals.

Younger kids will have great fun playing on the slide at the aviation-themed Kidport in Terminal C, and all kids will enjoy the view of the airfield from the observation deck, also in Terminal C. If you're in Terminal A, head for Gate 5, where the Tech Museum of Innovation has installed a mechanical contraption that sends small white balls through a maze of chutes and ladders.

Go into Town

A taxi ride to downtown San Jose can take anywhere from 10 to 30 minutes, depending on traffic, and cost from $15 to $20. Shuttle van trips begin at $12.

A free VTA/SJC Airport Flyer (route 10) runs from the airport to both the Santa Clara Caltrain Station and the Metro/Airport Light Rail station.

Other Information

If you need additional information about the San Jose International Airport, you can call 408-501-7600.

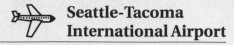 **Seattle-Tacoma International Airport**

Seattle, Washington
Airport Code: SEA
Web Address: http://www.seatac.org

Located halfway between the cities of Seattle and Tacoma, Seattle-Tacoma International Airport (SEA) is the primary air transportation hub of Washington State and the Pacific Northwest. It's my home-base airport, yet I always try to arrive early for flights just so I can visit favorite works of art and browse the shops.

Get Oriented

- Luggage carts rent for $1.50 throughout the airport and refund a token worth $.25 toward food and beverages at the airport when you return a cart to the rack. The racks also give you the option of donating your refund, on the spot, to a local charity.
- Lockers are located on the concourses, postsecurity.

In addition to a main terminal, SEA has four concourses (A, B, C, and D) and two satellites (North and South) accessible by an underground subway. Like many airports throughout the country, this airport is currently undergoing a vast expansion and renovation. Concourse A, for example, is being demolished, the main terminal is being expanded, and the subway system will undergo an overhaul. That means passengers might have to ride buses to the satellite terminals during various portions of the day and several airlines will be shifting gate areas.

All United flights leave from the North Satellite. Once Concourse A disappears, look for Frontier, Southwest, TWA, and US Airways to join Air Canada, Hawaiian Airlines, and Northwest in the South Satellite. Concourse B serves Continental, Delta, and Horizon, and Concourse C hosts Alaska, American, and some

Horizon flights. Concourse D is used mostly by Alaska Airlines. To get your bearings, ask for a terminal map at the information booth located in the plaza area behind the ticket counters in the main terminal.

Take Care of Yourself

►Eat

The main terminal houses a 24-hour cafeteria called Fresh Express as well as the more formal Carvery Dining Room, open daily until 9:30 PM. Liar's Seafood offers chowder and other ocean items (they'll even pack the food for travel), and Sweet Altitudes has ice cream, candy, and other sugar-laden pleasures.

Caffeine-dependent travelers (including most Seattleites) will find espresso stands in the main terminal, in every concourse, at a cart down in the baggage claim area, and out in the parking structure. In addition to those coffee shops, each concourse sports bars and a variety of sandwich and fast-food choices. China First Express is in Concourse B; TCBY, Juice Works, and C.J. Borg's Micro Brews is at the top of Concourse C. Cafeteria-style restaurants in the North and South Satellites have recently been upgraded and now offer everything from sushi and smoothies to bagels and cinnamon buns.

Best Healthful Nosh

Smoothies from Juice Works, just past security on Concourse C, or sushi from the food court in the South Satellite.

Best Sinful Snack

Ice cream or candy (by the piece or the pound) from Sweet Altitudes in the main terminal.

►Relax and Refresh

Quiet, out-of-traffic spots and comfortable seating can be found at both ends of the main terminal corridor and out at the ends of the concourses. A favorite spot for napping is the alcove seating area by the entrance to Concourse B. You can also try the meditation room on the main terminal's mezzanine level.

Stressed-out travelers can visit one of the airport's massage bars just past security near the entrance to Concourse C or in the North Satellite, where 15-or 30-minute massages are discounted during "Healthy Happy Hour" (9 AM–10 AM in Concourse C, 7 AM–8 AM in the North Satellite). Look for discount coupons in restaurants, shops, and information booths throughout the airport.

At Hairlines, a unisex barbershop/salon in the main terminal, you can get a manicure, haircut, shoeshine, or shave seven days a week.

There are no hotels on the SEA grounds, but a variety of hotels with pools and exercise facilities located just off-site offer day rates. Call to check on rates and amenities by using the phones at the information boards in the baggage claim area.

If you've got an hour or more, consider renting a portable DVD player and a film or two from the InMotion kiosk in the main terminal. If you're heading to an airport that also has an InMotion outlet, you can return the kit on arrival.

Sorry, smokers, SEA is a completely smoke-free airport.

Take Care of Business

You'll find data phones and Internet kiosks scattered throughout the airport, and a set of work cubicles with phones at the entrance to Concourse C. A business center, which rents fully equipped offices by the minute, has a branch in the center of the main terminal and is planning to open another outlet in the North Satellite. If you just need a notary or need to send a fax, mail a package, or get some clothes dry-cleaned, head for Ken's Baggage Storage, located in the baggage claim area between carousels 9 and 12. Ken's will also store dry and frozen food for you, and sell you a last-minute dog kennel, car seat, or shipping case for your rifle.

Explore the Airport

►Shop

The most interesting shops at SEA are those that offer Pacific Northwest regional specialties in the center of the main terminal.

The Museum of Flight store, for example, carries everything from airplane-emblazoned ties to model airplanes and other aviation-related toys. Outdoor Adventures features clothing and sports gear. You'll also find two well-stocked bookstores, Liar's Seafood, and the Northwest Marketplace, which offers Northwest wines, microbrewery beer, smoked salmon, Pendleton blankets, and blown glass.

Throughout the terminal, Starbucks and SBC coffee stands also carry a wide variety of coffee-related gift items.

Gift shops out in the concourses (with names such as Northwest Encounter and Northwest Rising) also feature books and a good variety of Northwest specialty items.

▶ Sightsee

In 1973 SEA became one of the first airports to buy and display art in the terminal. The first batch included work by major artists Robert Rauschenberg, Frank Stella, Robert Maki, and Louise Nevelson. In 1992 a dozen new pieces by Northwest artists were added, including Jim Green's water-fountain sound devices, humorous pop-can quilts by Ross Beecher (in the *bathrooms* by Gate B2 and Gate D5), and Eduardo Calderon's photographs of Ray Charles, Quincy Jones, and other jazz musicians whose careers were launched in Seattle. Ask the folks at the information booths located in the center of the main terminal "esplanade" (behind the ticket counters) for a map showing the locations of the artworks, or print out a list from the airport's Web site: www.portseattle.org/seatac/finding/exhibits.htm

Scattered throughout the terminals you'll also encounter temporary exhibits that highlight Northwest culture and local industries, which include everything from apples to airplanes. A favorite among locals is the glass exhibit featuring a wide variety of delicate and often whimsical pieces of contemporary work produced by artists associated with the Pilchuck Glass School. Up to 50 pieces are displayed in a quiet gallery located on the mezzanine level behind the ticket counters in the central plaza, or esplanade.

The Port of Seattle's airport police station prefers I don't share this, but upstairs in the main terminal there's a display of weapons and drug paraphernalia. They've got neatly arranged cases filled with assorted guns, razors, brass knuckles, and crafty drug-smuggling items. How did all this stuff get here? Most everything was confiscated at the airport's security checkpoints.

With all the windows at SEA, views of the runways are easily available, weather permitting.

► Play Around

The glass exhibit upstairs in the main terminal appeals to kids of all ages, as do several other pieces in the airport's permanent art collection. Youngsters also enjoy riding on the underground airport subway. Offer the kids a drink of water from one of Jim Green's "Talking Fountains" in Concourse B or Concourse C. Each emits a louder-than-normal gurgling fountain sound.

Go into Town

- You can call ahead for detailed ground transportation information from 5:30 AM to 2:00 AM: 206-431-5906.

Cab rides to downtown Seattle cost about $30 (but it's a flat $25 from downtown to the airport—go figure) and take about 20–40 minutes, depending on traffic. If you don't have much luggage, a Metro bus into town is a great deal for $1 on weekends and during off-peak weekday hours or $1.75 during peak hours. You can also get downtown for $21 via Shuttle Express, or for $8.50, on the Gray Line bus that stops at eight major downtown hotels. Corny jokes and tourist tips provided by the driver are free.

Other Information

If you'd like information about the airport before you arrive, call 206-431-4444 or 800-544-1965.

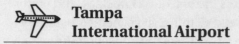 **Tampa International Airport**

Tampa, Florida
Airport Code: TPA
Web Address: http://www.tampaairport.com

Built in 1928 on 160 acres of barren pine woods 6 miles west of the Tampa city limits, Drew Field Municipal Airport was leased to the US government during World War II and served as a training facility for 120,000 combat aircrew members. Ownership of Drew Field reverted back to Tampa in 1945, and in 1952 the city officially changed the name to Tampa International Airport (TPA).

Get Oriented

- Luggage carts rent for $2. When you return a cart to the rack, $.25 is refunded.
- There are no lockers at TPA.

TPA is laid out in a wheel-and-spoke design with four satellite concourses (A, C, D, and F; there is no B), which are called "airsides" and are linked by an aboveground shuttle system to the main terminal, which is called the "Landside" Terminal. The Landside Terminal has three levels—transfer, ticketing, and baggage—with the transfer level housing shops, restaurants, and the helpful Travelers Aid booth.

Currently, Airside A serves America West, Continental, Northwest, and Southwest Airlines; Airside C serves Delta, Midwest Express, Trans World Airlines, and others; Airside D serves Air Canada, AirTran, United, and others; and Airside F serves American, US Airways, British Airways, MetroJet, and additional carriers.

Take Care of Yourself

►Eat

Highlights in the main terminal transfer level include fresh catches at the Wharf Seafood Restaurant, sandwiches at the Wall Street Deli, and breakfast, lunch, or dinner at T.G.I. Friday's. There's also a Starbucks (open 24 hours), which serves sandwiches, salads, and snacks. If you have time for a more leisurely dinner or champagne brunch, head for CK's Restaurant, the revolving rooftop eatery in the on-site Marriott Tampa Airport Hotel.

Best Healthful Nosh

Salads from T.G.I. Friday's in the main terminal.

Best Sinful Snack

Gummi-gators or alligators made of chocolate from the Florida Market shop in the main terminal.

►Relax and Refresh

Grab a chair by Starbucks in the main terminal for prime people watching, or snag a seat in an out-of-the-way corner of the ticketing level for a quick nap. For fresh air, head outside at the "Blue" baggage claim area on level 1 of the main terminal and take a seat by the fountains, or visit the rooftop patio at the Marriott. If you need total peace and quiet, go to the new 24-hour airport chapel located on the transfer level next to the shuttle exit from Concourse F.

For serious rejuvenation, book some time with the massage therapist on duty at the airport barbershop (open weekdays, 7 AM–7 PM; Saturdays, 9 AM–4 PM; Sundays, 11 AM–4 PM). Or check the current day rate at the Marriott Tampa Airport Hotel, which has an outdoor pool, a small health club, and exercise facilities. The hotel is connected to the terminal on the transfer level via a short, shop-lined corridor (813-879-5151).

Smokers can light up in the main terminal on the transfer level next to the "Blue" elevators; in Airside A near Gates 4, 9, and 15; in Airside F just past the security checkpoint (to the right); and in the bar/lounge areas of Airsides C and D.

Take Care of Business

• Phones with data ports are located throughout the airport.

If you need to take care of business, you'll find a business center in the walkway leading from the terminal to the Marriott Hotel. There's also a business center in the Marriott (813-874-6081).

Explore the Airport

►Shop

TPA has a retail shopping mall, called the Tampa Bay Galleria, on the transfer level of the main terminal building. In addition to a well-stocked 24-hour newsstand, an extensive bookstore (Authors Bookstore), and several sports-related shops, there's a sunglasses store, a leather-goods store, a Museum Company store, and a nice-smelling shop called Body Scentsations. Mindworks has a great selection of educational games, puzzles, and science projects, while AltiTunes has listening stations where you can hang out and sample music. And you can fill the empty space in your carry-on bags with beach souvenirs from the Florida Shop or the Florida Market shop.

►Sightsee

On the third level of the main terminal you'll find more than two dozen life-sized copper pelicans circling a 15-foot polished-copper Florida mangrove tree, courtesy of sculptor Roy R. Butler from Plantation, Florida. Even if you don't have bags to pick up, head to the baggage claim area to inspect the 22 enormous wool tapestries hanging behind the baggage carousels. These tapestries, depicting tranquil landscapes and waterscapes of Florida's gulf coast, were created by a team of two dozen weavers from Swaziland. There are also two large saltwater fish tanks in the baggage claim area full of colorful sea creatures.

In the airport chapel, located on the transfer level of the main terminal, you'll find a large glass work of art called "Light Passage" by Tampa artist Yvonne Barlog.

For a 360-degree view of the airfield, downtown Tampa, and the bay, visit the ninth floor of the short-term parking garage or the revolving rooftop restaurant in the Marriott Tampa Airport Hotel.

►Play Around

Kids enjoy riding the shuttles between terminals, peering through the telescopes conveniently placed at the ends of the concourses, or searching the airport for those metal birds. The saltwater aquariums in the baggage claim area should also prove both soothing and entertaining. At the educational toy store Mindworks, look for exhibits provided by the Tampa Museum of Science and Industry, or take the kids outside the "Blue" baggage claim area and let them play near the fountain.

Go into Town

A cab ride to downtown Tampa takes 10–20 minutes and costs about $14. Shared van services are available to all area hotels. If you want to try public transportation, Hillsborough Area Regional Transit (HART) buses stop at the east end of the "Red" baggage claim curbside.

Other Information

If you need more information about the Tampa International Airport before you arrive, call 813-870-8700.

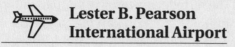 **Lester B. Pearson International Airport**

Toronto, Ontario, Canada
Airport Code: YYZ
Web Address: http://www.gtaa.com

Toronto's Lester B. Pearson International Airport (YYZ) began operation in 1938 as Malton Airport, on a large plot of farmland. In 1960, the airport was renamed Toronto International Airport, and it was retitled yet again in 1984 to honor Lester B. Pearson, the prime minister who had been on hand 20 years earlier to help celebrate the opening of Terminal 1. Pearson Airport is currently Canada's largest and busiest airport, and the 25th busiest airport in the world.

Get Oriented

- Luggage carts rent for $1 and are available throughout the terminals. Your dollar gets refunded when you return the cart to the rack.
- No lockers here, but there is a baggage check service in each terminal: in Terminals 1 and 2 at the Travel Store (on the baggage claim level) and in Terminal 3 at Canadian Locker on the arrivals level.

The Toronto airport has three terminals: 1, 2, and 3. Terminal 3 is the newest and roomiest; the older Terminals 1 and 2 will be consolidated into one new terminal by 2003.

Air Canada (which has its main hub here) and Canadian Airlines use Terminal 1 for international flights and Terminal 2 for domestic and "transborder" (Canada/US) flights. You'll find gates for US Airways and Delta in Terminal 1, for United in Terminal 2, and for TWA, Delta, and Northwest Airlines in Terminal 3.

To get between terminals, hop on one of the free shuttle buses that circle the airport. Once on the bus, it will take 5–10 minutes to get between terminals. Passengers with boarding passes may use the tunnel between Terminals 1 and 2.

Take Care of Yourself

►Eat

You'll find a nice variety of regional and national restaurants in Terminals 2 and 3. Highlights in Terminal 2 include the Mars Diner, a well-known Toronto deli with "comfort food," bottomless cups of coffee, and ice-cream desserts, and the Second City Alumni Bar & Grill, which offers a full menu and a continuous showing of archival film clips from SCTV (Second City Television), whose alumni include John Candy, Gilda Radner, Dan Akroyd, Catherine O'Hara, and others.

In the newer Terminal 3, the Swiss Chalet specializes in rotisserie chicken and other hearty food, and Shopsy's Deli & Bar, the Showtime Bar, and Pumpernickels serve up deli fare, hamburgers, and salads.

Best Healthful Nosh

Salads at the Swiss Chalet in Terminal 3, or crab cakes and shrimp cocktails in Terminal 2 at the Bluenose Bar & Grill in the domestic departures area.

Best Sinful Snack

Chocolate shakes from the Mars Diner in Terminal 2.

►Relax and Refresh

If you'd like to get out of the hustle and bustle, try the farthest ends of the lobby area in Terminal 3, where there are banks of chairs a bit out of the way. Or take the walkway across the street to the Sheraton Hotel and relax in their lobby.

For those seeking a bit more serenity, there are chapels in each terminal. In Terminal 1 you'll find the chapel on the lower level by the main elevators, and Terminals 2 and 3 each have a chapel on the departures level, next to the terminal's medical clinic.

Need a little pampering? Le Body Shop in Terminal 2 offers

face, neck, and hand massages and free beauty makeovers with certain levels of product purchases. The Hair-On-Salon (barber/beauty shop) is located on the lower level of Terminal 2 and, for just Can$15, or about US$9.75, you can get a day pass for the pool and health-club facilities at the Sheraton Hotel, which is connected to Terminal 3. The Sheraton also offers a day rate of Can$95 (about US$62).

If you need to smoke, you'll find ventilated smoking areas in most every food court and bar.

Take Care of Business

• Internet kiosks are located postsecurity in many of the gate waiting areas.

There are limited options at this airport for getting work done if you're not a member of one of the airline clubs. You can make copies and send faxes at the Travel Store in Terminal 2 on the arrivals level, but if you have more serious business needs, head over to the business center in the Sheraton Hotel, connected to Terminal 3.

Explore the Airport

►Shop

All three terminals have bookstores, well-stocked newsstands, gift shops filled with maple syrup in many forms, a Battery Plus outlet that sells all sorts of electronic items, and a branch of the souvenir and clothing shop called Oh Yes Toronto.

Terminal 3 has an appealing shopping "street," featuring The Great Canadian Bookstore, a PGA Tour Shop, a toy store, a branch of Roots Canada (sportswear), and Official Sports, which features souvenirs from the Toronto Maple Leafs and other local and regional teams. Design Trends, which also has an outlet in Terminal 2, carries watches, lamps, and a variety of trendy housewares.

In Terminal 2 you'll also find the Body Shop, a Chapters bookstore, a toy store, and several pushcarts filled with souvenirs and gifts.

►**Sightsee**

A chart hanging on the wall just outside the Second City Alumni Bar & Grill, in the departures level concourse of Terminal 2, features an incredibly long list of now well-known actors who spent time as cast members of *SCTV* in Toronto, Chicago, and several other cities.

In the Terminal 3 ticket lobby, across from the British Airways counter, there's an ornate, tubular chrome clock and a plaque commemorating the creation of a time capsule in 1991.

Looking ahead, the new terminal slated to open in 2003 will feature a wide array of artwork designed around aviation and flight.

Many gate areas face the runways, but if it's a nice day, head for the rooftop observation area in Terminal 1.

►**Play Around**

Nurseries for very young children, equipped with couches, toys, and play areas, are located on the lower level of Terminal 1 (by the elevators) and on the departures level of Terminal 3, across from the medical clinic and opposite the KLM counters.

If you've got older kids, be assured there's a bookstore and a toy store in each terminal, along with shops selling furry raccoon-tail hats in a variety of children's sizes. There's also a time capsule in the Terminal 3 lobby, and kids might have fun imagining what airport officials have stored away "way back" in the old days, circa 1991. Bring along some paper and see if the kids want to list their own time capsule ingredients.

Go into Town

The airport is located 16 miles northwest of downtown Toronto. A taxi ride to the downtown area will cost about Can$40 (about US$26), a shuttle bus ride will cost Can$13.75 (about US$9). The shuttle bus company, Pacific Western Airport Express, also offers senior citizens and students a 10 percent discount (800-387-6787; www.torontoairportexpress.com).

Other Information

Feeling sick? There are emergency medical clinics in each terminal: in Terminal 1 on the lower level, by the main elevators; in Terminal 2 on the departures level; and in Terminal 3 in the international departures area by the security checkpoint. The infirmary in Terminal 2 is larger than the other two centers and serves as a "walk-in" clinic for passengers. Services include chiropractic and massage therapy and pretravel immunizations.

If you need information before you arrive, call Terminals 1 and 2 at 905-676-3506 or Terminal 3 at 905-612-5100. On-site, don't be surprised if you find the information kiosks empty. Just keep your eyes peeled for one of the airport's uniformed "mobile customer service agents" and flag one down if you have a question.

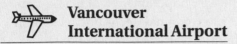 **Vancouver International Airport**

Vancouver, British Columbia, Canada
Airport Code: YVR
Web Address: http://www.yvr.ca

In 1928, locals were dismayed when Charles Lindbergh knocked Vancouver's "less than adequate" airport facilities. Oh, if he could see the place now. With the opening of a brand-new international terminal in 1996 and the remodeling of the 1960s-vintage domestic terminal, Vancouver International Airport (YVR) is not only a convenient place to catch a plane, it's also an art- and amenity-filled place to spend a few hours.

Get Oriented

- There is no charge to use a baggage cart.
- Baggage storage is available at CDS Baggage Storage, open 5 AM–12 midnight.

Vancouver International Airport has two main terminals, Domestic and International, connected by a short corridor dotted with services, seating, and a great kids' play area. In the International Terminal flights to and from the United States use gates in Concourse E, and all other international flights use the Concourse D gates. Flights within Canada use Concourses A, B, and C in the Domestic Terminal: Air Canada flights come and go from the Concourse A and B gates, and Canadian Airlines flights pull up at the Concourse C gates.

Take Care of Yourself

►**Eat**

The food court in the International Terminal offers sushi, pizza, noodles, burgers, deli sandwiches, and a nice upper-level seating area for those trying to get away from the crowds below. Table service is offered nearby at the Pacific Market Restaurant, the Jade Oyster Bar, and at the very popular Oriental Tea Garden, down the hall a bit by the international security checkpoint. Downstairs, in the international arrivals area, the Elephant & Castle Pub offers British pub fare, including ploughman's lunches.

In the Domestic Terminal your choices for table service include the Milestones Restaurant and Cheers Bar & Restaurant, both on the departure level. In the two food court areas on the departure level your choices include sushi, bagels, pizza, salads, juices, sandwiches, and burgers. There's also a brewpub, a doughnut stand, good coffee, and several fast-food outlets on the lower level, near the baggage claim areas.

Best Healthful Nosh

Juices, smoothies, or squeezes from the Juice Bar in the Domestic Terminal on the departure level.

Best Sinful Snack

Fresh fudge, truffles, or giant peanut-butter cups from the Rocky Mountain Chocolate Factory in the Domestic Terminal on the departure level.

►Relax and Refresh

To escape the airport scene, head for the comfortable seats in the lobby of the Fairmont Vancouver Airport Hotel, located right on top of the airport and accessible from the lobby of the International Terminal. If that's too upscale for you, join the folks napping in the seating area in the connecting corridor between the Domestic and International Terminals or stop in at the chapel, located on the lower level of the International Terminal.

If you find people watching relaxing and/or entertaining, grab a stool at the Starbucks coffee bar or the Jade Oyster Bar in the center lobby of the International Terminal. Both are near the giant jade-green bronze sculpture by Bill Reid ("The Spirit of the Haida Gwaii, the Jade Canoe") that sits in a sort of amphitheater setting with low wooden benches.

If you need to freshen up, you'll find a hair salon in the connecting corridor between the Domestic and International Terminals. The Fairmont Vancouver Airport Hotel (604-207-5200) has a day rate that runs upward from Can$90 (about US$58) and includes use of the swimming pool, hot tub, and exercise facilities. For a great deal, pass on the room and use the pool, hot tubs, showers, and workout facilities for just Can$15 (about US$8). The hotel also has a spa offering manicures, pedicures, facials, massages, and other anti–jet lag services.

Most areas of the airport are nonsmoking, but there are separately ventilated smoking rooms postsecurity in the Domestic and International Terminals and on the lower level of the Domestic Terminal near Stanley's Lounge. Smoking is also permitted in Cheers Bar & Restaurant, in the departure area of the Domestic Terminal.

Take Care of Business

- Most all phones at YVR have data ports, but the only Internet kiosk is located at Mailboxes Etc. in the ticket lobby of the Domestic Terminal.

A business center on the arrivals level of the International Terminal offers fax, copying, printing, and secretarial services as well as computer workstations and laptop hookups. Mailboxes Etc., located in the ticket lobby of the Domestic Terminal, offers postal services, as well as copying, Internet access, and computer workstation rentals.

There are several full-service bank branches (Royal Bank) scattered throughout the airport. ATMs are plentiful, but only before the security checkpoints. Some machines dispense Canadian dollars, some offer US bills, and others handle currency from 90 different countries.

Explore the Airport

►Shop

YVR has shop-filled "streets" on the departure levels of both the Domestic and International Terminals, all honoring the airport's street-pricing policy, which means prices here cannot exceed a shop's downtown prices.

Each terminal has a well-stocked bookstore, and a wide variety of shops selling smoked salmon, maple syrup, and other gift food items.

In the International Terminal, head to Kids' Place for toys, to the Mountain Style Shop for outdoor gear, and to Gifts of the Raven or Spirit of the North for artwork, crafts, and other gifts from British Columbia. Duty-free shops beyond the security checkpoints include a PGA Tour Shop, a wine store, and all sorts of food and gift shops.

In the Domestic Terminal, browse for clothing, books, jewelry, and other gift items at British Columbia & Beyond, and just try to restrain yourself at the Rocky Mountain Chocolate Factory shop. At the Fish Market (a small salmon, syrup, and gift food shop) I had a hard time choosing between the smoked salmon gift tin that featured a limited-edition carved native mask on the lid and the one that doubles as an authentic beating drum. I bought them both.

►Sightsee

Throughout the airport you'll find wonderful native art reflecting the Musqueam culture and people. The collection's centerpiece, a 12-foot-high, 10,800-pound cast bronze sculpture by Bill Reid titled "The Spirit of Haida Gwaii, the Jade Canoe," sits in the center of the departure level of the International Terminal. Behind Reid's masterpiece is the "Great Wave Wall," a glass installation by Lutz Hauschild that was inspired by the "Great Wave of Kanagawa" by the artist Hokusai.

In the arrivals hall you'll find large carvings by Susan Point, including the world's largest Coast Salish Spindle Whorl and two 17-foot-tall red-cedar Welcome figures. Large weavings by Musqueam weavers Debra Sparrow, Robyn Sparrow, Krista Point, Gina Grant, and Helen Calbreath hang nearby.

For more information about these artworks and others throughout the airport, stop by the information booth (the counter with a giant question mark overhead) in the Domestic Terminal.

You'll get the best views of airfield activities and the surrounding scenery from the glass-walled corridors in the International Terminal.

►Play Around

There are children's play areas both before and after the security checkpoints in both terminals and in the middle of the connecting corridor between the Domestic and International Terminals. A nursery in the connecting corridor is open 24 hours a day.

If kids ask politely the folks at the airport police desk (in the connecting corridor just down from the play area) will hand over a paper ambulance that kids can assemble and play with. At the information desk in the Domestic Terminal they hand out children's activity books.

Big kids (adults) might enjoy a game of pool at the Elephant & Castle Pub on the lower level of the International Terminal.

If it's a nice day, by all means take a walk in the park. Chester Johnson Park is located right next to the International Terminal, on the arrivals level between the terminal and the parking garage. It has a walking trail, three totem poles, a waterfall, and a reflection pool.

Go into Town

A taxi ride to downtown Vancouver will cost between Can$25 and Can$40 (about US$16–US$26) and can take up to half an hour. Customer service representatives, called "Taxi Hosts," are stationed by the taxi stands and can help you figure out how much your fare might be.

Shuttle vans (Can$10, or about US$6.50, one way; Can$17, or about US$11, round-trip) leave for downtown every 15 minutes until 10:30 PM. After that, until the last run just past midnight, they leave every 30 minutes. You can buy your tickets at the Tourism InfoCenter, the airport ticket office, or on the bus.

If you have lots of time, little luggage, and don't mind transferring, you can take the public bus downtown. Catch the #100 on the ground level of the Domestic Terminal and ask the driver where to switch.

Other Information

For more information about the airport before you arrive, call 604-276-6373.

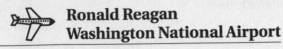 **Ronald Reagan
Washington National Airport**

Washington, DC (Arlington, VA)
Airport Code: DCA
Web Address: http://www.metwashairports.com/national

Back in the 1930s the merger of Washington Airport and Hoover Field created Washington-Hoover Airport, not far from the present site of the Pentagon. It was a curious alliance: one side of the airport bordered a highway with high-tension electrical wires, the other featured a tall smokestack. To make matters worse, a busy street (Military Road) crossed the single runway and guards had to be posted to flag down traffic during takeoffs and landings.

In 1941, President Franklin D. Roosevelt christened the safer and more user-friendly National Airport on a bend of the Potomac River just 4.5 miles south of Washington, DC. And in 1998, less than a year after the opening of the new Terminal B/C, designed by noted architect Cesar Pelli, the airport's name was officially changed from National Airport to Ronald Reagan Washington National Airport (DCA).

Get Oriented

- Baggage carts rent for $2 and are located throughout the terminals and in the Metro subway station stops. You'll receive a $.25 refund when you return your cart to the rack.
- Lockers are located behind the security checkpoints.

Midway, Northwest, and TWA still operate out of Gates 1–9 in the "old" (but to-be-updated) Terminal A, while all other airlines operate out of the new Terminal B/C, which is essentially one very long, three-tiered building with concourses called "piers." US Airways occupies the entire North Pier (Gates 35–45), while Air Canada, American, Midwest Express, and United use the Center Pier (Gates 23–34) just down the hall. The South Pier (Gates 10–22) is used by America West, Continental, Continental Express, Delta, and Delta Shuttle.

It can take up to 15 minutes to walk from one end of Terminal B/C all the way to Terminal A. The trip can be much longer however if, like me, you let yourself be lured into the enticing shops along the way.

Take Care of Yourself

► Eat

Highlights along the main corridor of Terminal B/C include Legal Sea Foods (outside the US Airways pier), T.G.I. Friday's (outside Gates 23–34), and the California Pizza Kitchen (by Gates 15–22). Branches of the Cheesecake Factory Bakery Café are located at either end of the departure level corridor and up on the ticketing level. Each concourse, or pier, also boasts a tavern and a food court offering bagels, hamburgers, tacos, and other fast-food fare.

Best Healthful Nosh

Oysters, steamed clams, or seafood salad at Legal Sea Foods, by Gates 34–44 (US Airways).

Best Sinful Snack

Candy by the ounce, the pound, or the box, from the Sweet Factory by Gates 15–22 (just before the walkway to Terminal A).

► Relax and Refresh

To get out of the hustle and bustle, head for the windows in the central waiting area in the "old" terminal (Gates 1–9) or turn your back on traffic and grab a seat facing the river view along the main corridor in Terminal B/C. For more privacy, head for the chapel, located across the hallway from the entrance to the South Pier (Gates 10–22).

There are no on-site health clubs or beauty salons, but men and women can get manicures at kiosks located at Gate 40 in Terminal B/C (North Pier, US Airways gates) or in the "old" Terminal

A, near the TWA/Northwest gate area. If you're here for a while and just must have clean clothes, there's a dry cleaners located on the baggage claim level of Terminal B/C.

There are no on-site hotels, but a wide variety of nearby hotels are accessible via shuttle bus and most offer day rates to travelers stuck at the airport and folks simply in need of a shower, a hot tub, or dip in the pool. "Just head for the hotel call board in baggage claim," suggest the folks at the information desk. "Call any hotel listed there under 'Crystal City' and ask for their best 'airport patron' deal."

Smokers must either go outside to light up or patronize one of the brewpubs that allow smoking: the Sam Adams Brewhouse in Terminal A or the Foggy Bottom Brew Pub in the connecting corridor between Terminals A and B/C, beyond security.

Terminal B/C also features well-marked "companion care" bathroom facilities, which offer privacy for those needing assistance.

Take Care of Business

- Phone stations with counter space and data ports are located by Gates 12, 33, and 36.

You can make copies, send faxes, get something notarized, or exchange foreign currency at one of the three Thomas Cook business service centers located near the entrance of each pier in Terminal B/C. You'll find Internet booths located just outside the business centers. The folks at the AT&T Wireless store in the center hall can also get you on the Web.

Explore the Airport

►Shop

National Hall, the long corridor on the concourse level in Terminal B/C, boasts a great selection of places to both shop and browse. There are two branches of Waldenbooks, a PGA Tour Shop, a wonderful jewelry and crafts shop (As Kindred Spirits), and branches of Brookstone, Wilsons Leather, the Disney Store,

Victoria's Secret, Easy Spirit (shoes!), and the Gap. National Geographic has a store here, as do the National Zoo and the Smithsonian Institution.

For regional DC souvenirs, stop by Capital Image or the US Capitol Historical Society shop. If politics is more your style, America! offers a set of towels "stolen" from the Lincoln Bedroom, all sorts of patriotic ties, socks emblazoned with pictures of the White House, and baby togs that say "Future President."

► **Sightsee**

Designed by noted architect Cesar Pelli, the multidomed new Terminal B/C is itself a work of art. The entire back wall of the terminal is a sheet of glass and more than 30 major artworks are incorporated as permanent parts of the building. Search out the stained-glass panels in the back wall, the giant mosaic medallions embedded in the floor, and the whimsical steel balustrades along the ticketing hall.

Ever wonder why airport ticket counters are so high? No one will tell me, but DCA obviously had wheelchair users and short folks like me in mind when they incorporated drop-down flaps into the front panel of every ticket counter in Terminal B/C. Don't be shy to ask a ticket agent to pop open an accessible writing table for you.

Pretty much anyplace by a window in Terminal B/C will be a good place to watch airfield activity, but to be sure you don't miss a thing, grab a seat at the end of any pier. There are also great viewing spots in Terminal A. And don't forget to keep a lookout inside as well: it's not unusual to spot a senator, congressperson, or cabinet member passing through.

► **Play Around**

National Hall, the airport's concourse level, has a wide variety of kid-oriented shops. So you and your well-behaved kids can while away oodles of hours in the Disney Store, the National Zoo Shop, the National Geographic store, or the Smithsonian Institution store and even learn some history or geography along the way. Older kids might enjoy browsing for souvenirs in Capital

Image or the America! shop. Or send them on an art tour of Terminal B/C, where 10 large and intriguing mosaic floor medallions and 20 other large-format artworks are incorporated into the architecture.

Go into Town

A taxi ride downtown to, say, the White House will cost about $15 and take anywhere from 15 to 30 minutes, depending on traffic. Shared shuttle rides (SuperShuttle) to downtown DC make the trip for about $8 per person.

If you don't have much luggage, the easiest, fastest, and certainly least expensive path downtown is via the Metrorail subway system. To get to the subway, simply walk across a covered pedestrian bridge or hop on an airport shuttle bus at any of the marked stops outside the terminals. Fares vary by stop and time of day, but should cost you $2 or less. Just remember that the Metro doesn't run round-the-clock and trains don't start running until 8 AM on weekends.

Other Information

If you need more information about the airport before you arrive, call the folks at the Travelers Aid desk: 703-417-1807.

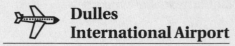 **Dulles
International Airport**

Washington, DC (Dulles, Virginia)
Airport Code: IAD
Web Address: http://www.metwashairports.com/dulles

Stars shone on Dulles International Airport (IAD) from the moment of its inception: President Dwight D. Eisenhower selected the site 26 miles west of the District of Columbia in 1958; the airport was named in honor of John Foster Dulles, one of the century's most eminent secretaries of state; and in November 1962, President John F. Kennedy was on hand for opening-day ceremonies.

Get Oriented

- Luggage carts rent for $2 and refund $.25 when you return a cart to the rack.
- Lockers are located postsecurity in the main terminal and in the concourses.

The most notable feature of Dulles is the soaring main terminal building designed by architect Eero Saarinen. A construction project to extend Saarinen's masterpiece was completed in 1996, and now Dulles consists of the main terminal (Gates M, H, and T) and two midfield terminals containing Concourses A, B, C, and D. Huge "mobile lounges," which will eventually be replaced by underground tunnels, take passengers from the main terminal to the midfield terminals. International arrivals pull up at the main terminal.

The main terminal serves some United Express flights at the T gates, and predominantly international carriers at the M and H gates. In the first midfield terminal, Concourse A serves United and United Express flights while Concourse B gates host Continental, Delta, Northwest, US Airways, Virgin Atlantic, and several other international carriers. In the second midfield terminal, you'll find Air Canada, Lufthansa, and United Air Lines in Concourse C and American, British Airways, Midwest Express, TWA, and several other airlines in Concourse D.

To get your bearings, head for one of the information booths located in the main terminal and on the lower baggage claim level (by the escalators).

Take Care of Yourself

▶ Eat

For a sit-down meal, your main choices are T.G.I. Friday's in the main terminal and in Concourse D. You can also pull up a seat at the Vintage Virginia Wine Bar in Concourses C and D, Samuel Adams Brewhouse in Concourses B and D, or the Old Dominion Brewing Company in Concourse B and in Concourse C at Gates 11 and 19.

For a quick bite, visit the concessions along the concourses or in the food court in the main terminal, where you can grab a window seat and keep an eye on the activity outside. Highlights in the concourses include Vie de France in Concourses C and D, and Panda Express in Concourse D.

Best Healthful Nosh

Salads from T.G.I. Friday's in the main terminal and in Concourse D.

Best Sinful Snack

Ben & Jerry's ice cream in Concourse B.

▶ Relax and Refresh

Before you spend hours cramped in an airplane, stroll around the wide-open spaces of Eero Saarinen's landmark main terminal building, or grab a seat with some legroom and relax. For a truly quiet spot, visit the 24-hour chapel in Concourse B. To freshen up, head for restrooms away from busy gate areas, or try the newer restrooms at the far end of the baggage claim areas in the main terminal. There is also a pair of "secret" restrooms in the main terminal: take the escalator down to the A gates and make a sharp left turn; the restrooms are at the end of the hallway, tucked right under the escalator.

If you have a bit more time, grab a shuttle and head over to the Washington Dulles Airport Marriott, located on the airport property. Day rates are available, depending on current occupancy, and include access to the hotel's health and exercise facilities (703-471-9500).

Take Care of Business

- The Lounge Café/Cyberflyer on the upper floor of the main terminal (west end) has two Internet hookups. In Concourse B, log on at Gates 22 and 43; in Concourse C at Gates 6, 16, and 27; and in Concourse D between Gates 18 and 20 and between Gates 24 and 26.

There are five Thomas Cook business service centers at Dulles: two in the main terminal (east and west), one in Concourse B, and one each in Concourses C and D. Services include foreign-currency exchange, faxing, photocopying, and a notary public. Hours are 7 AM–9 PM daily.

Explore the Airport

►Shop

Street pricing is in effect at Dulles, which means prices here are no higher than what you'd pay in a mall. So you can wait until you get to the airport to purchase a miniature Washington Monument, or a souvenir with the current president's mug on it. For something a bit different, browse the patriotic gifts at the America! shop near Gate B24.

You'll find bookstores in the main terminal (Benjamin Books) and in Concourses B and D (Waldenbooks). There's a Liz Claiborne outlet in Concourse B, as well as a Sweet Factory, a Bally leather goods shop, and a Sunglass Hut. In Concourse C look for AltiTunes (CDs and small electronics), and a variety of gift shops and kiosks. In Concourse D, you'll find Wilsons Leather, Brookstone, another AltiTunes outlet, and several more gift shops. All the Hudson News shops carry books, but the Hudson News Euro Café in Concourse B has a wider selection as well as a coffee shop.

► Sightsee

Without a doubt, the main attraction at Dulles is the main terminal itself. Once described as "a hammock slung between columns of concrete," the glass building with the swooping roof was designed as the "airport of the future" by noted Finnish-born architect Eero Saarinen. Saarinen's architectural goal was to find "the soul of an airport" in an age when jet travel was still something travelers dressed up for. He wanted to capture the spirit of flight and invoke a feeling of soaring. Since the building itself is an award-winning work of art, airport officials have been hesitant to add paintings, sculptures, or other artwork that could interrupt the structure's lines.

On a clear day you get a nice view of the Blue Ridge Mountains of Virginia. In the main terminal, just beyond the security offices, an observation deck circles the restaurant and food court. In Concourse B, head for the north side of the terminal for a good view.

► Play Around

There is a children's play area in Concourse C, but kids will have more fun riding the mobile lounges between concourses or hanging out at the observation deck in the main terminal and watching planes come and go.

Go into Town

- To review all your transportation options, call Washington Flyer at 888-927-4359.

Washington Dulles Airport is 26 miles from downtown Washington, DC. A taxi ride takes about 40 minutes and ranges from $35 to $47. Cab rides to many other destinations in metropolitan Washington and suburban Maryland will take about the same amount of time and cost the same, but if you are heading to northern Virginia or parts of southeastern Maryland, build in more time and expect to pay a bit more. Other transportation options include a Washington Flyer bus to downtown ($16), a shared shuttle van ($22), or a bus to the nearest Washington Metro station ($8), located 10 miles away.

Other Information

To find out more about Dulles International Airport before you arrive, call 703-572-2700.

So why are the vehicles that go back and forth between the main terminal and the midfield concourses called "mobile lounges" instead of buses or moving waiting rooms? Because, when they were first introduced, hostesses actually served cocktails to travelers on their way out to the airplane! Those days are long gone, but with service like that, who'd really care if they ended up stuck at the airport?

Appendix

Airports Listed by Code: The following list includes the airports described in this guide, code first. For a complete list of 630 airport codes worldwide, check www.faa.gov/aircodeinfo.htm

ALB: Albany, NY
AMS: Amsterdam, Netherlands
ATL: Atlanta, GA
AUS: Austin, TX
BDL: Hartford, CT
BNA: Nashville, TN
BOS: Boston, MA
BUR: Burbank, CA
BWI: Baltimore, MD
CDG: Paris, France—Roissy– Charles de Gaulle
CLE: Cleveland, OH
CLT: Charlotte, NC
CMH: Columbus, OH
CVG: Cincinnati, OH
DCA: Washington, DC— National
DEN: Denver, CO
DFW: Dallas, TX
DTW: Detroit, MI
EWR: Newark, NJ
FLL: Fort Lauderdale, FL
HNL: Honolulu, HI
IAD: Washington, DC—Dulles
IAH: Houston, TX
IND: Indianapolis, IN
JFK: New York, NY—Kennedy
LAS: Las Vegas, NV
LAX: Los Angeles, CA
LGA: New York, NY— LaGuardia

LGW: London, England— Gatwick
LHR: London, England— Heathrow
MCO: Orlando, FL
MEM: Memphis, TN
MIA: Miami, FL
MSP: Minneapolis, MN
MSY: New Orleans, LA
ORD: Chicago, IL
ORY: Paris, France—Orly
PDX: Portland, OR
PHL: Philadelphia, PA
PHX: Phoenix, AZ
PIT: Pittsburgh, PA
RDU: Raleigh-Durham, NC
RNO: Reno, NV
SAN: San Diego, CA
SEA: Seattle, WA
SFO: San Francisco, CA
SJC: San Jose, CA
SLC: Salt Lake City, UT
SNA: Santa Ana, CA (Orange County, CA) John Wayne Airport
STL: St. Louis, MO
TPA: Tampa, FL
YUL: Montreal, Quebec, Canada
YVR: Vancouver, BC, Canada
YYZ: Toronto, Ontario, Canada

About the Author

Frequent traveler HARRIET BASKAS is an award-winning radio producer and writer. She reviews airports for the Expedia.com travel Web site and reports on unusual museums, boomer issues, and other topics for National Public Radio, Expedia Radio, Marketplace, and a variety of other public and commercial radio programs. She is also the author of *Museums of the Northwest* (Sasquatch Books, 1999) and the co-author (with Adam Woog) of *Atomic Marbles and Branding Irons: A Guide to Museums, Collections and Roadside Attractions in Washington and Oregon* (Sasquatch Books, 1993).